Classical Memories/Modern Identities
Paul Allen Miller and Richard H. Armstrong, Series Editors

Humanism and Classical Crisis

Anxiety, Intertexts,
and the Miltonic Memory

Jacob Blevins

THE OHIO STATE UNIVERSITY PRESS • COLUMBUS

Library of Congress Cataloging-in-Publication Data
Blevins, Jacob, 1970–
   Humanism and classical crisis : anxiety, intertexts, and the Miltonic memory / Jacob Blevins.
      p. cm. — (Classical memories/modern identities)
   Includes bibliographical references and index.
   ISBN-13: 978-0-8142-1241-7 (cloth : alk. paper)
   ISBN-10: 0-8142-1241-7 (cloth : alk. paper)
   ISBN-13: 978-0-8142-9344-7 (cd-rom)
   ISBN-10: 0-8142-9344-1 (cd-rom)
1. Literature, Modern—17th century—History and criticism. 2. Literature, Modern—15th and
16th centuries—History and criticism. 3. Classical literature—Influence. 4. Humanism.
5. Milton, John, 1608–1674—Criticism and interpretation. I. Title. II. Series: Classical memories/
modern identities.
   PN721.B57 2013
   809'.031—dc23
                          2013021106

Cover design by AuthorSupport.com
Type set in Adobe Garamond Pro
Text design by Juliet Williams

9 8 7 6 5 4 3 2 1

For Catherine
my most beautiful memory

Contents

Acknowledgments

I would like to express my sincere gratitude to the U.S. and U.K. Fulbright Commissions for their early support of this project. I also owe thanks to those at Cardiff University, who allowed me access to their wonderful university back in 2006. I would particularly like to thank Martin Kayman for a lunch conversation with me about his concerns over the notion of "influence." His thoughts on the subject have remained with me throughout my writing of this book. I would like to thank Catherine Belsey for her initial support of my project; her endorsement, I am sure, carried substantial weight with the Fulbright selection committee.

David H. J. Larmour and Diana Spencer published an altered version of Chapter 2 in their *The Sites of Rome: Time, Space, Memory* (Oxford: Oxford University Press, 2006). Their early comments and suggestions helped shape the direction of the book as a whole. Thanks to *Intertexts* and the *Andrew Marvell Newsletter* for publishing other sections of this study. Eugene O'Connor, Paul Allen Miller, Richard Armstrong, and the anonymous readers of my manuscript at The Ohio State University Press, I cannot thank you enough for your careful attention and ultimate support of this book. I could not be more pleased to have it published by The Ohio State University Press.

I would also like to thank my friends and colleagues at McNeese State, especially Keagan LeJeune, Ray Miles, Amy Fleury, Rita Costello, Wendy Whelan-Stewart, Dafydd Wood, Scott Goins, and Bob Cooper; your influence manifests itself in all areas of my personal and professional life. I also owe a tremendous debt to John Wood, who taught me to see the beauty and wonder of art. John may reject many of the theoretical principles of this book, but his influence is present in all that I do. I am very grateful to John Metoyer for his permission to use his photograph for the cover.

Finally, I would like to thank Alison, my wife, and my two children, who have given me more than I could ever imagine.

Introduction

This book's argument rests on two primary assertions. The first is that the act of literary appropriation of classical texts and culture during the early modern period, in its various manifestations, is primarily the result of a psychical process of identity construction and only secondarily a matter of historical literary development.[1] The historical and cultural forces that influence literary appropriation *are* intricately connected to the methods and practices of *imitatio*. However, the phenomena of "influence" and "imitation" in literature are historical only insofar as history shapes and influences the psychical processes of subjectivity. There is no historical marker, whether it is a law, a political movement, or a previous work of art, that is not first processed through the sieve of the psyche before it can be recast in the form of a new literary expression. We cannot even begin to understand the ideological pressures that might direct literary filiation without first understanding the way those ideologies and literary memories are processed by the psyche. The traditional approach to the study of liter-

---

1. Throughout this book, I use the term "psychical" as opposed to "psychological," primarily because the term "psychological" is so closely linked to psychology as a discipline or clinical practice. Lacan viewed the field of psychology as extremely problematic: "Psychology properly so-called is effectively a science of perfectly well-defined objects" (Seminar 3, 243); "To look for the real that psychoanalysis deals with in the psychological is the principle of a radical deviation. Every reduction, every attempt to return, as they say, or of the exhaustion of psychoanalysis in some pscyhologism . . . is the negation of psychoanalysis" (Seminar 12, 16.06.65, p. 2).

ary imitation and influence has tended to begin with the historical, with the modes and operations of practice, with available texts, with the reading habits of authors, and with the previous models of genres and themes—all of which do find a place in the current study. But to locate the significance of such textual negotiation, to identify how texts and the act of writing itself actually function for writers, one must approach intertextuality as fundamentally a part of a psychical process, and any given text as a kind of amalgamation of psychical influence. In a general sense, this has been a core idea in psychoanalytic criticism since Freud, but such an approach has not been adequately considered in the area of literary appropriation. That is the starting point of this study.

Some clarification of the terms "influence" and "imitation" as they are understood and utilized in this book is necessary, particularly as they relate to a psychoanalytic approach to literary appropriation. The notion of influence is troublesome in many ways, especially as it has been used by previous critics, Harold Bloom most notably. There is a certain nebulous quality to the concept of influence; it is both difficult to define and even more difficult to analyze systematically. Bloom tried, and other critics have followed with varying success. Still, influence itself, whether one is considering literary influence or the influences of history and ideology, represents an infinite source of psychical stimuli impacting the manifestation of subjectivity, and that manifestation seems virtually unmappable. Imitation on the other hand is something quite different. It is an active process, an actual literary act by which an author appropriates a text or group of texts and assimilates them into a new creative act, a new literary self-projection. Imitation is not only identifiable but is measurable within given criteria. Critics have tended either to paint a canvas of influence in very broad strokes that yields little useful analysis or to focus so much on the technical intricacies of literary imitation that the underlying ideological, literary, and psychical forces that drive the creation of a literary consciousness get lost. From a psychical standpoint, literary influence is akin to the vast influence of individual experience that shapes a particular subject's self-fashioning; imitation represents the acts and behaviors that can give us insight into the origins of influence that construct the subject and that subject's sense of self.

The second underlying assertion of this study is that literary appropriation is not a stable act. Generally speaking, writing essentially functions as a mode of either self-expression or self-representation, and psychically such representation of the self or of the self's perception of the world is seldom, if ever, "stable." Even narrative discourse, from a Bakhtinian perspective, is dialogic in nature and is the result of multiple narrative discourses converging on the narrative text.[2] The concept of *convergence* is key to this approach. Voices are not separated out into well-packaged categories but rather engage one another, begging for response, reinterpretation, reevaluation, and finally reexpression. Even within a narrative text, intertextuality shapes any voice heard, and that is the principle of literary imitation outside an individual text as well. This sounds simple enough; however, once voices and ideologies converge, textual tension must result as writers attempt to integrate one "voice" into another, one ideological position into another. Therefore, the instability to which I refer is the result of competing ideologies, competing voices, that must be negotiated psychically within the text in order for the writer to create. The competition could be explicit, as when the *Beowulf* writer must find a medieval Christian heroism within the pagan shame culture of the Germanic tribes; the result is a text that at times seems jarring, disjointed, a literal battlefield for cultural exchange. Similarly, such explicit instability resides in the medieval *Ovid Moralisé*, in which Ovid's *Metamorphoses* is violently redefined in terms of Christian allegory. At other times, that competition is subtler, a slight variation of a myth or an anachronistic image that actually calls attention to itself as inorganic to the world of the work. In some ways, the author's ability to integrate two worldviews into a text is a testament to that author's literary talents, but the tension is even more pronounced in such integration. That tension is the origin of poetic identity and of the voice of that identity.

As mentioned above, the one approach to literary appropriation that has addressed these two assumptions is Harold Bloom's theory of the "anxiety of influence" put forth in his seminal work of the same name.[3] Bloom's ideas concerning literary history were arguably the most provocative approach to literary imitation and literary tradition since T. S. Eliot's "Tradition and the Individual Talent" (1919), and Bloom's ideas regarding the psychical origins of literary creation are the foundation of the current study. Bloom certainly did not invent the idea that the relationship between a writer and the writers that came before is important, but he observed that the nature of that relationship resembles a more elemental psychical construction, specifically the Freudian relationship between a son and his father. Still, Bloom was not even the first "critic" to sense some kind of familial relationship

---

2. See Bakhtin's *The Dialogic Imagination: Four Essays,* ed. Michael Holquist, trans. Caryl Emerson and Michael Holquist (Austin: University of Texas Press, 1982). Taken together, these essays lay out Bakhtin's notion of dialogism and heteroglossia. Bakhtin saw language, particularly as expressed through novelistic discourse, as dialogic, or multivoiced. See also his work *Problems of Dostoevsky's Poetics,* trans. Caryl Emerson (Minneapolis: University of Minnesota Press, 1984).

3. Harold Bloom, *The Anxiety of Influence* (Oxford: Oxford University Press, 1973).

among works of literature. In classical Rome, Seneca the Younger, writing specifically about imitation, states:

> This is what our mind should do: it should hide away all the materials by which it has been aided, and bring to light only what it has made of them. Even if there shall appear in you a likeness to him who, by reason of your admiration, has left a deep impress upon you, I would have you resemble him as a child resembles his father, and not as a picture resembles its original; for a picture is a lifeless thing.[4]

In the Renaissance, Petrarch in a letter to Boccaccio picked up and expanded on this same idea:

> A proper imitator should take care that what he writes resemble the original without reproducing it. The resemblance should not be that of a portrait to the sitter—in that case the closer the likeness is the better—but it should be the resemblance of a son to his father. Therein is often a great divergence in particular features, but there is a certain suggestion, what our painters call an "air" most noticeable in the face and eyes, which makes the resemblance. As soon as we see the son, he recalls the father to us, although we should measure every feature we should find them all different. But there is a mysterious something there that has this power. Thus we writers must look to it that with a basis of similarity there should be many dissimilarities. And the similarity should be planted so deep that it can only be extricated by quiet meditation. The quality is to be felt rather than defined. Thus we may use another man's conceptions and the color of his style, but not his words. In the first case the resemblance is hidden deep; in the second it is glaring. The first procedure makes poets, the second makes apes.[5]

Of course neither Seneca nor Petrarch would comment on any psychical crisis that a writer/son has with an actual source/father, but finding such a father/son relationship an appropriate metaphor for the act of literary imita-

---

4. *Epistulae Morales*, 84.8–9, quoted and translated in Thomas M. Greene, *The Light in Troy: Imitation and Discovery in Renaissance Poetry* (New Haven, CT: Yale University Press), 95–96. My general practice in this study is to give extended prose passages only in translation; extended verse passages will be provided in both the original language and translation.

5. *Familiarium rerum libri* 23.19, quoted and translated by Greene, *The Light in Troy*, 95–96. See also Carol Everhart Quillen, *Rereading the Renaissance: Petrarch, Augustine, and the Language of Humanism* (Ann Arbor: University of Michigan Press, 1998) 134.

tion quite naturally leads, at least in a post-Freud (and a post-Bloom) era, to the psychical implications.

Despite the fact that Bloom's theory opens up the psychical significance of literary identity—and for that, Bloom's contribution is indispensable—the usefulness of Bloom himself, particularly for a study dealing with classical appropriation in a postclassical age, is problematic (despite his continuous claims that he is developing a "practical criticism").[6] On the most basic level, Bloom never accounts for the tremendous impact the classical world had on subsequent writers. Neither *Anxiety of Influence* nor Bloom's work *A Map of Misreading* looks beyond the immediate precursors of the writers discussed. The anxiety of *tradition* is largely missing from Bloom's approach; it is the direct anxiety of a named precursor that is the root of a writer's anxiety and his attempt at rewriting his models. Bloom's basic assertion is that writers suffer an Oedipal "anxiety" with regard to their predecessors, or their "literary fathers," and these literary fathers are typically specific writers who take on that Freudian father role (Spenser for Milton, Milton for Wordsworth, and so on). As a result, literature is a series of "misreadings" of earlier texts as poets ("strong poets" he calls them) attempt first to undermine and eventually to overcome their "fathers'" position of superiority. Bloom summarizes his own theory as follows:

> Poetic Influence—when it involves two strong, authentic poets—always proceeds by a misreading of the prior poet, an act of creative correction that is actually and necessarily a misinterpretation. The history of fruitful poetic influence, which is to say the main tradition of Western Poetry since the Renaissance, is a history of anxiety and self-saving caricature, of distortion, of perverse, willful revisionism without which modern poetry as such could not exist.[7]

The root of Bloom's reductionism lies in his attempt to transfer the literalness of Freudian psychoanalysis to his theory of literary tradition. In Bloom's reading of Freud, the father (and presumably the mother, who is not accounted for in Bloom's model) is a real entity, an individual with whom the developing psyche directly comes into contact. Therefore, in a Freudian-based concept of literary influence, Bloom looks for that real

---

6. Bloom continuously claims he is providing a practical criticism for reading poetry: "This book [*A Map of Misreading*] offers instruction in the practical criticism of poetry, in how to read a poem, on the basis of the theory of poetry set forth in my earlier book, *The Anxiety of Influence*." Bloom, *A Map of Misreading* (New York: Oxford University Press, 1975), 1.

7. Bloom, *The Anxiety of Influence*, 30.

entity, an actual identifiable writer whom the writer must overcome (just as the developing son must overcome his father's position of superiority). Bloom never does show exactly how the Freudian "mother" figure fits in (as the initial object of desire), nor does he ever really give an adequate definition of what a "strong poet" is—nor why the "strong/weak" binaries are needed at all. Also, he never really addresses the meaning of "authentic poets," the potential danger in reducing influence to "two" figures, the valorization of the "western canon," or the seemingly absent female poet. And why is this necessarily a *post*-Renaissance phenomenon? Bloom fails to discuss any of these issues. Perhaps the most troublesome element of Bloom is the reductive claim that "poems . . . are neither about subjects nor about themselves . . . they are necessarily about other poems."[8] Ultimately, Bloom's simplified understanding of Freud and his attempt to develop a binary father/son paradigm of literary imitation and influence close the door on many of the ideological, social, and structural elements that affect the writer's self-projection and acts of literary creation.

Some critics have definitely taken Bloom's ideas to more "practical" ends: Sandra Gilbert and Susan Gubar in *The Madwoman in the Attic* (1979) and more recently—and even more important to our current interest in the manifestation of the classical world in subsequent literary expression—Thomas Hubbard in *The Pipes of Pan* (1998). However, it is Thomas Greene's *The Light in Troy* (1982) that gives us the most substantial and useful Bloomian application to classical reception, especially in the early modern period.[9] Greene more carefully considers both the power of classical *imitatio* during the Renaissance and the role that *imitatio* plays in the tenuous constructions of history, the present moment, and the self:

> Imitation acts out a passage of history that is a retrospective version or construct, with all the vulnerability of a construct. It has no ground other than the "modern" universe of meanings it is helping to actualize and the past universe it points to allusively and simplifies. It seeks no suprahistorical order; it accepts the temporal, the contingent, and the specific as given. But it makes possible an emergent sense of identity, personal and cultural, by demonstrating the viability of diachronic itineraries. (19)

Greene asserts that the literary recreation of a (literary) history "fabricates a context that is itself of course subject to alteration, distortion, anachro-

---

8. Bloom, *A Map of Misreading*, 18.
9. Hubbard cites Greene several times in his book *The Pipes of Pan* (Ann Arbor: University of Michigan Press, 1998), most notably on p. 247.

nism," one that "provides only a semblance of rootedness"; however, that fabricated context is significant because "it represents a limited means, a human means, for dealing with the force of rupture" (18). A *human* means for dealing with rupture is a *psychical* means for dealing with the anxiety of fragmentation. Like the current study, Greene's is primarily a revision of, or supplement to, Bloom. Greene, responding to Paul de Man's statement that "the writer cannot renounce the claim to being modern but also cannot resign himself to his dependence on predecessors,"[10] believes that "it is precisely this dilemma which heuristic imitation quite consciously confronts and builds deliberately into the literary work. It points to a dependence which it then overcomes by a declaration of conditional independence."[11] The humanist poet is not "a neurotic son crippled by a Freudian family romance, which is to say he is not in Harold Bloom's terms Romantic. He is rather like the son in a classical comedy who displaces his father at the moment of reconciliation."[12] Greene understands the psychical implications of Bloom for classical appropriation, but he also recognizes the need for a more expansive understanding of identity formation and the role "worldview"—both the perceived past and present—plays in the identity formation of a writer.

Greene's categorization of Renaissance *imitatio* is much more practical than Bloom's so-called revisionary ratios, and the categories Greene articulates account for much more than simple poetic misreading; however, Greene's approach is also problematic on several levels. He defines different modes of imitation that factor into both an examination of textual manipulation and ideological pressure, something Bloom does not do. Especially relevant to the present discussion are Greene's definitions of "reproductive/sacramental," "eclectic," "heuristic," and "dialectical" imitation. Reproductive (or sacramental) imitation occurs when the writer sees no separation between himself and the single, "original" text that is being revered; eclectic imitation is the indiscriminate use of a blend of "sources" as if previous literature were a stockpile of topoi; in heuristic imitation the writer recognizes separation and difference between the worldviews of the original and his own work but seeks to reconcile those differences; and in dialectical imitation the separation and difference are not only left unresolved but are

---

10. Paul de Man, *Blindness and Insight: Essays in the Rhetoric of Contemporary Criticism* (Minneapolis: University of Minnesota Press, 1971), 162.

11. Thomas M. Greene, "Resurrecting Rome: The Double Task of the Humanist Imagination," in *Rome in the Renaissance: The City and the Myth*, ed. P. A. Ramsey (Binghamton, NY: Medieval and Renaissance Texts and Studies, 1982), 41.

12. Ibid.

actually exploited. The manner in which writers appropriate the classics in Greene's model is immensely helpful; but Greene, like Bloom, gives too much priority at times to the single precursor: "Most long poems also tend to reach out to a single privileged predecessor and bind themselves to that authenticating model with particularly intricate knots."[13] Although that statement is not entirely untrue, writers such as Milton, when they invoke classical models, tend more often to engage a codified tradition than a privileged predecessor. Greene does not simplify the relationship as radically as Bloom does, but he seems to focus at times on the particulars of *imitatio* (the allusions themselves and from whence they come) rather than on the power of the literary system that codifies those particulars. More troublesome in Greene's model is the lack of accounting for more contemporary psychoanalytical thought. Although he critically engages the implications of deconstruction on reception, in a study that emphasizes the relationship between history and the self, modes of self-projection, psychical and ideological ruptures, the anxiety of identity, and the pressures of ideological determinacy, the complete silence regarding thinkers like Jacques Lacan and Louis Althusser seems deafening. Although Greene's critical instincts suggest much about Lacanian psychoanalysis and Althusserian theories of cultural ideology, his complete failure to discuss the implications that post-Freudian psychoanalysis might have for his essentially psychoanalytic approach to literary history and literary identity (essential both in Bloom's original model and in his revision of Bloom) makes his work incomplete at the very least.

So while problems with Bloom abound, and Greene's insightful and more sophisticated revision of Bloom is, to a large degree, incomplete, there remains the reality that imitation and influence are substantial factors in the production of literature, that "anxiety" about a writer's own identity within tradition seems valid in a general sense, and that psychoanalytic approaches to identity formation are relevant to understanding that anxiety. This study proposes that rereading Bloom (and Greene) through a Lacanian lens can further help to validate Bloom's basic ideas about poetic history. Such a rereading can also suggest possibilities of a "non-reductive" version of Bloom as well various methods needed for a more holistic approach to influence that still focuses on the importance and significance of anxiety as a guiding force for the production of literary texts, especially those humanist texts that are grounded in Renaissance classicism. I am not proposing that we should ultimately reduce literary imitation and influence to a Lacanian "structure"

---

13. Greene, *The Light in Troy*, 51.

(such a structure, in any context, the later Lacan himself would reject); however, understanding what a Lacanian reformulation of Bloom might look like can give us a certain perspective on a psychoanalytical approach to literary history that can be useful when considered in broader terms—as I hope to show as this study progresses.

The question remains, why emphasize the classical world and early modern identity? There are so many discursive interplays between various literary periods, cultures, and self-representation in both Western and non-Western literary traditions that focusing on this one cultural "moment" and the history of its making might seem arbitrary. Certainly, one could apply the principles of this study to Greek and Roman, pre- and postromantic, Western and non-Western, or modern and postmodern convergences of literary voice as well; however, the specific impact of the classical world on the early modern conception of the self has a particular relevance. First, the Renaissance is truly *early* modern; it is a period of transition between the ancient (and medieval) world and the modern world as we think of it today. So many of the modern notions of the self, of the mind, of philosophical and scientific inquiry—and of course literary expression—can be traced directly to the early modern period, and the early modern understanding of the classical world as a source of authority and a necessary, but flawed, model of cultural sophistication and identity makes this period a kind of adolescent stage of Western identity. Second, the weight of the classical world is still being felt, still being carried through our modern development. That past is threaded throughout our philosophies, sciences, arts, politics—even our entertainment. We can neither fully accept that past nor abandon it; its influence has remained an unconscious core of our modern identity. In *Civilization and Its Discontents* (1930) Freud suggests the idea of a timeless unconscious, one that even seems to transcend the individual's ego to become part of a cultural unconscious. He imagines Rome itself as a "psychical entity," one that undergoes a kind of psychical development that we constantly interpret and reinterpret, and presumably integrate into our own constructions of ourselves in relation to the historical moment:

> Now let us, by a flight of imagination, suppose that Rome is not a human habitation but a psychical entity with a similarly long and copious past— an entity, that is to say, in which nothing that has once come into existence will have passed away and all the earlier phases of development continue to exist alongside the latest ones.[14]

---

14. Sigmund Freud, *Civilization and Its Discontents,* ed. and trans. James Strachey (New York and London: Norton, 1961), 17.

Freud's vision of Rome as the eternal city is one that mirrors the unconscious itself; the identity of Rome is both ancient and modern, and this identity is constantly in flux as we define this city by both its material reality (i.e., its ruins) and our own ideologically charged reinterpretation of those material remains. Richard Armstrong has carefully explored Freud's personal "compulsion for antiquity," but Freud's own compulsion can be said to mirror the *Western* compulsion for the classical past, the "memory work" that is always at play in building a present through an attempted return to the past.[15] However, what is clear, both in Freud himself and in Armstrong's discussion of Freud, is that the classical world is both the past and the present, both real and imagined—always exerting its pressure, its influence, its history, on our current identity and its own. And this fact was never more apparent than in the early modern period.

Despite my belief that Bloom, Freud, and Lacan all contribute to an understanding of subjectivity that can, and should, be considered closely in an evaluation of poetic identity and literary filiation, I do not intend to reduce literary history to a specific Bloomian, Freudian, or Lacanian reading. However, such an academic inquiry cannot ignore their theories of the unconscious, of identity, of projection, or of a psychical understanding of history; therefore, these three thinkers play an important role in this study. What I ultimately argue here is that for the Renaissance, the "looking back" to antiquity—its art, literature, philosophy, politics, nationalism— was, on the one hand, the primary source for a growing focus on self-identity and a secular world founded on introspection of the self; on the other hand, antiquity was the unattainable "Other," the object of a desire the Renaissance could never completely satisfy, a lack that could never be filled, but one that could also never be accepted. The classical world became a material reminder of past greatness as well as a symbol of Renaissance selfhood and cultural sophistication, but for humanists it also represented the source of a dialectic that both glorified and negated classicism. I argue that the classical world was temporally and ideologically foreign, but it was also integral to humanist identity formation. For the Renaissance to be something different, something progressive, humanist ideology also had to equip itself with methods of exposing a lack in the very myth it valorized. Ultimately, the fissures and ideological gaps humanists hoped to expose reveal the inherent ruptured characteristics of the classical texts themselves.

---

15. Richard H. Armstrong, *A Compulsion for Antiquity: Freud and the Ancient World* (Ithaca, NY: Cornell University Press, 2005).

In chapter 1, I explore the fundamental theoretical basis for my study of this "classical crisis" during the Renaissance. In particular, I look to Jacques Lacan and his views of identity formation as a supplement to Bloom's Freudian model of literary history and Greene's work on Renaissance imitation. Lacan offers a more nuanced discussion of anxiety than Bloom does. The manner in which anxiety interacts with fissures in a subject's self-projection I consider in terms of a writer's attempt to self-project within a formalized literary tradition and dominant ideological forces, the two of which are often at odds.

In chapter 2, I look at specific representations of the city "Rome" as a symbol of the classical world during the early modern period. What begins to emerge is an image of a Rome in ruins. Italian humanists literally excavated the ruins of Rome around them, which included, in a sense, the actual manuscripts of classical texts. Writers, too—Joachim du Bellay, Ben Jonson, and William Shakespeare—all present Rome as a kind of ruinous past that somehow must be reconstructed in their own images. After a close reading of du Bellay's *Les Antiquitez de Rome* (1558), as well as several of Shakespeare's and Jonson's so-called Roman plays, certain conclusions can be drawn. What I propose is that for humanists, the remnants of the classical world—monuments, coins, manuscripts, and mythology—serve as a kind of unstable physical or tangible connection to the "idea" of Rome. Humanists needed the greatness of Rome to be the source of their own identity (i.e., their own greatness), but those stones and fragmented texts were not *really* the actual Rome they sought; each artifact serves as what Lacan might call an *objet a,* artifacts of memory and identity, the accessible, but fragmented piece of a "wholeness" that can never be attained.

In chapter 3, I look at how classical texts are made the focus of writers' self-construction during the early modern period; I consider specifically the French poets Pierre de Ronsard and du Bellay, the English lyric poet Andrew Marvell, and the group known as the "sons of Ben." The split subject that emerges in the French poets hovers between an ideological emphasis on the vernacular and a perceived mythological authority of classical allusion. These poets cannot forgo the classical, even in their attempts at establishing a uniquely French voice, but their need to subvert the ancient world on which they draw also plays out in their poetry in ways that emphasize a crisis of poetic identity. Andrew Marvell provides an interesting English case study in the problems of invoking both myth and language as he self-translates his own Latin poem in "The Garden" and "Hortus." Building on arguments I have made elsewhere concerning the complexity of imitation in the seventeenth century (*Catullan Consciousness and the Early Modern Lyric*

[2004]), I demonstrate that the "sons of Ben" simultaneously revere and desecrate the models that they use, but theirs is a more confident undermining of sources. In their use of Catullus, for example, seemingly superficial allusions are systematically used against the authority of the sources themselves. In fact, a trend begins to emerge whereby the closer the imitation, the further removed from the original contexts the allusions seem to be. Horace's *carpe diem* is stripped—often violently—from its context, and then transferred (and transformed) into a masculine, Cavalier discourse. My ultimate argument in chapter 3 is that poetic identity *must* be constructed in these ways. The poets here must reveal and expose the gaps in their classical predecessors in order for their own poetry, their own poetic identity, to exist. For critics, an understanding of the early modern process of poetic identity comes about only through an understanding of how such identity relates to the classical texts to which these writers do violence.

Chapter 4 is the first of two chapters that engage John Milton as an extended case study of the crisis of poetic identity. Although Milton is frequently considered a kind of perfect Christian humanist because of his ability to combine the classical and the Christian, he represents humanism's classical crisis at its most volatile—but richest—point. A close reading of Milton's texts and sources supports this assessment. Milton's work, in this reading, proves to be a battleground for a literary tradition Milton *needs* in order to validate his own place in that tradition, and a *Christian* tradition that reinforces Milton's sense of self as a seventeenth-century man of God. As a result, Milton's corpus is constructed using a method of classical imitation that is always in flux, constantly reflecting on and revising both its models and, more importantly, its own previous imitation of those models. In chapter 4, I analyze a selection of Milton's early work in Latin and English: his Latin elegies, the "Nativity Ode," and his famous pastoral elegy, *Lycidas*. Examining Milton's work closely in relation to his sources (Roman elegists in general and, in the case of his pastoral model, Virgil and Theocritus in particular), we find that Milton's imitation is not stable, but a constantly fluctuating poetic consciousness that fights to be both part of the grand (classical) tradition and an autonomous voice of seventeenth-century religious ideology.

Chapter 5 demonstrates that in his major works—*Paradise Lost, Samson Agonistes,* and *Paradise Regained*—Milton develops "heroism" as a guiding principle and perhaps his most significant theme. However, he displays vastly different notions of heroism in these works. The manifestations of the Christian "hero" in *Paradise Lost* and *Samson Agonistes* are formed from and then positioned against the "classical" hero of antiquity as Milton tries both to conform to "tradition" and also to create a new Christian hero that reflects the deep-rooted religious ideologies of seventeenth-century England. Ultimately, the conflictive interplay between the past and the present causes Milton to abandon classical allusion per se and to move toward a more structural understanding of the classical hero, one that can finally be grounded in antiquity while displaying Milton's own sense of Christian sacrifice and suffering. The relationship Milton forms with his "classical history" can be seen as a fundamental mode of self-fashioning, of a subject formation that is part of Lacan's notion of the Symbolic, as Milton strives to become part of the very "system" of literary history.

In the epilogue, I continue this discussion, showing that *Paradise Regained* is a fundamental abandonment of the past and a sign that Milton's text has slipped firmly into a Symbolic self-positioning. I argue that this humanist crisis of imitation and influence is a crisis of identity formation, and that the identity in question is not separate from the classical world but rather an extension of it. Just as Rome is perceived as a natural progression from Greece, so is Renaissance Europe a natural progression from Rome. Humanism is, I reemphasize, the classical world *reborn,* but since literal rebirth is impossible, since Rome of the past—the "real," classical Rome—is dead and buried, it must be reconstructed from fragments, recreated in the imagination, psyche, and ideological realties of a different world. In addition, I consider the implications this general approach to literary filiation might have in other periods and in other contexts. The search for identity for writers is an ongoing quest, and as long as that is the case, the quest will be rooted in crisis.

Chapter 1

The Convergence of Voice, The Artifacts of Memory

Theoretical Orientations[1]

Tradition is a matter of much wider significance. It cannot be inherited, and if you want it you must obtain it by great labour. It involves, in the first place, the historical sense, which we may call nearly indispensable to anyone who would continue to be a poet beyond his twenty-fifth year; and the historical sense involves a perception, not only of the pastness of the past, but of its presence; the historical sense compels a man to write not merely with his own generation in his bones, but with a feeling that the whole of the literature of Europe from Homer and within it the whole of the literature of his own country has a simultaneous existence and composes a simultaneous order. This historical sense, which is a sense of the timeless as well as of the temporal and of the timeless and of the temporal together, is what makes a writer traditional. And it is at the same time what makes a writer most acutely conscious of his place in time, of his contemporaneity.

—T. S. Eliot, "Tradition and the Individual Talent"

Anxiety and the Lack of Lack

One of the most obvious shortcomings in Harold Bloom's theory of influence is that the key concept, "anxiety," is never systematically or analytically dealt with. In Bloom, anxiety is never truly defined or discussed as a clinical, psychical response; it is presented vaguely and abstractly. Greene

---

1. Portions of this chapter previously appeared as "Influence, Anxiety, and the Symbolic: A Lacanian Rereading of Bloom," *Intertexts* 9.2 (2006): 123–38.

unfortunately follows Bloom's lead in this regard. However, both Freud and Lacan discuss anxiety in much greater detail than either Bloom or Greene suggests. Freud's early work on anxiety presents it as a primarily libidinal, physiological response to unsatisfied sexual desire, but Freud himself later recognized the psychical scope of anxiety.[2] In fact, Freud considered anxiety to be a crucial point of psychical analysis as a whole: "The problem of anxiety is a nodal point at which the most various and important questions converge, a riddle whose solution would be bound to throw a flood of light on our whole mental existence."[3] Although Bloom may have picked up on the significance of anxiety's power in the study of literary identity and tradition, he does not seem interested in the more subtle distinctions in Freud's account of anxiety, including the differences between automatic and signal anxiety, the latter of which is connected to the disintegration of the self, the former a kind of frontline anxiety that alerts the subject to the possibilities of that disintegration.[4] To take Bloom's theory of the anxiety of influence to its natural Freudian end, the possibility that the writer could be completely devoid of a poetic identity (i.e., a disintegrated self) is automatic anxiety, and the anxieties that are produced or rather played out within the textual negotiations with predecessors are the signal anxiety that suggests, albeit unconsciously, the possibility of an empty poetic consciousness, a voice that lacks the creative power of those precursors.

Like Freud, Lacan also understood the significance of anxiety and its function in the construction and projection of the ego. Lacan's reinterpretation and reformulation of Freud's model of human psychical development are now well known; however, a brief—and necessarily simplified—overview will help establish this study's context, particularly with regard to how anxiety functions within a subject's (writer's) desired (literary) self-projection and the realities of a Symbolic manifestation of lack. Since Bloom's model is based on the Freudian development of the psyche and the "family romance" that ensues, how Lacan reconceptualizes those developmental stages has implications for a reconceptualized Bloomian reading.[5] Lacan

---

2. See Sigmund Freud, *Inhibitions, Symptoms, and Anxiety*, vol. 20 of the Standard Edition (1929), in *The Complete Psychological Works of Sigmund Freud* (New York: Norton, 1990).

3. See Freud's *Introductory Lectures on Psycho-Analysis*, The Standard Edition (1916–17), 16: 393.

4. See Jean Laplanche and J. B. Pontalis, *The Language of Psychoanalysis* (London: Hogarth Press, 1974), 198.

5. My reading of Lacan is more Freudian than many other recent commentaries on Lacan, such as those by Žižek, Lyotard, and others. Not only is understanding Lacan's Orders in a Freudian context necessary for a reconceptualization of Bloom, but Lacan's principles had a Freudian foundation and thus can best be understood by returning them to Freudian origins, at least ini-

suggests that three orders constitute the psyche. The Imaginary Order represents the state in which an infant's self-identity is defined wholly by his/her biological dependence on the mother and the perception of preverbal images; ultimately, the Imaginary becomes the source of a preverbal self-recognition, the narcissistic manner in which the self wishes to project itself. The Mirror Stage for Lacan represents the beginning of this self-recognition, the understanding that the self is separate, literally, from the mother, and that certain things (*objet a*)—sounds, human waste, the mother's touch, and so on—are also separate from the physical self. In other words, self-representation to and for the self alone is recognized as unsustainable.[6] There is an outside reality that makes self-projection a communicative process. This creates a sense of lack and a desire to regain the security of a self whole in itself. However, with this recognition, there is an Imaginary castration that takes place, and the child then moves into the father-dominated Symbolic Order. In this stage, the psyche is inevitably affected by language as well as social rules and conventions, signifiers that can only denote and suggest the self-projection and identity desired in the Imaginary; this is identified by Lacan as the "Law of the Father." The Symbolic Order is characterized by fragmentation, difference, and the desire to repossess the security of the isolated self-knowledge of the Imaginary Order and now to situate that desire within the "law" of the Symbolic. Finally, the Real Order represents the remote, "unutterable" part of the psyche that exists beyond both the specular existence of the Imaginary and the linguistic existence of the Symbolic and contains those strong emotional feelings associated with birth, death, and sexuality. The absolute unity of the "Real" is largely inaccessible to the individual, manifesting itself only in fleeting moments of joy and pain, called "jouissance."[7] Our very existence within

---

tially. Numerous summaries of the Lacanian Orders have been offered, none of which are identical. See Dino Felluga, "Modules on Lacan: On the Structure of the Psyche," in *Introductory Guide to Critical Theory,* January 31, 2011, Purdue University, December 2, 2011, http://www.purdue.edu/guidetotheory/psychoanalysis/lacanstructure.html; Paul Allen Miller, *Subjecting Verses: Latin Love Elegy and the Emergence of the Real* (Princeton, NJ: Princeton University Press, 2003), 5–6; M. Keith Booker, *A Practical Introduction of Literary Theory and Criticism* (New York: Longman, 1995), 35–37; Jacques-Alain Miller, "Translator's Note," in Jacques Lacan, *The Four Fundamental Concepts of Psychoanalysis,* ed. Jacques-Alain Miller and trans. Alan Sheridan (New York: Norton, 1981), 279–80; and Fredric Jameson, "Imaginary and Symbolic in Lacan: Marxism, Psychoanalytic Criticism, and the Problem of the Subject," *Yale French Studies* 55–56 (1977): 338–95.

6. Lacan discusses the Imaginary Order and Mirror Stage throughout his career. His foundational early study on the Mirror Stage is "The Mirror Stage as Formative of the Function of the I," in *Ecrits* (New York: W. W. Norton 2006), 75–81. See Elisabeth Roudinesco, "The Mirror Stage: An Obliterated Archive," in *The Cambridge Companion to Lacan,* ed. Jean-Michel Rabaté (Cambridge: Cambridge University Press, 2003), 25–34.

7. On these glimpses into the realm of the Real, Lacan comments: "The real may be represented by the accident, the noise, the small element of reality, which is evidence that we are not dream-

the Symbolic and our self-identity rest within the conflict between isolation and fragmentation, and a desire for our Imaginary self, which is pitted against the distance of the Real.[8] While Freud, at least for Bloom, gives us the literal family romance of the son, mother, and father, Lacan ultimately sees these stages as more representative, more metaphorical. The mother becomes not the actual mother, but the isolation of the Imaginary. The father, whose place the Freudian male wishes to overtake, is now the structural system into which the subject must enter and take a place.[9] The Symbolic is fragmentary, because a "true" self-projection is impossible within the referential system of language and social power structures.

Like Freud, Lacan saw the immensity of anxiety within his model of development. Freud called anxiety the "nodal point" that, when examined, could offer insight into the whole of "mental existence." Lacan dedicated an entire seminar to the topic of anxiety, *L'Angoisse* (1962), in which he refers to anxiety as precisely the point "where you will find waiting everything that was involved in my previous discourse and where, together, there await a certain number of terms which may appear not to have been sufficiently connected up for you up [*sic*] to the present. You will see on this terrain of anxiety how, by being more closely knotted together, each one will take its place still better."[10] Lacan suggests here that his discussion of anxiety shows

ing. But, on the other hand, this reality is not so small, for what wakes us is the other reality hidden behind the lack of that which takes the place of representation—this, says Freud, is the *Trieb*" (*Four Fundamental Concepts*, 60). Jacques-Alain Miller describes the Real as "the ineliminable residue of all articulation, the foreclosed element, which may be approached, but never grasped: the umbilical cord of the symbolic" (*Four Fundamental Concepts*, 280). For further discussions of the Lacanian Real, which have been prolific and varied, see Slavoj Žižek, *Interrogating the Real* (London: Continuum, 2005); Catherine Belsey, *Culture and the Real* (London: Routledge, 2005); and Rex Butler, *Jean Baudrillard: The Defence of the Real* (London: Sage, 1999), who offers a different perspective on Lacan's Real than Žižek does, calling Žižek "brilliant . . . provocative" but "less Lacanian, than he claims" (53). See also Miller, *Subjecting Verses;* and Bruce Fink, *The Lacanian Subject: Between Language and Jouissance* (Princeton, NJ: Princeton University Press, 1996).

8. See Miller, "Translator's Notes," 279–80; Booker, *A Practical Introduction*, 35–37; Miller, *Subjecting Verses*, 5–6; Sean Homer, *Jacques Lacan* (New York: Routledge, 2005); Fink, *The Lacanian Subject;* Dylan Evans, *An Introductory Dictionary of Lacanian Psychoanalysis* (London: Routledge, 1996); Ellie Ragland-Sullivan, *Jacques Lacan and the Philosophy of Psychoanalysis* (Urbana: University of Illinois Press, 1986).

9. See Lacan, *The Psychoses, 1955–1956: The Seminar of Jacques Lacan, Book 3*, ed. Jacques-Alain Miller, trans. Russell Grigg (New York: Norton, 1997), 96: "The Oedipus complex means that the imaginary, in itself an incestuous and conflictual relation, is doomed to conflict and ruin. In order for the human being to be able to establish the most natural of relations . . . a third party has to intervene, one that is the image of something successful, the model of some harmony. . . . There has to be a law, a chain, a symbolic order, the intervention of the order of speech, that is, of the father. Not the natural father, but what is called the father."

10. All translated passages from *L'Angoisse* are from Cormac Gallagher, *The Seminar of Jacques Lacan X: Anxiety* (London: Karnac Books, 2002). Consistent with the original manuscripts, I will cite excerpts by lecture date. This quote is from November 14, 1962 (11.14.62).

many of his other concepts in a clearer light; likewise, his other concepts help us to understand anxiety. And indeed, in *L'Angoisse,* Lacan has much to say about the *objet a,* the Imaginary, castration, the Real, object relations, and the identification of the ego. Even before the 1962 seminar, Lacan frequently cited the significance of anxiety, particularly Freud's concept of signal anxiety:

> Anxiety is not a sort of energy that the subject has to apportion out in order to constitute objects. . . . Anxiety is always defined as appearing suddenly, or arising. To each of the objectal relations there corresponds a mode of identification of which anxiety is the signal. The identifications . . . precede the ego-identification. But even when this latter will have been achieved, every new re-identification of the subject will cause anxiety to arise. . . . Anxiety is a connotation, a signal, as Freud always very clearly formulated it, a quality, a subjective colouration.[11]

Still, *L'Angoisse* is the most complete treatment of anxiety by Lacan, and although much of the seminar is concerned with elements of clinical treatment that are not directly applicable to the current study,[12] there are a few key aspects of his seminar on anxiety that are relevant here. First of all, for Lacan, anxiety arises not because of lack, but because of a lack of lack. In other words, when lack is not recognized, when the subject is too secure in his/her self-positioning, anxiety is the result. As Charles Shepherdson puts it, "For Lacan . . . if anxiety arises it is rather because lack has not yet been instituted for the subject . . . it [anxiety] is rather the first incarnation of a lack that opens the field in which language will find its place. . . . Lacan argues that anxiety is the index of an Other that is too close or too full; it indicates not a lack to be overcome, but a lack that has not been fully established, and requires elaboration in order to be secured."[13] Transferring this idea to the Bloomian model, writers do not suffer anxiety because they cannot overcome an Other, but rather because they do not understand the gap (and the resulting lack) that exists between themselves and that Other.

---

11. *Freud's Papers and Techniques, 1953–1954: The Seminar of Jacques Lacan, Book 1,* ed. Jacques-Alain Miller, trans. John Forrester (New York: Norton, 1988), 68–69.

12. For the most complete critical treatment of Lacan's seminar on anxiety, see Roberto Harari's *Lacan's Seminar on Anxiety: An Introduction* (New York: Other Press, 2001). Although Harari characterizes his book as "an introduction," his work is a thorough and comprehensive commentary on the seminar.

13. Shepherdson, foreword to *Lacan's Seminar on Anxiety,* xlviii n. 21.

Also central to Lacan's anxiety is the role of the object for the subject seeking to fill the gap of an anticipated identity castration (the loss of the perceived self within the Imaginary). What Lacan proposes is that the subject ultimately fixates on objects that are negotiable, that is, they can be exchanged, emulated, battled, and perhaps even overcome:

> Along the plane of the primary identification, the original miscognition of the subject as a whole in his specular image, then the transitivist reference which is established in his relationship with the imaginary other, his fellow, which makes him always badly separated out from this identity with the other and introduces here mediation, a common object which is an object of rivalry, an object, then, whose status is going to begin from the notion of belonging or not: it belongs to you or it belongs to me. In this field, there are two sorts of objects, the ones that can be shared, and those which cannot be. Those which cannot be, when I see them involved all the same in this domain of sharing, with the other objects, whose status rests entirely on rivalry, this ambiguous rivalry which is at the same time emulation but also agreement, they are priceable objects, they are objects of exchange. (*L'Angoisse* 1.9.63)

When the subject fails to recognize the true lack, the true separation between itself and the Other,[14] objects, the *objet petit a,* function as placeholders that subvert or conceal the presence of lack (i.e., they create a lack of lack in the subject).[15] For writers who strive for that autonomous poetic voice, previous texts become these Lacanian objects, and regardless of whether or not the writer embraces these objects or rejects them, "the ambiguous rivalry which is at the same time emulation" facilitates the operations of intertextuality and exposes the underlying anxiety that exchange with the objects works to hide.

---

14. Lacan identifies this inexpressible, unattainable Other as "the essential object which is not an object any longer, but this something faced with which all words cease and all categories fail, the object of anxiety par excellence." *The Ego in Freud's Theory and in the Technique of Psychoanalysis, 1954–1955: The Seminar of Jacques Lacan, Book II* (New York: W. W. Norton & Company, 1991), 164. Lacan also discusses anxiety in *Seminar IV: Object-Relations,* 1956/57; *Seminar VIII: Transference,* 1960/61; and, later, *Seminar XXII: 'R-I-S,'* 1975/76.

15. "In so far as it is an *objet a* reduced, of its nature, to a punctiform, evanescent function, it leaves the subject in ignorance as to what there is beyond the appearance." Lacan, *Four Fundamental Concepts,* 77.

Anxious Influence and a
Lacanian Reconceptualization of Bloom

Bloom suggests that the literary precursor represents an Oedipal father figure whom the strong poet must battle and overcome, but considering some
of these basic Lacanian concepts, I would suggest that writers—*initially, as
readers*—are first joined to their precursors in a manner reminiscent of the
Lacanian Imaginary Order. In the most basic form of literary self-representation, there is no differentiation between the writer and the source. The
reader, who is in a sense in a preverbal state (a prewritten state) projects
himself or herself organically onto the text. Images, themes, allusions, all
are fed to the writer by a mother figure, not an Oedipal father. However,
eventually the writer realizes that those things he imitates are not his own,
that his own self-image, temporally and ideologically, is different and separate from his "literary mother," and literary projection is a communicative
act that requires entry into a referential system—of language, of tradition,
of conventions. It is at this point that he moves into a Symbolic realm,
in which he must deal with the fragmentation and ideological differences
between his own work and that of his predecessors. Poetic individuality,
which will always be defined by some sense of lack, and the overcoming
of anxiety (or desire)—which is caused by a desire to hold a position of
significance, to be a signifier in the structure of literary tradition—can be
achieved only by conforming to the laws of literary convention and tradition, of which even his predecessors are a part. The Real Order is the
inarticulable place of absolute unity, pure creation, distant from both the
image of self projected in the Imaginary and the referential subjectivity of
the Symbolic. The Real contains for the writer those deep intense drives for
creation and the fear of being obsolete, and the writer's *jouissance* manifests
itself in literature when the joy of literary creation or the fear of obsoles-
cence (i.e., a literary death) becomes, regardless of dominant themes explicit
in the work, the focal point of the poet. The Real, the possibility of a pure
creation beyond the limitations of language and structure, is the force that
drives writers to write and whose distance is the ultimate source of those
writers' anxiety.

With this Lacanian perspective on the Bloomian model, the critic can
approach imitation and influence as an anxious process of defining a poetic
self within the conflict caused by the desire for both separation from and
dependence on predecessors. Bloom states that all poetry is about previous poetry; this, again, is an overstatement. Poetry, like all discourse, is
constructed from other discourses—including the religious, social, political,

and sexual discourses of any given culture, each of which has the ability to function as a "master signifier" that impacts a subject's understanding of all signifiers. Still, like Bloom, I would assert that the poetry of others is always present. For any poet to self-project, he must be both "like" and "unlike" his predecessors. He recognizes that without his predecessors his work is lacking, but in order to be a true autonomous "subject" he must also identify a lack in his predecessors and attempt to fill that lack with his own poetry. When he fails to identify or to deal with that lack, anxiety is the result.

The risk in such an approach, as in Bloom, is to reduce poetic history, imitation, and influence to a single psychical structure. But Lacan hardly allows for such reductionism, since the entire notion of the self in the Symbolic is illusionary, is dictated by a conception of self based on difference and signifiers leading endlessly to other signifiers, a fact that also illustrates the subject's continued presence in the Imaginary as well. The Symbolic is not just a single system of signifiers, but *systems* of signifiers, all of which must be negotiated by the self in an attempt at self-construction. Like everyone else, writers must enter into numerous ideological systems that often conflict with one another, and writers have the added discursive system of "genre" or "convention," which governs the existence of both the writer *and* his predecessors. The original connection and unity writers-to-be have with their predecessors exist in the Imaginary; the attempt at positioning one's own work among those predecessors can exist only in the Symbolic. The Symbolic is where Bloom's "strong poet" must exist.

I would suggest that there is a moment of unconscious recognition that a reader/writer experiences regarding his own separateness and distance from previous literature. It can be said that in a sense all writers, before they are an entity called a "writer," are joined to literature by the act of reading (of "viewing" in the case of drama and film, of "hearing" in the case of the oral tradition, etc.). The "needs" of the reader are met by the other, by that literature they read—pleasure, pity, fear, catharsis. However, when one begins to "write," the original union is broken, like the child who gazes in the mirror and recognizes his own "self" and his own disconnect with the mother. At that moment, the individual identifies himself as a "writer," but typically the beginner's own writing is inadequate; writing does not meet those needs in the same way that reading did. The writer attempts to reunite with the original by imitating; his work is derivative, is an attempt at recreating what he valued, what he needed, originally from the source. He mistakenly believes that his own writing is his poetic self. Being derivative, however, makes it difficult to express what he needs (now, what he *demands*) from the source. Even now, when the writer reads there is an evident gap, a lack in both the other's work as well as his own: the lack in his own exists because it cannot "do" what the other work does, and the lack in the other exists because it cannot fill the lack in the writer's own work. The experience of literature for the writer is now different from that of the "reader"; pleasure, fear, pity, all the needs that the work of literature originally met, now become the very things that should show the writer that he is different and separate. Ultimately, the desire that is born is not for anything specific (it cannot be to have the original oneness the reader felt with the text, which would now be impossible), but it is to hold a place in the very system of literature, to be his own signifier in the chain of signifiers that makes up the literary tradition—the system itself makes that seem possible. T. S. Eliot in "Tradition and the Individual Talent" suggests the same:

> No poet, no artist of any art, has his complete meaning alone. His significance, his appreciation is the appreciation of his relation to the dead poets and artists. . . . The necessity that he shall conform, that he shall cohere, is not onesided; what happens when a new work of art is created is something that happens simultaneously to all works of art which preceded it. The existing monuments form an ideal order among themselves, which is modified by the introduction of the new (the really new) work of art among them. The existing order is complete before the new work arrives. (15)

For the writer, this is entry into a Symbolic mode of identity formation; this is the point where the writer's identity roots itself in the conventions and traditions of genre, which validate the writer's work, and in the ideological circumstances that construct self-identity within a given cultural and social context. It is not a specific source (i.e., other) with which the poet must contend; rather, the poet must contend with establishing his work's place and value within the system—and for that poet working in the Symbolic, such security within that system always seems to be a structural possibility.

So we return to Bloom's "strong poet" and the assertion that the anxiety of influence exists when a poet attempts to position himself in tradition while at the same time breaking from it—a process necessary in the Symbolic realm of self-construction. Bloom's definition of the strong poet (and again it is not a strong definition) is this: strong poets are "major figures with the persistence to wrestle with their strong precursors, even to the death."[16] Bloom must not have sensed what is an essentially poststructuralist element in that definition: a strong poet is one who positions himself

---

16. Bloom, *Anxiety of Influence*, 5.

against a strong precursor, who, consequently, must position himself against a strong precursor, who, consequently, must. . . . This same basic idea is one of the real strengths of contemporary theories of poetic intertextuality: that literary influence is not as much source-oriented as it is an endless chain of sources with no ultimate source at all. This is where Bloom fails. He always suggests that there is a single source, a single literary father with whom the strong poet battles. But an individual precursor and the poems he writes are nothing more than the *objet a,* the illusionary, seemingly attainable object that falsely represents the true, unquenchable desire of the poet. According to Bloom, the poet uses "tropes" as his "defense" against his anxiety over belatedness and his battle to elevate himself above his own time. The weapons the young poet uses are misprision, misinterpretation, and the misreading of previous strong poets. The problem with Bloom's analysis is that misprision, misinterpretation, and misreading can occur only if we (or rather the writers themselves) assume there is a correct reading at all. Either consciously or unconsciously the writer would have to "know" what the correct reading of the previous text is and then subvert that reading. Consistent with Freud's idea that the boy wants to overtake the father, Bloom chooses to focus on the writer's need to move *away* from the predecessor by implementing these various misreadings. But as I have already suggested, those other writers more accurately represent the Lacanian mother figure to whom the writer would like to return—if he only could. Anxiety is at least as much caused by the inexpressible, unperceived lack of union with the Other as it is the desire to move away from it. The writer does not misinterpret in order to subvert; he repositions himself and his own work, because he must. This is suggested by Lacan himself when he speaks of the patient recalling the history of his own self-making: "She relates in the present origins of her own person. And she does this in a language that allows her discourse to be understood by her contemporaries and that also presupposes their present discourse."[17] Ideological and discursive differences are part of what makes union impossible. Anxiety is the result of a writer's inability to be "like" a predecessor because difference, both literary and ideological, is what legitimizes the writer within the system itself. The writer cannot return to the original, cannot have the union he first had with the precursor; he therefore goes after the structural position of the precursor, which he sees as a center to the structure itself. Consider Lacan's own statement regarding imitation of Freud: "The point here is not to imitate him [Freud]. In

---

17. *Ecrits,* trans. Bruce Fink (New York: Norton, 2006), 212. All subsequent quotes from *Ecrits* come from this edition.

order to rediscover the effect of Freud's speech, I won't resort to its terms but rather to the principles that govern it" (*Ecrits* 241). This is basically the state of our writer within the Symbolic: rediscovery comes not through imitation per se but through the principles of the precursor's own existence, the precursor's structural place in literary history. Ultimately, there is no center, no central meaning to a text as Bloom sees it, nor is there a central position in literary history at all. A belated poet's reading of a strong precursor is not a misinterpretation; it is an ideological gap, one that makes it impossible to be both like and unlike the predecessor.

Still, somehow strong writers, writers writing from the Symbolic, *must* be both like and unlike their predecessors—at least to a degree. They must be part of the tradition, which means they base their poetic identity on those who wrote before them, but they must be original, current, and they have to be as much part of their own historical moment as their precursors were part of theirs. Where does this leave the "strong poet"? First, it leaves him genres, systems of discourse that establish specific qualities to which he must adhere, but from which he can also deviate. Second, the strong poet has to move among his own historical moment, be part of the "law" that dictates his identity within his own culture. A center of poetic influence is impossible, since it is the structural position of the precursor—not the precursor itself—that is the object of desire, and it is the failure to recognize the essential lack in that object that is the source of the anxiety.

In addition to the evaluation of *specific* allusions and references to precursors, we must recognize that the primary discursive structures within which poets work are tied closely to genre and tradition. Genre, along with the conventions that make it up, represents the "law" of poetic identity; it is that "law" that is the true father figure. Genre is the structure that defines the place of both the writer and his precursors. As I have already proposed, the writer cannot have the union with a precursor that he initially had as a reader, so the writer strives to be the structural equal—or even superior—to all precursors. Genre supplies the means of establishing the precursor's imminence, it supplies the means of recognizing lack in the precursor, and it ultimately provides the current poet with a means to be both like the other and the filler of the ideological lack in that other. Genre provides the system that allows such negotiation to take place. Without the various generic discourses, the poetic ego would suffer complete separation from the past, from tradition, and such separation would make it impossible for the writer to have an identity within literary tradition at all. The "law" of any given genre allows for enough individual movement within the genre that poetic self-identity can be established once the lack in others who have also existed in that genre has been exposed, and it is a gap waiting to be filled by the new poet and his own ideological present. Therefore, critics must realize that more than with sources or direct allusions, a writer's engagement with the literary structure itself says more about a writer's engagement with his predecessors than any direct reference could. My primary purpose here is not so much to provide a Lacanian system of interpretation or to specifically critique Bloom and Greene through Lacanian psychoanalysis as it is to use Lacan as a supplement to realize more fully the implications of Bloom and Greene for Renaissance humanism.

Humanism and the Ideologies of the Self

The term "humanism"—as a cultural, intellectual, and artistic concept—was not commonly used until the early nineteenth century, but there were without question dominant ideological forces that governed Renaissance attitudes toward the self—primarily Christianity, but also a new secular humanism and an entire period of political thought and revision of that thought.[18] In fact, these ideologies and the construction of the Renaissance self were closely aligned. Although Louis Althusser's conception of "ideology" is sometimes vague, and its connection to the "self" from a psychoanalytic approach undefined, Althusser did recognize that some relationship between the unconscious and ideology exists—even though he clearly declined the invitation to define that relationship—and it is ultimately a relationship that proves relevant for an understanding of Renaissance humanism:

> I have stopped short (quite clearly) before the question that interests you about the "relations" between ideology (or concrete ideological formations) and the unconscious. I have said that there must be some relation there, but at the same time I forbade myself from inventing it—considering that

---

18. There has been substantial work on Renaissance humanism over the years. See, for example, Douglas Bush, *The Renaissance and English Humanism* (Toronto: University of Toronto Press, 1939); Myron P. Gilmore, *The World of Humanism* (New York: Harper, 1952); Karl H. Dannenfeldt, ed., *The Renaissance: Medieval or Modern?* (Boston: D. C. Heath, 1959); Hans Baron, *The Crisis of the Early Italian Renaissance: Civic Humanism and the Republican Liberty in an Age of Classicism and Tyranny* (Princeton, NJ: Princeton University Press, 1966); Denys Hay and Nicolai Robinstein, eds., *The Age of the Renaissance* (New York: McGraw-Hill, 1967); Robert Weiss, *The Dawn of Humanism* (New York: Haskell, 1970); Paul O. Kristeller, *Renaissance Thought and Its Sources* (New York: Columbia University Press, 1979); Jessica Wolfe, *Humanism, Machinery, and Renaissance Literature* (Cambridge: Cambridge University Press, 2004).

it was for me a problem provisionally without solution, for myself or perhaps not only for myself—for myself in any event.[19]

Despite Althusser's unwillingness to assert exactly what the relationship
is, his writings often suggest the implications of ideology for a psychoanalytic approach to examining the ideological forces that shape cultural self-
consciousness; he closely aligns the imaginary consciousness of the individual and the dominant ideologies that guide that consciousness:

> We observe that the ideological representation of ideology is itself forced
> to recognize that every "subject" endowed with a "consciousness" and
> believing in the "ideas" that his "consciousness" inspires in him and freely
> accepts, must "*act* according to his ideas," must therefore inscribe his own
> ideas as a free subject in the actions of his material practice.[20]

Althusser suggests that the individual's own consciousness functions within
a given ideological position while the very material actions that result from
the ideology give the subject a sense of self. He also suggests the presence
of a "cultural consciousness" as individuals collectively function within an
ideology that both guides individual actions and serves as a system through
which individuals are initiated into the dominant culture.

Despite the fact that Althusser was friends with Lacan, attended his
seminars, corresponded regularly with him, and in fact seemed to be influenced greatly by him, a fundamental connection between the function of
ideology and Lacan's idea of the Symbolic has been undervalued. Lacan's
notion of the Symbolic was literally the subject's entry into the system of
language (and what Lacan associated with the Law of the Father), but in a
larger sense the Symbolic represents the subject's participation in the various discursive patterns of ideology, the discourses that allow the ego to
enter into society and to assume the place of others in that cultural system. Micaela Janan, in *When the Lamp Is Shattered: Desire and Narrative
in Catullus,* asserts that Plato, Freud, and Lacan all propose the notion of a
divided self, and, for Catullus, Janan finds an intricate interplay between the
psychical workings of "desire" and the presence of Roman social values that
unavoidably are sought after, tested, undermined, and then reconstructed
as desire meanders through the speaker's attempts to fill the gaps in identity

---

19. Quoted in Louis Althusser, *Writings on Psychoanalysis: Freud and Lacan,* ed. Olivier Corpet
and François Matheron, trans. Jeffrey Mehlman (New York: Columbia University Press, 1996), 4–5.

20. Althusser, "Ideology and Ideological State Apparatuses," in *Lenin and Philosophy and Other
Essays,* trans. Ben Brewster (New York: Monthly Review Press, 1971), 167–68.

and find a projection for torn desires he cannot reconcile.[21] Despite Janan's sometimes difficult theoretical framework, she does demonstrate, through Lacan, that psychical desire is linked closely to the positioning of a cultural ideological system, which possesses as many inherent gaps and fissures as the unconscious itself. Beyond language—or perhaps as an extension of language—ideology is at the heart of the Symbolic, and ideology governs the subject's conception of himself/herself and the cultural consciousness of society as a whole. Total deviation from ideology is not a viable option, for it is in the seemingly secure place of the Symbolic that the fragmented self finds some feeling of wholeness—even though that feeling is ultimately illusionary. The medieval Christian ideological domination from which humanists sought to escape could not be replaced by an actual humanistic secularism, but it could be psychically realigned with a perceived classical ideology that provided humanists with a secular component to their fundamentally Christian self-identity.[22]

The model of the unconscious that Lacan provides illustrates a subject unconsciously grasping for both the unwavering wholeness that the Real might provide and the psychical journey back to the specular, Ideal-I of the Imaginary Order, and from the collective consciousness of the humanist program, Rome functions as that Other that can never be realized. Just as Lacan describes the analysand digging into his own past and bringing back "in the present the origins of her person'" (*Ecrits* 212), Renaissance humanism attempted to return to the classical origins of its own making. Lacan utilized the methodology of historicism in order to better understand the behavioral action of the patient—incidentally in a manner not dissimilar to Althusser's discussion, quoted above, of the relationship between the subject's material actions and the ideological system that governs them. Lacan states: "The unconscious is the chapter of my history that is marked by a

---

21. Micaela Janan, *"When the Lamp Is Shattered": Desire and Narrative in Catullus* (Carbondale: Southern Illinois University Press, 1994).

22. One concept in Lacan that is relevant to the psychical function of ideology is that of the Phallus, or Master Signifier. The Phallus represents complete lack, but its influence overshadows all signifiers; its impact on the signification of all symbols is pervasive, but unidentifiable ("On The Signification of the Phallus," in *Ecrits*, 575–84). As a result, subjects seek to replace the Master Signifier with ideological substitutions that are treated in the Symbolic as that lost Phallus: God, political idealism, and so on. Žižek is particularly interested in this aspect of Lacan for his political philosophy, as Matthew Sharpe and Geoff Boucher discuss: "[For Žižek] in Psychoanalytic terms, the Symbolic is not centred on the 'signification of the phallus'—that is, on a master signifier. The signifier is what the psychotic subject lacks. Instead, the psychotic compensates by building an imaginary replacement for the missing master signifier—some image of God or a Master supposedly filled with Meaning and capable of directly manipulating the Real." Sharpe and Boucher, *Žižek and Politics* (Edinburgh: Edinburgh University Press, 2010), 121.

blank or occupied by a lie." He writes that the body (like monuments), childhood memories (like archival documents), and "heroicized" traditions and legends of the self all help the analyst to see the subject's history and to discover the truth of the subject's own making (*Ecrits* 215):

> What we teach the subject to recognize as his unconscious is his history—in other words, we help him complete the current historicization of the facts that have already determined a certain number of the historical "turning points" in his existence. But if they have played this role, it is already as historical facts, that is, as recognized in a certain sense or censored in a certain order.
>
> Thus, every fixation at a supposed instinctual stage is above all a historical stigma: a page of shame that one forgets or undoes, or a page of glory that obliges. . . . Obligation perpetuates in symbols the very mirage in which the subject found himself trapped. (*Ecrits* 217)

For humanism, Rome is a central part of the history of its own making, and like the analysand lying on the analyst's couch, realizing the buried ruins of his/her ego, humanists began to see literally the buried ruins of Rome and the textual discoveries of its own self-construction. The humanist instinct to associate himself with the past is finally a mirage of the Symbolic. Still, the Christian humanist had to justify a return to the pagan past by staying firmly rooted in the Christian present, and the lost world of classical Rome served paradoxically as both the source of a desired connection as well as a validation of this *new* Rome in all its symbolic power as the stronghold of a new Europe based firmly on papal authority. In a most insightful examination of the "double-task" of the humanist resurrection of ancient Rome, Greene succinctly identifies the crux of this humanist dilemma and thereby illustrates the inherent anxiety in the "Humanist program":

> One can detect the implicit duality of the Humanist program. There is first the archaeological impulse downward into the earth, into the past, the unknown and recondite, and then the upward impulse to bring forth a corpse whole and newly restored, re-illuminated, made harmonious and quick. This duality is present at all points on the spectrum of Humanist activity.

Although Greene does indeed scratch the surface of the classical crisis inherent in humanism, such a binary vision overly simplifies that humanist program and the fluid anxiety that haunts it. From a Lacanian perspective, both the digging into and building up of the humanist ego are part of the same exercise: to find self-identity amid a self-consciousness constantly being confronted by opposing ideological forces. Materially and ideologically, the building up, tearing down, resurrecting, and burying are all functions of a self struggling to find its place in the material present, in the dominant ideology, in the Symbolic. For the humanist, Rome functioned as the perceived center of a broken self.

Chapter 2

The Renaissance, Rome, and Humanism's Classical Crisis[1]

> Thou stranger, which for *Rome* in *Rome* here seekest,
> And nought of *Rome* in *Rome* perceiu'st at all,
> These same olde walls, olde arches, which thou seest,
> Old Palaces, is that which *Rome* men call.
> Behold what wreake, what ruine, and what wast.
>
> —Joachim du Bellay, *Les Antiquitez de Rome*
> (1558), trans. Edmund Spenser (1591)

Despite the critical tendency to view the Renaissance in Europe as a great awakening of autonomous selfhood, Renaissance humanism was as much about conflict as self-discovery.[2] Ideological tensions during the Renaissance abounded, none more significant than humanism's obsession with classical culture amid very contemporary economic, religious, and political changes. The gaze back to antiquity—its art, literature, philoso-

---

1. A version of this chapter was initially published as "Staging Rome: The Renaissance, Rome, and Humanism's Classical Crisis," in *The Sites of Rome: Time, Space, Memory,* ed. David H. J. Larmour and Diana Spencer (Oxford: Oxford University Press, 2007), 271–94.

2. Various recent approaches to humanism have implicitly and explicitly challenged this somewhat old-fashioned view of the Renaissance. Jonathan Dollimore, *Radical Tragedy: Religion, Ideology, and Power in the Drama of Shakespeare and His Contemporaries,* 3rd ed. (Durham, NC: Duke University Press, 2004), in his discussion of "essentialist humanism" with regard to attitudes toward Renaissance tragedy, illustrates the politically subversive nature of humanism; Ernesto Grassi, *Renaissance Humanism: Studies in Philosophy and Poetics* (Binghamtom, NY: Medieval and Renaissance Texts and Studies, 1988), takes a Heideggerian view of the Renaissance; and Gian Mario Anselmi, *Le frontiere degli umanisti* (Bologna: CLUEB, 1988) approaches the humanist program from a fundamentally Marxist view. See also Grassi, *Heidegger and the Question of Renaissance Humanism* (Binghamton, NY: Medieval and Renaissance Texts and Studies, 1983); and Leonard Barkan, *Transuming Passion: Ganymede and the Erotics of Humanism* (Stanford, CA: Stanford University Press, 1991).

phy, politics, nationalism—was, on the one hand, the primary source for a growing focus on self-identity and a secular world founded on introspection of the self; on the other hand, antiquity was the unattainable "Other," the object of a desire the Renaissance could never completely satisfy, a lack that could never be filled. Classical Rome became both a material reminder of past greatness and a symbol of Renaissance selfhood and cultural sophistication, but for humanists classical Rome and Roman identity also represented the source of a dialectic that both glorified and negated classical "Romanness." Classical Rome was temporally and ideologically foreign, but it was also integral to humanist identity formation. Humanism existed only in its relationship to the concept of "Rome" as a place, a cultural center, but for the Renaissance to be something different, something progressive, humanist ideology also had to equip itself with methods of exposing a lack in the very myth it valorized.

Although a substantial body of scholarship addresses the Renaissance fascination with Rome, none of that work, I believe, has adequately dealt with the psychic conflict between humanists and their rediscovery and literary representation of Rome.[3] Materially, textually, and ideologically, there existed a "classical crisis," and at the center of that crisis, serving as a primary locus of anxiety, was the reality of a ruined Rome, a Rome that in one sense had to be recovered and restored, but ultimately replaced. Just as Renaissance archaeologists and mapmakers had sought to uncover the buried ruins of Rome and to interpret the "truth" of Rome (and consequently the "truth" of themselves) from the material fragments of Rome's past, Renaissance writers also attempted to uncover Rome by appropriating Latin texts that centered on "place" and Roman ideology, and then to create a fictitious Rome that served to validate classical Rome as a center of cultural supremacy. However, those literary representations of Rome were often subverted and altered, thus exposing a lack that could be filled only by humanists' own mythological constructions of a new Europe, one that was still definitively Christian. At times, these writers recreate Rome in Europe's

---

3. Two notable exceptions are Greene, "Resurrecting Rome"; and Margaret W. Ferguson, "'The Afflatus of Ruin': Meditations on Rome by du Bellay, Spenser, and Stevens," in *Roman Images*, ed. Annabel Patterson (Baltimore and London: Johns Hopkins University Press, 1984), 23–50. Ferguson actually characterizes du Bellay's relationship to ancient Rome and his hopes for a contemporary adoption of Roman qualities as an essentially Freudian "family romance" (26–27). Barkan also addresses the connection between Rome and the Oedipal family romance in *Transuming Passion* (1991). For more studies of the Renaissance fascination with ancient Rome, see Cyril Bailey, ed., *The Legacy of Rome* (Oxford: Clarendon Press, 1923); and Philip Jacks, *The Antiquarian and the Myth of Antiquity: The Origins of Rome in Renaissance Thought* (Cambridge: Cambridge University Press, 1993).

own image, depicting Rome as a mere reflection of contemporary European cultural centers. The various humanist processes of appropriation illustrate the ideological struggle in justifying a present with a past that, by necessity, had to be shown as somehow incomplete.

Just as Rome's material ruins were excavated, authors textually excavated the works of Latin authors—Roman historians, poets, and playwrights—and the fissures that emerge in those Latin texts allowed a humanist reinvention of Rome's mythic past and its material, ruinous present.[4] Writers such as Joachim du Bellay respond directly to the ruins of Rome, grieving over the loss of ancient Rome's great past but recognizing that that greatness suffered from its own lack, its own self-destructive qualities. English playwrights "play out" the very psychical crisis of the humanist in their Roman plays as they depict a Rome whose great history becomes the site of tremendous anxiety for the Roman characters in the plays. Ben Jonson and William Shakespeare offer up characters that use Rome as the locus of Roman identity, but there remains a recognition that Rome's failures will lead to the literal ruining of Rome and what Rome represents. These works, and the constant dialogue between humanism and its Roman other, demonstrate a fragmented sense both of Rome and of the humanist "self" during the period; they demonstrate the instability not only of Roman myth, but of the very ideologies that attempt to possess it.

Rome's Ruins and the Resurrection of the Secular Self

For Italian humanists in the fourteenth and fifteenth centuries, ancient Rome was all around them, and it hardly comes as a surprise that those men would begin to map, catalogue, excavate, and ultimately reconstruct (if only mentally or academically) those material ruins.[5] Many of the scholars of the period saw the reconstruction of classical Rome as a means of validating a movement away from medieval religious ideology toward a new secular

---

4. Catharine Edwards addresses the appropriations and reappropriations of Rome by Romans themselves as well as by later thinkers and writers, in *Writing Rome: Textual Approaches to the City* (Cambridge: Cambridge University Press, 1996). Edwards identifies such inherent contradictions in the views of Rome of Roman writers and consequently in later appropriations of the myth of Rome from those writers. See also Edwards, *Roman Presences: Receptions of Rome in European Culture* (Cambridge: Cambridge University Press, 1999).

5. One of the most insightful, informative, and recent studies of Renaissance archaeology and antiquity is Leonard Barkan's *Unearthing the Past: Archaeology and Aesthetics in the Making of Renaissance Culture* (New Haven, CT and London: Yale University Press, 1999).

sense of self.[6] Giovanni de Matociis, also known as Giovanni Mansionario (d. 1337), sketched the heads of Roman emperors from Roman coins.[7] Cristoforo Buondelmonti traveled to the Aegean islands in 1420 and drew careful renditions of the ruins he took to be those of Troy. Giovanni Dondi (*Iter Romanum*, 1375) and Leon Battista Alberti (*Descriptio Urbis Romae*, 1434) examined ruins to understand and praise their technical characteristics. Poggio Bracciolini, in the early fifteenth century, wished to make an archaeological examination of Rome's stone walls and various sites of antiquity, and, perhaps even more importantly, he expressed deep concern about the destruction of these ruins and the opportunity to access the sites firsthand. Pirro Ligorio, a quintessential "Renaissance man," scoured the ancient ruins as he produced his own architecture, paintings, and even sketches of Rome.[8] The fact is that Rome's material past and present captivated these men and supplied them with a pre-Christian history of their own making; however, the very sites they examined became symbolic of something greater, and their subsequent loss, their slow destruction, a sign of degeneration and lack.

While many of these scholars focused on recreating the material past, others focused on what the monuments and remnants of Rome meant for their own contemporary Rome. The various sites of Rome became the symbolic embodiment of Rome's power: the greatness of its people, its institutions, and its culture. Petrarch was fascinated with the actual physical ruins of Rome, but he was less interested in the topographical or archaeological reconstruction of Rome (although his writing uses a vast amount of imagery relating to the physical remains) than in the symbolic nature of classical Rome as an ideological link to the past. He praises the institutions of classical Rome, its military, and its valuing of *pietas*. Most important, Petrarch

---

6. Riccardo Fubini, *Humanism and Secularization: From Petrarch to Valla* (Durham, NC: Duke University Press, 2003); originally published as *Umanesimo e seccolarizzazione de Petrarca a Valla* (Rome: Bulzoni, 1990). Fubini specifically addresses, in various contexts, the coexistence of religious fervor and a new secular drive during the Italian Renaissance that undermined established ideological constructs. See also Carlo Caruso and Andrew Laird, eds., *Italy and the Classical Tradition: Language, Thought, and Poetry* (London: Duckworth, 2009); Mary A. Papazian, ed., *The Sacred and Profane in English Renaissance Literature* (Newark: University of Delaware Press, 2008); Stephen A. McKnight, *Sacralizing the Secular: The Renaissance Origins of Modernity* (Baton Rouge: Louisiana State University Press, 1989); and Roberto Weiss, *The Spread of Italian Humanism* (London: Hutchinson, 1964).

7. Matociis was also the first to identify the existence of two "Plinys."

8. See Caroline Vout, "Sizing Up Rome, or Theorizing the Overview," in Larmour and Spenser, *The Sites of Rome*, 295–322. Also, for an intensive biography of Ligorio, consult David R. Coffin, *Pirro Ligorio: The Renaissance Artist, Architect, and Antiquarian* (University Park: Pennsylvania State University Press, 2003). Also Barkan, *Unearthing the Past, passim*.

sees in Rome's ruins the opportunity to praise a model on which the society of his day could fashion its own sense of self and society.[9] Similarly, Giovanni Cavallini in his *Polistoria de Virtutibus et Dotibus Romanorum* (ca. 1343–52) glorifies ancient Rome as the pinnacle of human achievement: "Verum et si omnium gentium [h]istoriae revolvantur, nullarum gentium gesta clarius elucescunt quam gesta magnifica Romanorum."[10] And of course Flavio Biondo, in both *Roma Instaurata* (1446) and *Roma Triumphans* (1459), examines all aspects of Roman antiquity and on the basis of the archaeological relics attempts to recreate the entire spectrum of ancient Rome and to show that Roman *virtus* is the source of Rome's greatness as well as of its ultimate ruin.[11] In addition, despite Rome's ultimate failure, Biondo believes, Roman virtues can still provide contemporary Christian society with a social model that, viewed through a Christian lens, can be even more successful than its ancient source.

All these humanists shared a goal—the reconstruction of and the *reconnection* with the past. While rediscovering a material Rome clearly facilitated and fed the humanist program, there was the reality that the grandeur and glory of classical Rome was now lost, never to be regained, but only replaced by a *new* Rome that centered on the papacy and Christian doctrine. Regardless of all the remarkable archaeological and artistic rediscoveries, it was perhaps the feeling of loss, the presence of and inability to accept that lack, that most haunted the humanist and drove him to return to the excavations, again and again, in search of unity with his cultural past; the more of Rome that was uncovered, the greater the gap between past and present and the greater the desire to search even deeper into the ruins. The humanists' inability to recognize fully the scope of the gap that existed between the two worlds on which they were basing their identity was the source of their anxiety and crisis. Lacan throughout his seminar on anxiety negotiates the paradoxical relationship between difference and sameness, and he proposes that it is indeed "anxiety" that occupies the gap between

9. For a fuller discussion of Petrarch's view of ancient Rome, see David Galbraith, "Petrarch and the Broken City," in *Antiquity and Its Interpreters*, ed. Alina Payne, Ann Kuttner, and Rebekah Smick (Cambridge: Cambridge University Press, 2000), 17–26; Greene's extensive examination of Petrarch in *The Light in Troy*, 104–46; Angelo Mazzocco, "The Antiquarianism of Francesco Petrarca," *Journal of Medieval and Renaissance Studies* 7 (1977): 203–24; and Roberto Weiss, *The Renaissance Discovery of Classical Antiquity* (Oxford: Blackwell, 1969).

10. Quoted in Mazzocco, "Rome and the Humanists: The Case of Biondo Flavio," in Ramsey, *Rome in the Renaissance*, 186. The quote originally appeared in *Polistoria de Virtutibus et Dotibus Romanorum*, Biblioteca Apostolica Vaticana MS, Rossiano 728, fol. 1. A new edition, with a bibliography, and indices of the *Polistoria* is now available: Giovanni Cavallini, *Polistoria*, ed. Marc Laureys (Stuttgart: B. G. Teubner, 1995).

11. See Mazzocco, "Rome and the Humanists," 189–90, for a discussion of this paradox.

the two. Lacan attributes anxiety to the subject's disassociation from the Other and the subject's failure to recognize the fundamental lack inherent in the fragmented but accessible object(s) (*objet a*) that the subject mistakenly takes for the Other.[12] Anxiety, then, is the result of that missing "lack," a false sense of wholeness that keeps desire, in a state of fantasy, focused on the material *objet a* rather than on the Other it cannot possess. As Roberto Harari states in his discussion of Lacan's seminar, "Anxiety irrupt[s] when the object *a* is on the verge of falling away."[13] Furthermore he suggests that for Lacan it is when the illusionary relationship between the subject and the *objet a* begins to unravel that anxiety comes to bear; anxiety emerges when the disconnected relationship between the *objet a* and the Other is brought to light and the subject's own relationship to the Other (which has been delusively fashioned on the *objet a*) is in doubt. The material ruins of Rome represent the initial *objet a* of the humanist psyche, particularly for those early Italians like Cavallini and Biondo. Ultimately, piece by piece, the archaeological remains demonstrated how fragmented the past really was and how truly distant in time ancient Rome was. Physical recovery revealed the ruins, the *objet a*, the artifacts of memory, to be literally "on the verge of falling away." The fragments of the past on which the humanist gaze was fixed were not classical Rome; they were pieces of a past greatness that humanists tried to shape into their own being. Bracciolini feared the loss of those ancient ruins (both the "real" physical loss and, perhaps more important, the conceptual/psychical loss) because unconsciously he knew that without the artifacts of memory, his very being would be threatened: these ruins were the only connection to the ideological valorization of Rome as the origin of the humanist self. Admittedly, Italian humanists at the very least had their "heritage" and reality of "place" to hold on to; that is, they could at least say, "Rome is my home, and these things buried beneath my feet are mine and are part of me, are part of this place of which I am a part." Even that is illusionary, however, and it was perhaps that illusion that sometimes kept Italians from recognizing and acknowledging the gaping distance between themselves and the past Rome they valorized; later humanists in France, England, and other places—who were not only temporally distanced from classical Rome, but spatially as well—often were more aware of their difference and distance from classical Rome.

---

12. For one of Lacan's more thorough discussions of the *objet a*, see "Of the Gaze as *Objet Petit a*" (1978). The simplest way to understand the function of the *objet a* is as a seemingly attainable signifier of the unattainable Other.

13. Roberto Harari, *Lacan's Seminar on "Anxiety": An Introduction*, trans. Jane Lamb-Ruiz (New York: The Other Press, 2001), 231.

Although many of these humanists suggest an actual *loss* amid their praise, admiration, and perceived recovery of ancient Rome, none provides as concise an examination of the great sense of anxiety and despair over what the ancient ruins lack as Joachim du Bellay does in *Les Antiquitez de Rome* (1558).[14] The Frenchman du Bellay spent four years in Rome, and the result was a deep obsession with what Rome was and had become, and where his own France was situated in the grand scheme of Western culture.[15] *Les Antiquitez* depicts both du Bellay's awe over and disappointment in the Roman ruins. Although he clearly wishes to praise Rome—"chanter / Les sept Costaux Romains, sept miracles du monde" (2.13–14),—a real sense of loss, destruction, and regret is also present. Most notable perhaps is the paradox of a modern Rome that does not really represent ancient Rome:

> Nouveau venu qui cherches Rome en Rome,
> Et rien de Rome en Rome n'apperçois,
> Ces vieux palais, ces vieux arcz que tu vois,
> Et ces vieux murs, c'est ce que Rome on nomme.
> Voy quell orgueil, quelle ruine. (3.1–5)[16]

---

14. Edmund Spenser published his well-known translation of *Les Antiquitez, Ruines of Rome,* in 1591. For studies addressing Spenser's translation of du Bellay, see Hassan Melehy, *The Politics of Literary Transfer in Early Modern England* (Farnham, UK and Burlington, VT: Ashgate, 2011), 75–138; Anne Lake Prescott, "Spenser (Re)Reading Du Bellay: Chronology and Literary Response," in *Spenser's Life and the Study of Biography,* ed. Judith Anderson, Donal Cheney, and David A. Richardson (Amherst: University of Massachusetts Press, 1996); M. L. Stapleton, "Spenser, the *Antiquitez de Rome,* and the Developments of the English Sonnet Form," *Comparative Literature Studies* 27 (1990): 259–74; and A. E. B Coldiron, "How Spenser Excavates Du Bellay's *Antiquitez;* or, The Role of the Poet, Lyric Historiography, and the English Sonnet," *Journal of English and Germanic Philology* 101.1 (2002): 41–67.

15. For a fine study of du Bellay, his travels to Rome, and his attitudes toward classical Rome and contemporary France, see George H. Tucker, *The Poet's Odyssey: Joachim du Bellay and the "Antiquitez de Rome"* (Oxford: Clarendon Press, 1990). Particularly relevant to the present discussion is Tucker's chapter "The Quest for Rome, in Rome" (55–104). See also Wayne A. Rebhorn, "Du Bellay's Imperial Mistress: *Les Antiquitez de Rome* as Petrarchist Sonnet Sequence," *Renaissance Quarterly* 33.4 (1980): 609–22; Eric Macphail, "The Roman Tomb or the Image of the Tomb in Du Bellay's *Antiquitez,*" *Bibliothèque d'Humanisme et Renaissance* 48.2 (1986): 359–72; Eric MacPhail, *The Voyage to Rome in French Renaissance Literature* (Saratoga, CA: ANMA Libri, 1990); Françoise Giordani, "Utilisation et cescription de l'espace dans *Les Antiquitez de Rome* de Joachim du Bellay," in *Du Bellay et ses sonnets romains,* ed. Yvonne Bellenger (Paris: Champion, 1994), 19–46; Hassan Melehy, "Du Bellay's Time in Rome: The *Antiquitez,*" *French Forum* 26.2 (2001): 1–22; Melehy, *The Poetics of Literary Transfer,* 17–74.

16. The French text of *Les Antiquitez* is from Richard Helgerson's edition, *The Regrets* (Philadelphia: University of Pennsylvania Press, 2006), and is cited by poem and line number. The verse translations are from Spenser's 1591 translation in *The Poetical Works of Edmund Spenser,* ed. J. C. Smith and E. De Selincourt (London: Oxford University Press, 1950).

Thou stranger, which for *Rome* in *Rome* here seekest,
And nought of *Rome* in *Rome* perceiu'st at all,
These same olde walls, olde arches, which thou seest,
Old Palaces, is that which *Rome* men call.
Behold what wreake, what ruine.

Here, the Rome with which humanists longed to reconnect is full of "orgueil," is a "ruine," and has become the "proye au temps" (3.8). The desired Rome is not the Rome of the present, regardless of its name. Du Bellay illustrates here the Lacanian concern regarding "difference" and "sameness," that regardless of the desire to be the same as the object of that desire, the Symbolic Order (particularly considering its linguistic structure) is ultimately structured on difference rather than sameness. Renaissance Rome is both the same as Rome and different from Rome: "Sacrez costaux, et vous sainctes ruines, / Qui le seul nom de Rome retenez" (7.1–2). The dual nature of a Rome that is both the same and different is played out often in du Bellay's sequence and proves to be the primary source of his anxiety. He states that "Rome suele pouvoit à Rome ressembler / Rome seule pouvoit Rome faire trembler" (6.9–10), "Rome n'est plus" (5.5), and "Le corps de Rome en cendre est devallé, / Et son esprit rejoinder s'est allé / Au grand esprit de ceste masse ronde" (5.9–11). For du Bellay, Rome becomes a specter raised from the dead, but it also becomes a kind of Platonic ideal, its remnants only a faint manifestation of its perfection.

Du Bellay's grief over the "death" of Rome in Rome and his implicit praise of and desire for ancient Rome aside, the humanist program demanded also that a lack be identified in the very object it desired. Du Bellay suggests two essential causes of Rome's failure, the first being the susceptibility to time: "proye au temps." The decline of Rome's greatness and the remaining rubble are subjected to the destruction of time. While this clearly suggests that Rome possessed an inherent vulnerability, the passive nature of such destruction does not exactly undermine the status of Rome itself:

Afin qu'ayant rangé tout pouvoir sous sa main
Rien ne peust ester borne à l'empire Romain:
Et quie si bien le temps destruit les Republiques

Le temps ne mist si bas la Romaine hauteur,
Que le chef deterré aux foundemens antiques. (8.9–13)

To th' end that hauing all parts in their power,
Nought from the Romane Empire might be quight,
And that though time doth Commonwealths deuowre,
Yet no time should so low embase their hight,
That her head earth'd in her foundations deep.

Du Bellay states that it is the work of the "Palles Esprits" that has left Rome as the dusty field ("pouldreuse plaine," 15.14) that now remains. Still, the weakness of Rome, the inability of Rome to outlast the reach of time—the initial lack in Rome itself—is at least tempered by the ability of Rome to recreate itself in its new Christian identity: "Mist ce pouvoir es mains du successeur de Pierre, / Qui sous nom de Pasteur, fatal à ceste terre, / Monstre que tout retourne à son commencement" (18.12–14). Du Bellay has here connected the history of a civilization founded by shepherds with the new shepherd (Peter) who resurrects the city itself after time has devoured the initial incarnation of Rome's identity: "Et ces braves palais dont le temps s'est fait maistre, / Cassines de pasteurs ont esté quelquefois" (18.13–14). The emergence of Peter both validates the lack of Rome and makes possible the ability of Rome to persevere through the severity of time. This is quite different from the perspective of someone such as Joseph Hall, who makes it clear that Peter's church has further destroyed the greatness of Rome, not saved it:

When once I think if carping Aquine's sprite
To see now Rome were licenced to the light,
How his enraged ghost would stamp and stare
That Caesar's throne is turned to Peter's chair.
To see an old shorn losel perched high
Crossing beneath a golden canopy,
The whiles a thousand hairless crowns crouch low
To kiss the precious case of his proud toe;
And for the lordly fasces borne of old,
To see two quiet crossed keys of gold,
Or Cybele's shrine, the famous Pantheon's frame,
Turned to the honour of Our Lady's name. (*The Virgidemiae* 4.7.10–20)

Hall's perception and ridicule of this new Catholic Rome is set *against* the classical standard, the true greatness and power of the ancient Roman identity. Du Bellay, in contrast, mourns the loss of the ancient authority but finds some solace in the return to "son commencement," its foundations as a shepherd-built city. The difference lies in the fact that while Hall implicitly defines himself in terms of the past, du Bellay feels the crisis of identity that the rupture between past and present creates, and he therefore constructs a consciousness that attempts to fill that rupture with a new valorization of the present.

While du Bellay finds Rome's initial lack to be its susceptibility to time, he ultimately must find a more fundamental lack, a more active locus of Rome's self-destruction. That Rome is simply subject to time does not adequately give rise to and allow for the valorization and prioritization of du Bellay's present. Not only has Rome faded into ashes, but it has done so by its own hand: "et comme / Celle qui mist le monde sous ses loix / Pour donter tout, se donta quelquefois, / Et devint proye au temps, qui tout consomme" (3.5–8). Although "time" may have been the general culprit of Rome's demise, du Bellay finds flaws in the very fabric of what ancient Rome was, even calling Rome, with its eventual troubles, a Pandora locked away: "Le tenoit clos, ainsi qu'une Pandore" (19.8). He also suggests that Rome possessed a pride and arrogance that directly led to violence and civil war, both of which contributed to Rome's ultimate fall:

> Tel encor' on a veu par dessus les humains
> Le front audacieux des sept costaux Romains
> Lever contre le ciel son orgueilleuse face:
>
> Et telz ores on void ces champs deshonnorez
> Regretter leur ruine, et les Dieux asseurez
> Ne craindre plus là hault si effroyable audace. (12.9–14)

> So did that haughtie front which heaped was
> on those seuen Romane hils, it selfe vpreare
> Ouer the world, and lift her loftie face
> Against the heauen, that gan her force to feare.
> But now these scorned fields bemone her fall,
> And Gods secure feare not her force at all.

The pride and violence of Rome are part of its "premier discord" (22.11), and the very seeds of its existence will be returned to and engulfed in the Chaos of its own identity: "Au ventre du Caos eternellement closes" (22.14). Ancient Rome may have been great, indeed the pinnacle of human achievement and therefore worthy of emulation, but still Rome's destruction was built into itself:

Mais le destin debrouillant ce Caos,
Où tout le bien et le mal fut enclos,
A fait depuis que les vertus divines

Volant au ciel ont laissé les pechez,
Qui jusqu'icy se sont tenus cachez
Sous les monceaux de ces vieilles ruines. (19.9–14)

But destinie this huge Chaos turmoyling,
In which all good and euill was enclosed,
Their heauenly virtues from these woes assoyling,
Caried to heauen, from sinfull bondage losed:
But their great sinnes, the causers of their paine,
Vnder these antique ruines yet remaine. (261–66)[17]

The Christian connotations here are obvious—"vertus divines," "le bien et le mal," "les pechez"—and this passage suggests the ultimate crisis of the humanist psyche: to turn back to a classical Rome that was fundamentally lacking the Christian ideological structure that formulated the Renaissance self, but to a Rome that was also necessary for a new secular construction of that self. Even with the immense praise, admiration, and sadness over the ruins and the admitted loss of ancient Rome, only by identifying a lack in those objects and what they represent could the Renaissance psyche be made to feel secure. (Regardless of his great love of classical Rome and his numerous compositions in Latin, du Bellay in his *Les Regrets* even renounces Latin in favor of his own French tongue.)[18]

Despite the grief over and preoccupation with what Rome was and what it has become, du Bellay's closing poem in the sequence demonstrates that everything in *Les Antiquitez* functions ultimately as a means for him to find his own consciousness and voice as a Frenchman. In this final poem, the speaker addresses his own verse and questions whether his own words will succumb to the same fate as the ruins of Rome:

---

17. G. W. Pigman addresses the issue of Rome's destruction in du Bellay in "Du Bellay's Ambivalence towards Rome in the *Antiquitez*," in Ramsey, *Rome in the Renaissance*, 321–32.

18. For a discussion of du Bellay's sadness at being in Rome and his preference for his native land and language, see William B. Clark, "Letters from Home: The Epistolary Aspects of Joachim Du Bellay's 'Les Regrets,'" *Renaissance Quarterly* 52 (1999): 140–79. Similarly, in England, both Francis Meres in *Palladis Tamia* (1598) and Thomas Carew in "The Excellencie of the English Tongue" (1595–14?) praise the Latin language and the writers Rome produced, but they attempt to validate "English" as a worthy and necessary substitute; these essays are included in *Elizabethan Critical Essays*, vol. 2, ed. George Gregory Smith (Oxford: Oxford University Press, 1904), 285-94; 308-24.

Esperez vous que la posterité
Doive (mes vers) pour tout jamais vous lire?
Esperez vous que l'oeuvre d'une lyre
Puisse acquerir telle immortalité

Si sous le ciel fust quelque eternité,
Les monuments que je vous ay fait dire,
Non en papier, mais en marbre et porphyre,
Eussent gardé leur vive antiquité.

Ne laisse pas toutefois de sonner
Luth, qu'Apollon m'a bien daigné donner:
Car si le temps ta gloire ne desrobbe,

Vanter te peuls, quelque bas que tu sois,
D'avoir chanté le premier des François,
L'antique honneur du peuple à longue robbe. (32.1–14)

Hope ye my verses that posteritie
Of age ensuing shall you euer read?
Hope ye that euer immortalitie
So meane Harpes worke may chalenge for her meed?
If vnder heauen anie endurance were,
These moniments, which not in paper writ,
But in Porphyre and Marble doo appeare,
Might well haue hop'd to haue obtained it.
Nath'les my Lute, whom *Phoebus* deignd to giue,
Cease not to sound these olde antiquities:
For if that time doo let thy glorie liue,
Well maist thou boast, how euer base thou bee,
That thou art first, which of thy Nation song
Th'olde honour of the people gowned long.

The anxiety about Rome's decay is here transformed into the speaker's anxiety about his own poetry, about his own ability to project a secure and stable consciousness that is distinctly French. However, that consciousness is rooted in the instability of ancient Rome. Such a connection—such a dependence—is the source of the speaker's desire to actually have a voice, but also the source of the fear that his own voice could be subject to the same fate as Rome's ruins. If marble and porphyry ruins cannot survive, then what hope does the speaker's own poetry have? In relation to the greatness of Rome, his verse is humbled—"quelque bas que tu sois"—but by being the first, "le premier des François," to sing of Rome's "antique honneur" he positions himself to take on the structural equivalent of Rome's sites, to have his work do for the posterity of France what those stone marvels did for Rome.

Along with the walls and the crumbled traces of ancient streets, humanists sought out also the *textual* ruins of Rome's past. In fact, while the physical monuments perhaps instilled awe and regret, it was the distant "voices" of Roman writing that ultimately drove the humanist spirit. Certainly, on one level ancient texts were no different from other archaeological ruins. Like the Renaissance archaeologists who tried to make sense of and to understand the material remnants before them, numerous transcribers and editors were faced with a similar task of recovering the ancient texts they encountered. Most ancient manuscripts had survived into the Renaissance through the labors of often careless hands. Renaissance editors therefore had to wade through a vast textual labyrinth that consisted of fragments, errors, and doubtful attributions. Classical texts did indeed largely exist as "ruins" to be excavated.[19] Their material presence, like that of their stone counterparts, was a visible sign of Rome's past and seen as a gateway for a humanist return to that past. Even including those ancient texts that had survived more or less intact, the classical corpus as a whole, with all its missing texts and authors, was regarded by humanists as something that was now fragmentary and incomplete.

Although texts existed in their material reality (they were indeed tangible "things" capable of being restored, altered, or admired for the objects that they were), these written ruins also contained the intangible, ideological voices that served as a more accessible site of appropriation for humanists. Roman texts—despite their often fragmented forms—became the source for ideological connections with humanism's classical Other. Writers such as Cicero became the benchmark of Renaissance sophistication. His work was extensively read, its form and technique adopted as the model of Renaissance Latin prose, and whether in the classroom or at court, Cicero was *the* source for sophisticated cultural discourse.[20] Still, eventually it was

---

19. For one example of this, see Julia Haig Gaisser's *Catullus and His Renaissance Readers* (Oxford: Clarendon Press, 1993) for an in-depth study of the history of Catullus' texts during the Renaissance.

20. For Cicero's presence in the Latin School curriculum, consult Robert Black, *Humanism and Education in Medieval and Renaissance Italy: Tradition and Innovation in Latin Schools from the Twelfth to the Fifteenth Century* (Cambridge: Cambridge University Press, 2001), *passim;* for Cicero's influence in the public sphere, see Ronald G. Witt, "Civic Humanism and the Rebirth of

not as much the work of Cicero as it was the *idea* of Cicero that aided in the construction of the humanist identity. Again, the works themselves were certainly important, but they and the humanist valorization of their author ultimately served as the supreme *objet a;* if one could become like Cicero, one's identity as a humanist would be whole. But, as we have seen, since anxiety stems from failing to recognize the lack that exists in the *objet a* (i.e., the literary source), only by exposing the lack in that source could a true humanist identity begin to emerge. A writer like Cicero had to be shown as a flawed model of Renaissance selfhood, and his importance for the humanist eventually had to be both affirmed and negated. As William J. Bouwsma observes in *The Waning of the Renaissance,* "By the later sixteenth century, scholars were able increasingly to identify conflicts among the various schools of ancient philosophy, and some humanists read the classics less as sources of timeless truths than as revelations of individual personalities and of their own times."[21] But it was more than "ancient philosophy" per se; it was a lack in the entire body of classical culture that was exposed—or at the very least exposed as a body that was incomplete, indefinite. Montaigne, for example, regarded the classics merely as a source of information, not of identity: "[A reader should] pass everything [from the classical world] through a sieve, and lodge nothing in his head on mere authority and trust."[22]

---

the Ciceronian Oration," *Modern Language Quarterly* 51 (2001): 167–84. See also Virginia Cox and John O. Ward, eds., *The Rhetoric of Cicero in Its Medieval and Early Renaissance Commentary Tradition* (Leiden: Brill, 2006); Carlos Montes Serrano, *Cicerón y la cultura artística del Renacimiento* (Valladolid: Universidad de Valladolid, Secretariado de Puplicaciones e Intercambio Editorial, 2006); Christian Mouchel, *Cicéron et Sénèque dans la rhétorique de la Renaissance* (Marburg: Hitzeroth, 1990); E. B. Fryde, *Humanism and Renaissance Historiography* (London: Continuum, 1984); Hans Baron, *Cicero and the Roman Civic Spirit in the Middle Ages and Early Renaissance* (Manchester: Manchester University Press, 1938).

Although much work has been done on the Renaissance reliance on Cicero, Montaigne made statements against the idolization of Cicero during the period: "We know how to say: 'Cicero says thus; such are the morals of Plato; these are the very words of Aristotle.' But what do we say ourselves? What do we judge? What do we do? A parrot could well say as much." (Nous sçavons dire: Cicero dit ainsi; voilà les meurs de Platon; ce sont les mots mesmes d'Aristote. Mais nous, que disons nous nous mesmes? que jugeons nous? que faisons nous? Autant en diroit bien un perroquet.) "I would rather be an authority on myself than on Cicero." (J'aymerois mieux m'entendre bien en moy qu'en Ciceron.) *The Complete Essays of Montaigne,* trans. Donald M. Frame (Stanford, CA: Stanford University Press, 1958), 100, 822. See Kenneth Gouwen's article on Erasmus' similar position that imitators of Cicero are like "apes": "Erasmus, 'Apes of Cicero,' and Conceptual Blending," *Journal of the History of Ideas* 71.4 (2010): 523–45.

21. William J. Bouwsma, *The Waning of the Renaissance, 1550–1640* (New Haven, CT: Yale University Press, 2000), 35.

22. Quoted in Bouwsma, *The Waning of the Renaissance,* 36. Montaigne consistently made statements warning against unoriginal imitation: "I do not speak the minds of others except to speak my

The result of such a recognition—that ancient texts were not authoritative and that the humanist himself had to enter into a system that validated his own authority—was innovative methods of imitation and appropriation.[23] Montaigne's reading "through a sieve" is a far cry from early humanists such as Giovanni Villani whose valorization and imitation of classical texts were quite reproductive and sacramental:

> On that blessed pilgrimage in the holy city of Rome, [in 1300] I saw the great and ancient things of that place and read the histories and great deeds of the Romans written by Virgil, Sallust, Lucan, Titus Livy, Valerius, Paul Orosius, and other masters of history who wrote things great and small, of the deeds and achievements of the Romans, and also of foreign peoples in the whole world. In order to preserve the past and provide a model for those who are to follow, I emulated this style and form, just like a disciple, although unworthy of doing such a thing.[24]

Such a need to ground identity in the classics and Roman myth ultimately had to be usurped by a realization that great deeds of the past were often destructive and that imitating these models had to supply something that was lacking in the original.

The result of such a "double reading" of Rome's ruins is an inescapable conflict within the humanist self. The stone buildings, monuments, streets, and texts *were* there, always reminding humanists that the past was present in their own history and that they could never completely join nor completely flee from that past. The humanist agenda had to exist fully within the Symbolic realm; it had to reconstruct itself within the very cultural structure of which Rome was a part, had to become a "new" Rome and usurp the very qualities it sought to emulate. Imitation of all things Roman had to be validated by its relationship to Rome, but Rome also had to be negated in order for the new culture to take its place. Rome had to be

---

own mind better." (*Je ne dis les autres, sinon pour d'autant plus me dire.*) "He who follows another follows nothing." (*Qui suit un autre, il ne suit rien.*) "The bees plunder the flowers here and there, but afterwards they make of them honey, which is all theirs; it is no longer thyme or marjoram. Even so with the pieces borrowed from others; he will transform them and blend them to make a work that is all his own, to wit, his judgment." (*Les abeilles pillotent deçà delà les fleurs, mais elles en font apres le miel, qui est tout leur; ce n'est plus thin ny marjolaine: ainsi les pieces empruntées d'autruy, il les transformera et confondra, pour en faire un ouvrage tout sien: à sçavoir son jugement. Son institution, son travail et estude ne vise quà le former.*) *The Complete Essays of Montaigne,* trans. Frame, 108, 111.

23. See especially Greene, *The Light in Troy.*
24. Giovanni Villani, *Cronica,* ed. F. G. Dragomanni (Florence, 1844–45), 2: 39.

embraced and then quickly cast out from the humanist psyche; Rome had to be present, but only in the form of dead and wasted ruins scattered across the Renaissance landscape.

Rome on the English Stage

Although the Renaissance literary manifestations of Rome are many and exhibit a myriad of forms, the depictions of Rome on the stage are particularly reflective of the psychical underpinnings of the humanist program. In England, for example, the so-called Roman plays of writers such as Ben Jonson and Shakespeare effectively capture the psychical crisis inherent in humanism, and the nature of the dramatic genre lends itself to an analysis of that crisis. Most striking perhaps is drama's need to physically recreate place; Rome must be physically reinvented on the stage. Acts and scenes in the Roman plays are consistently set in "the streets," "the Colosseum," "the senate." As a result there is a physical recreation of Rome's presence, a manifestation of Rome as an active, yet unheard participant in the drama. In addition, this silent presence suggests the physical reality of Rome in the humanist landscape, ruins that exist but whose "voice" is reconstructed by those who examine and excavate those ruins. In fact, the very attempt to recreate a Rome on the stage—with set designs, fabricated armor, and characters establishing physical context through their speech—is itself an untruth; it is a largely fragmented, illusionary conception of Rome that thus, in a sense, mimics the nature of the actual physical ruins themselves. The audience is asked to remove itself imaginatively from its own space and place, and to suspend disbelief, to accept that what it is witnessing is a "true" Rome. Although this may be considered simply an experience of "literary imagination," it still suggests the humanist reality that the Rome they believe they see and know is not Rome at all, but rather an illusion of Rome, one constructed from bits and pieces of what Rome was and what their own current space *is*.

Aside from the tenuous nature of Rome's space on the stage, within the plays themselves there is nearly always an ideological struggle between a past Rome and a changing present Rome, and the characters actively seek out an understanding of what it means to be "Roman" and how their place within Rome is validated. In their Roman plays both Jonson and Shakespeare depict Romes in conflict, and even more importantly, Romes in ruin. The Rome on the stage is ideologically fragmentary in nature. Both the "place" created on the stage, which is constructed by means of arranged sets and limited space, and the very ideological uncertainty about what Rome is are illusionary. In Jonson's *Catiline,* for example, there is a fundamental reality that the perceived grandeur of Rome is threatened and that Rome risks falling into ruins. Cicero's version of the Catilinarian conspiracy was well known in the Renaissance, and the story itself has a dualistic quality that proves indicative of the humanist identification with Rome: Cicero himself represents everything "great" about Rome, but the conspiracy he describes shows the tenuous nature of Rome's greatness, of Rome's wholeness. Jonson's dramatization of this conspiracy illustrates the need to find a Roman precedent for England's own political turmoil,[25] but it also identifies the fractures in the humanist idealization of Rome. In the opening lines of *Catiline,* for instance, the audience is instantly presented with a Rome that is in danger of being reduced to a ruinous state; the ghost of Sylla recognizes the danger of the Catilinarian conspiracy to Rome's existence:

> Dost thou not feel me, Rome? Not yet! is night
> So heavy on thee, and my weight so light?
> Can Sylla's ghost arise within thy walls,
> Less threatening than an earthquake, the quick falls
> Of thee and thine? Shake not the frighted heads
> Of thy steep towers, or shrink to their first beds?
> Or as their ruin the large Tyber fills,
> Make that swell up, and drown thy seven proud hills? (1.1.1–8)

Not only is Rome being asked questions that Rome itself can never answer, but the implication is that the state of Rome is dependent on the answers that only a reconstructed view of Rome by outsiders can ultimately provide. In other words, the questions are being addressed to a Rome that is now gone, and as a result the answers about Rome's own fate can be supplied only by an outsider, by a humanist's reconstruction of Rome's past. Although the greatness of Rome, the Other with which the characters constantly try to connect, is always present, the image of Rome in Jonson also mirrors the physical ruins that were the Renaissance reality:

---

25. See Michael McCanles, *Jonsonian Discriminations: The Humanist Poet and the Praise of True Nobility* (Toronto: University of Toronto Press, 1992); Katharine Eisaman Maus, *Ben Jonson and the Roman Frame of Mind* (Princeton, NJ: Princeton University Press, 1984); B. N. Luna, *Jonson's Romish Plot: A Study of Catiline and Its Historical Context* (Oxford: Oxford University Press, 1976); and Warren L. Chernaik, "Ben Jonson's Rome," in *The Myth of Rome in Shakespeare and His Contemporaries* (Cambridge: Cambridge University Press, 2011), 108–34.

> leaue Romes blinded walls
> To embrace lusts, hatreds, slaughters, funerals,
> And not recouer sight, till their owne flames
> Do light them to their ruins. (1.1.63–66)

Such an attitude, that Rome will feed the flames of its own ruin, was exactly how du Bellay came to terms with the lost Rome he experienced during his time in Italy—that Rome was like a Pandora's box. Still, paradoxically, it is only through the ruins left behind that the humanist might cast his gaze on that past. Like this double gaze of the humanist, Catiline represents the potential of a broken Rome while Cicero and Sallust, the primary sources for the incident, represent Rome at its height. The humanist had to come to terms with both.

In *Sejanus*, too, Jonson shows the dualistic reality of Rome and the conflict between past and present. As with Catiline's conspiracy, the attempt by Sejanus to rise up against Tiberius and thereby destroy the current state of Rome indicates a Rome that is lacking the strength to withstand change; said another way, the threat itself denotes some lack. As Lucius Arruntius, supporter of Agrippina, speaks of past times and the play's current Rome, he echoes the humanist concern about Rome's degeneration:

> Times? The men,
> The men are not the same . . .
>   . . . .
>   . . . Those might spirits
> Lie raked up with their ashes in their urns,
> And not a spark of their eternal fire
> Glows in a present bosom. All's but blaze,
> Flashes, and smoke, wherewith we labour so,
> There's nothing Roman in us; nothing good,
> Gallant or great. . . . (1.1.87–88, 97–103)

This view of Rome is consistent with how humanists looked at a past Golden Age Rome that had vanished, that had turned into memories and ruins. Projected onto this "Roman" speaker is the humanist realization that their Roman model was no longer attainable.

Likewise, early in *Sejanus*, when the emperor Tiberius looks back to the past, he actually mentally materializes those past deeds into monuments and physical remnants:

These things shall be to us
Temples and statues, reared in your minds,
The fairest and most during imagery:
For those of stone or brass, if they become
Odious in judgement of posterity,
Are more contemned, as dying sepulchers, Than ta'en for live monuments.
    (1.484–90)

Jonson's materialization of Rome's history sets up the image of Rome truly in ruins, the same kind of ruins du Bellay found in the material reality of Renaissance Rome. Tiberius begins to recognize his own weakness: "For myself, / I know my weakness, and so little covet / (Like some gone past) the weight that will oppress me" (3.124–26). Sejanus immediately reminds Tiberius that recognizing such weakness—recognizing lack—is what leads to ruin:

But Rome, whose blood,
Whose nerves, whose life, whose very frame relies
On Caesar's strength, no less than heaven on Atlas,
Cannot admit it [weakness] but with general ruin. (3.128–31)

Of course, ultimately it is Sejanus himself who would cause the ruin of Caesar. Sejanus earlier envisioned turning Caesar's "house" into buried ruins:

Work then, my art, on Caesar's fears, as they
On those they fear, till all my lets be cleared:
And he in ruins of his house, and hate
Of all his subjects, bury his own state. (2.399–402)

This, again, is the potential for Rome in the play. Once the lack, the potential for ruin, is recognized, the wholeness, the greatness Rome represents, comes into question. The only remedy from a humanist standpoint—and it is a remedy that is characteristic of humanism—is to fill that lack with something else.

Sejanus, as the senators observe, is finally the one who is left in ruins: "Now you lie as flat / As was your pride advanced" (5.735–36), but it was Caesar's own flaw that allowed it. Sertorius Macro, who sees in the fall of Rome the ruins of Rome to come, articulates the humanist opportunity for creating a new Rome, a chance to fill the lack in *this* Rome with something fresh:

If then it be the lust of Caesar's power
To have raised Sejanus up, and in an hour
O'erturn him, tumbling down, from height of all
We are his ready engine: and his fall
May be our rise. It is no uncouth thing
To see fresh buildings from old ruins spring. (4.744–50)

The final three lines of this passage encapsulate the humanist need to build a Renaissance present that amends the greatness of the Rome that came before. The senators praise Macro as a hero: "Praise to Macro, that hath saved Rome / Liberty, liberty, liberty. Lead on, / And praise Macro, that hath saved Rome" (5.736–39); and it is Arruntius who best articulates the inevitability of Rome's ruins rising again through Macro:

I prophesy, out of this Senate's flattery,
That this new fellow, Macro, will become
A greater prodigy in Rome, than he
That now is fallen. (5.740–43)

Rome's past is indeed the foundation of what will come, but identifying the flaws that lead to ruin provides Macro (and ultimately humanism) with the lack that allows his own Rome—his own Roman identity—to be realized.

Like Jonson, Shakespeare also dramatizes the humanist conception of a battling past and present Rome, particularly in *Julius Caesar*. Drawn primarily from translations of Plutarch, Shakespeare's play reflects the psychical dilemma facing humanism on multiple levels. First, as has been frequently noted, Shakespeare chooses a Roman precedent for dealing with fundamentally English political issues. The very crux of Shakespeare's play, Brutus' desire to save Rome from the tyranny of a "monarch," is a timely issue for England during the late sixteenth century. The legitimacy of divine right, of monarchy based on either tradition or power, was being called into question (to some degree this issue culminates with John Milton's *The Tenure of Kings and Magistrates* [1649], in which Milton argues a monarch should be removed, even killed, for the good of the commonwealth). Shakespeare certainly addresses this issue in his English history plays, but the early use of "Rome" as a model that shows conflict and "grandeur threatened" epitomizes the humanist need to validate the European present with Rome's past.[26] And the need to either reclaim the past or move beyond a past now in ruins proves to be a primary theme.

In Shakespeare, Caesar represents the grandeur of a past Rome undermined by a present Rome, represented by Brutus, and it is a present that is ideologically different. Brutus does not despise Caesar but recognizes that Caesar must be torn down in order for a new Rome to be built. The state of Rome under Caesar is similar to that of du Bellay's Rome as a "wreake" and "ruine": "What trash is Rome? / What rubbish and what offal?" (1.3.108–9). This description by Cassius is also echoed by Antony as he mourns the loss of Caesar:

> O mighty Caesar! Dost thou lie so low?:
> Are all thy conquests, glories, triumphs, spoils,
> Shrunk to this little measure? Fare thee well! (3.1.148–50)[27]

Caesar's wife Calpurnia in her prophetic dream sees the fate of Caesar as that of an exploited monument. Caesar, describing his wife's dream to Decius, states:

> She dreamt to-night she saw my statue,
> Which, like a fountain with an hundred spouts,
> Did run pure blood; and many lusty Romans
> Came smiling and did bathe their hands in it. (2.2.76–79)

Calpurnia recognizes one fate of Rome in the dream; Decius another:

---

26. For studies dealing with Shakespeare and his view of Rome, see Chernaik, *The Myth of Rome*; Maria Del Sapio Garbero, *Identity, Otherness, and Empire in Shakespeare's Rome* (Farnham, UK and Burlington, VT: Ashgate, 2009); Barbara L. Parker, *Plato's Republic and Shakespeare's Rome: A Political Study of the Roman Works* (Newark: University of Delaware Press, 2004); Charles Martindale and A. B. Taylor, eds., *Shakespeare and the Classics* (Cambridge: Cambridge University Press, 2004); Margaret Tudeau-Clayton, *Jonson, Shakespeare, and Early Modern Virgil* (Cambridge: Cambridge University Press, 1998); Coppélia Kahn, *Roman Shakespeare: Warriors, Wounds, and Women* (London and New York: Routledge, 1997); Geoffrey Miles, *Shakespeare and the Constant Romans* (Oxford: Clarendon Press, 1996); Charles Wells, *The Wide Arch: Roman Values in Shakespeare* (New York: St. Martin's, 1993); Robert S Miola, *Shakespeare's Rome* (Cambridge: Cambridge University Press, 1983); Paul A. Cantor, *Shakespeare's Rome, Republic and Empire* (Ithaca, NY: Cornell University Press, 1976); Derek Traversi, *Shakespeare: The Roman Plays* (Stanford, CA: Stanford University Press, 1963); and Paul Dean, "Tudor Humanism and the Roman Past: A Background to Shakespeare," *Renaissance Quarterly* 41.1 (1988) 84–111.

27. All quotations are taken from *The Riverside Shakespeare*, ed. G. Blakemore Evans, 2nd ed. (Boston and New York: Houghton Mifflin, 1997) and are cited by act, scene, and line numbers.

This dream is all amiss interpreted:
It was a vision fair and fortunate.
Your statue spouting blood in many pipes
In which so many smiling Romans bath'd,
Signifies that from you great Rome shall suck
Reviving blood, and that great men shall press
For tinctures, stains, relics, and cognizance.
This by Calpurnia's dream is signified. (2.2.83–90)

These two interpretations of the dream point to the dilemma of human-ism's entire identification with Rome. With Caesar as the model of an old Rome to be admired, praised, and emulated, Caesar is ultimately cast down for what he lacks, and what he lacks (a more republican system of rule) is what Brutus and his supporters need to establish as their own self-identity. Humanism looked at classical Rome in both ways: Rome was the source of self-consciousness, but it had to be destroyed, left in ruins, for that self-consciousness to seem complete. Antony himself, grieving the loss of Cae-sar, states: "Thou art the ruins of the noblest man / That ever lived in the tide of times" (3.1.256–57); and as he thinks of revenge, he hypothesizes:

But were I Brutus
and Brutus Antony, there were an Antony
Would ruffle up your spirits, and put a tongue
In every wound of Caesar, that should move
The stones of Rome to rise and mutiny. (3.226–30)

Also like Jonson, Shakespeare ultimately offers no true reconciliation of the dualistic quality of Roman consciousness in the play. The fact is that all the characters struggle to come to terms with a vision of Rome that is idealized but not *realized*. Stated another way, the characters on both sides of the con-spiracy—Brutus, Cassius, Antony—understand there is something lacking in the Rome they have in front of them, that Rome either is in ruins or has the potential to fall into ruin. They all struggle to find their place in a per-ceived center of "Romanness" that is illusionary. Some characters, such as Antony, return to the past to fill the lack in the present Rome; others, such as Brutus, look toward the future and the destruction of the object (i.e., Caesar) that represents that past. As for the humanist, the characters must both bury and rebuild Rome and what it represents; destruction and rebirth are part of the same search for wholeness.

When Bloom wrote of the "anxiety of influence," he focused almost entirely on the Freudian relationship of a single author with a single literary precursor. However, the anxiety inherent in identity formation spills over into much more than just literary imitation. When individuals base their conception of self on the remnants of a cultural Other, they are ultimately left with the crisis of validating themselves with an Other that must be shown to be incomplete. Without identifying that lack, consciousness experiences tremendous anxiety over its total dependence on that Other it can never possess. All that remains are the remnants of that Other—the *objet a*, the "other"—but those remnants, those ruins of the Symbolic, are illusionary, flawed, and must finally be shown to fail to provide wholeness. Humanists did indeed see Rome around them: in the landscape, in their cities, in the texts they read and wrote. However, this Rome was not the Rome of their present; it was a Rome that existed only in ruins. Still, those ruins were the source of the humanist consciousness; they were the tangible *objet a* that could lead the Renaissance back to a unity with a Roman world now gone. These remains were the source of a dialectic that called for an affirmation and a negation of what it was they represented. The humanist could never be Rome—whatever that meant—so he had to undermine the very objects he admired. He had to show that those ruins represent the ruinous qualities of Rome, and only by recognizing *that* could a true self-consciousness be constructed. These individuals had to enter into the Symbolic Order of self-making, in which their very existence depended on identifying the lack in the Other now gone and filling that lack with a new sense of self that could transcend that Other and place the humanist world in the structural position of its Roman Other.

Although such a crisis was at the center of the humanist agenda as a whole, we begin to see literary representations of that crisis. Du Bellay explicitly looks to the ruins he must both praise and mourn; they represent a past greatness that must be emulated, but their material presence proves lacking, destructive, and a barrier to a new consciousness and sense of self. Even the ideological reproductions of Rome in the Roman plays of Jonson and Shakespeare reflect and project the humanist anxiety over dismissing the very thing that made the humanist what he was, but still those plays illustrate a vision of Rome in ruins and the difficulty—however inevitable—of burying that which is necessary in order to overcome. Those works illustrate a dualistic Rome, one that is both worthy of conservation as well as constantly in danger of being left in ruins. Projected onto the figures of the past, the anxiety over a perceived reality of Rome—a history of the self on the verge of falling away—consumes the characters, regardless of their initial ideological position. Catiline/Cicero, Sejanus/Tiberius, Brutus/Antony—the depictions of these figures mirror the humanist's two paradoxical needs: to preserve Rome and to tear it down. As the traditional views of Renaissance humanism have attested, classical Rome was indeed central to humanism and the development of Western culture, but not so much in what it provided as in what it lacked.

Chapter 3

Anxiety and Constructions of the Text

Dialogues with a Classical Past

> The authoritative word demands that we acknowledge it, that we make it our own; it binds us, quite independent of any power it might have to persuade us internally; we encounter it with its authority already fused to it. The authoritative word is located in a distanced zone, organically connected with a past that is felt to be hierarchically higher. It is, so to speak, the word of the fathers. Its authority was already *acknowledged* in the past. It is a *prior* discourse.
>
> —Mikhail Bakhtin, "Discourse in the Novel," in *The Dialogic Imagination;* emphasis in original

*E*ven with the recognition that the classical world manifests itself as a key locus of identity formation, and that writers such as du Bellay, Shakespeare, Jonson, and others reflect the general sense of anxiety that results from an indefinite and alien place within that locus, the problems of allusion and imitation per se are still present. A major problem with previous scholarship regarding classical reception is the failure of critics to deal adequately with the differences between imitation and influence and their respective subtleties. These concepts are often conflated, resulting in an awkward and hazy understanding of the relationship between writers and their predecessors. No one was guiltier of this conflation than Harold Bloom. More recently, Charles Martindale has addressed the issue of conflation, acknowledging the danger of misunderstanding the nature of influence as it relates to the study of allusions:

It is not sufficient to show a vague general similarity with some other text, nor is allusion the same as "influence," about which, given the mysterious alchemy of poetic creation, there must always be a large matter of uncertainty. Allusion implies conscious design by the writer, and, if the writer is playing fair, should be to something which a properly informed reader has a reasonable chance of recalling.[1]

Martindale is absolutely correct here. Allusion and imitation do suggest active strategies of poetic creation, while "influence" is a phenomenon that is harder to understand. Be that as it may, Martindale underestimates the importance of "influence" as it affects and determines the processes of imitation—regardless of the difficulty in finding certainty in such influence. Imitation is something that the writer *actively does;* influence is something that *happens to* the writer. Both are substantial and significant elements in literary identity.

Once again, we are led to psychical principles that seem to be a natural fit for a study of poetic creation—particularly one focusing on Renaissance humanism and its classical origins. Generally speaking, in psychoanalysis analyzing the patient begins with identifying what he/she *actively does,* and then trying to identify and understand what has *happened to* that patient to motivate those actions. In other words, there is a natural difference *with* but also a connection *to* what the individual actively does and what has influenced the individual, and thus his/her actions. In literary terms, then, it might be said that we look first to the techniques of poetic creation (which include imitation and allusion); but ultimately we must turn to the broader issues of literary influence and the ideological pressures of cultural identity to understand fully the origins and dynamics of imitation.

Lyricism and the Processes of Identity in the French *Pléiade*

Tracking the influence of Latin lyric poetry during the Renaissance is a particularly difficult task. Perhaps as much as any other genre, lyric poetry of the period was the product of a diverse set of ideological and literary sources. Although the French troubadour poetry of the Middle Ages, which to a substantial degree was developed in the tradition of Ovid, provided

---

1. Charles Martindale, *John Milton and the Transformation of Ancient Epic* (Bristol: Bristol Classical Press), 1.

inspiration for the early Italian lyricists, once Petrarch arrived on the literary scene classical poetry became a kind of hidden, often unidentifiable presence. Certainly Petrarch himself was greatly influenced by classical writers, but the Petrarchan poets to follow felt the classical world more often intermediately through Petrarch himself—and even then only superficially.[2] This kind of multilayered influence is not surprising and is, in fact, rather typical of any literary connection to the past. Petrarch's influence was so pervasive, however, that writers who wanted to return to the genre's classical roots had to differentiate themselves from him; indeed, they frequently had to become anti-Petrarchan in their lyric tone.[3] This differentiation involved a very strange process of both imitation and literary identity. Petrarch managed to distance himself and the genre from the classical world; he found a humanist "voice" that at least was perceived as original and his own, but imitators of Petrarch then had to identify some deficiency, some lack in the Petrarchan mode itself. To do that, they often returned to the classical world, and in such a return, they were faced once again with the classical crisis of the humanist literary program. My purpose in this section is not to discuss the vast influence of Petrarch and the subsequent "anti-Petrarchan" mode, but to examine the classical presence in the most classical of the lyric poetry of the period. Critics must always remember that Petrarchism represented a somewhat closed generic system against which writers often attempted to position themselves, and classical imitation proved one way to do just that.[4]

There is no better Continental example of the return to classical literature than the work of the French *Pléiade*.[5] This group of humanists, which

---

2. See Lynn Enterline, *The Rhetoric of the Body from Ovid to Shakespeare* (Cambridge: Cambridge University Press, 2000); Margaret M. McGowan, *The Vision of Rome in Late Renaissance France* (New Haven, CT: Yale University Press, 2000); and M. L. McLaughlin, *Literary Imitation in the Italian Renaissance: The Theory and Practice of Literary Imitation in Italy from Dante to Bembo* (Oxford: Clarendon Press, 1995).

3. I discuss this aspect of early modern lyric poetry in *Catullan Consciousness and the Early Modern Lyric* (Aldershot, UK: Ashgate, 2004).

4. For discussions of Petrarchism as a lyric model, see Blevins, *Catullan Consciousness;* Gordon Braden, *Petrarchan Love and the Continental Renaissance* (New Haven, CT: Yale University Press, 1999); Ignacio Enrique Navarrete, *Orphans of Petrarch: Poetry and Theory in the Spanish Renaissance* (Berkeley: University of California Press, 1994); Thomas P. Roche, *Petrarch and the English Sonnet Sequences* (New York: AMS Press, 1989); Stephen Minta, *Petrarch and Petrarchism: The English and French Traditions* (Manchester: Manchester University Press, 1980); Thomas M. Greene, "Petrarch and the Humanist Hermeneutic," in *Italian Literature: Roots and Branches,* ed. Giose Rimanelli and Kenneth J. Atchity (New Haven, CT: Yale University Press, 1976), 201–24; Ernest H. Wilkins, "A General Survey of Renaissance Petrarchism," *Comparative Literature* 2.4 (1950): 327–42.

5. For a few good studies on the French *Pléiade,* see Louisa Mackenzie, *The Poetry of Place: Lyric, Landscape, and Ideology in Renaissance France* (Toronto: University of Toronto Press, 2011);

included Pierre de Ronsard, Joachim du Bellay, Pontus de Tynard, Jean-Antoine de Baïf, Guillaume Desautels, Etienne Jodelle, and Jean de La Péruse, seemed dedicated to the revival of classical lyricism, and although these poets would certainly not escape the influence of the Petrarchan mode, they appeared to base their poetic identity on their connection to Catullus, Ovid, Horace, and others from the classical world. However, what seems clear about this group of poets is that despite their return to the classics, their literary program is very much concerned with validating and legitimizing their identity as *French* poets.[6] Their emphasis—and dilemma—seemed to be that they wanted to return to the classical tradition, but only as it could be articulated and improved on in their native French tongue.

Du Bellay, as I have noted previously, argued for the value of the French language, and the need to recast the classical world in his own French image was at the very least an unconscious attempt to identify a lack in the classical Other and to replace it with a new and improved classical tradition. The strange tension that existed in the French identity (caused by the need to be both classical and French) was felt at a very fundamental level of French criticism and was nowhere more apparent than in du Bellay's *Deffence et illustration de la langue françoyse* (1549).[7] There is constant vacillation in *Deffence* between du Bellay's praise for and criticism of classical language

Jo Ann Della Neva, *Unlikely Exemplars: Reading and Imitating beyond the Italian Canon in French Renaissance Poetry* (Newark: University of Delaware Press, 2009); David Coward, *A History of French Literature: From Chanson de Geste to Cinema* (Oxford: Blackwell, 2002); Claude Faisant, *Mort et résurrection de la Pléiade* (Paris: H. Champion, 1998); Guy Demerson, *La mythologie classique dans l'oeuvre lyrique de la Pléiade* (Geneva: Droz, 1972); and Grahame Castor, *Pléiade Poetics: A Study in Sixteenth-Century Thought and Terminology* (Cambridge: Cambridge University Press, 1964).

Much earlier than even the French *Pléiade,* there was a group of Italian writers, the Chariteean Petrarchans (which included Serafino d'Aquilano, Benedetto "Il Chariteo" Gareth, and Antonio Tebaldi), known for their shift away from Petrarch toward the classical lyricists Catullus, Propertius, Tibullus, Ovid, and others. Speaking of Gareth, Patricia Thomson, in "Wyatt and the School of Serafino," *Comparative Literature* 13 (1961): 289–315, states that his work "is no servile copy of the sonnets to Laura. . . . His strong predilection for the pagan love poets, Propertius, Tibullus, Catullus, Ovid, and Horace, modified the attitude toward the love theme derived from Petrarch" (290). See also Giovanni Parenti, *Benet Garret detto il Cariteo: Profilo di un poeta* (Florence: Olschki, 1993); and Alessandro Tortoreto, *Lirici Cortigiani del Quattrocento: Il Chariteo, il Tebaldeo, l'Aquilano* (Milan: Leonardo, 1942).

6. See William J. Kennedy, *The Site of Petrarchism: Early Modern Sentiment in Italy, France, and England* (Baltimore: Johns Hopkins University Press, 2003); Timothy Hampton, *Literature and Nation in the Sixteenth Century: Inventing Renaissance France* (Ithaca, NY: Cornell University Press, 2001); James B. Atkinson, "Naïveté and Modernity: The French Renaissance Battle for a Literary Vernacular," *Journal of the History of Ideas* 35.2 (1974): 179–96.

7. For a recent discussion of du Bellay's *Le Deffence,* see the first section of Hassan Melehy, *The Poetics of Literary Transfer,* 17–71; see also Greene, *The Light in Troy,* 220–41; and Margaret W. Ferguson, "The Exile's Defense: Du Bellay's *La Deffence et illustration de la langue François,*" *Publications of the Modern Language Association* 93.2 (1978): 275–89.

and culture. As his purpose is to validate French as a worthy tongue, he must position his personal and national justification within the broader humanist valorization of the classical world:

> If our language is neither as rich nor as copious as either Greek or Latin, it should not be imputed to any defect in the language, as if it could ever be deficient or sterile on its own. It should rather be attributed to the ignorance of our forefathers who, as someone said of the ancient Romans, had more regard for noble actions than for fine words, preferring to leave for posterity examples of valour sooner than wise sayings. (Willet, *Poetry & Language*, 1.3.45)[8]

Latin, particularly, represents a kind of linguistic perfection, one that formed because Romans quickly "trimmed off the useless branches and restored it by replacing them with sound, domestic growths, masterfully derived from the Greek language" (1.3.45). Still, despite his praise of the model itself, du Bellay still criticizes "those ambitious idolaters of Greek and Latin, who, even if they were Pytho, goddess of persuasion herself, would not believe that anything valid could be expressed except in a foreign language not understood by a commoner" (1.4.46). This idea of a "common," vernacular language is important to du Bellay and his ultimate insinuation that his own French can be better—more accessible, more ideologically relevant—than those classical models. However, in order to validate, to situate the identity of his French language, he still must locate himself and his language within that classical origin: "Let he who wishes to enrich his language set about imitating the finest Greek and Latin authors" (1.8.51). He even justifies his own praise of French by citing Cicero's praise of Latin over Greek (1.12.62).

In *Les Regrets*, du Bellay shows us the speaker's celebration of his home and time, but that speaker can only valorize them by somehow dismissing the authority of Rome. As we have seen, however, he must first praise the thing he must eventually dismiss:

> Heureux qui, comme Ulysse, a fait un beau voyage,
> Ou comme cestuy là qui conquit la toison,

---

8. I use Laura Willet's translations of the French essays in *Poetry & Language in 16th-Century France: Du Bellay, Ronsard, Sebillet* (Toronto: Centre for Reformation and Renaissance Studies, 2003); however, the poems quoted below are taken from Hope Glidden and Norman R. Shapiro, eds., *Lyrics of the French Renaissance: Marot, Du Bellay, Ronsard* (New Haven, CT and London: Yale University Press, 2002); I also include verse translations from Glidden and Shapiro for longer passages.

Et puis est retourné, plein d'usage & raison,
Vivre entre ses parents le reste de son aage.

Happy the man who, like Ulysses, went
Sailing afar; or him who won the fleece,
Then, wise and worldly grown, returned to Greece,
Amongst his own, to live and die content. (31.1–4)

Here, Ulysses is established as the prototype for the centripetal man, who returns to his own home, family, and friends after his worldly experience and conquered hardships. But Ulysses and his world are immediately undermined, as the speaker wishes to return to his own home. Still, compared to the Greek, the speaker's home is a "pauvre maison," but one that the speaker loves more than the marbled ruins or salty breeze of Rome:

Plus me plaist le sejour qu'ont basty mes ayeux,
Que des palais Romains le front audacieux:
Plus que le marbre dur me plaist l'ardoise fine,

Plus mon Loyre Gaulois que le Tybre Latin,
Plus mon petit Lyré que le mont Palatin,
Et plus que l'air marin la doulceur Angevine.

More do I love the home my father made
Than Rome's bold palaces, in pride arrayed:
More do I love fine slate than marble rare;

More than their Tiber do I love my Loire;
Their Palatine, more my Liré by far;
And more than sea's salt breeze, Anjou's soft air. (31.9–14)

The speaker manages to pay tribute to Rome and then to subvert that praise by returning spatially to contemporary France, to his birthplace (Liré), and to the gentle, sweet air of Anjou.

Du Bellay's rhetoric is not surprising, but such discourse once again illustrates that even in the most basic sense, the humanist can only confirm his own self by defining his relationship to that classical Other. Somehow, French had to be part of and distinct from its classical predecessors. He paradoxically criticizes "idolaters of Greek and Latin" by referencing the Greek goddess Pytho. He defends his own rhetoric in French by situating it among

Cicero's Latin examples. Du Bellay strives to find an autonomous presence for himself, for French, for his culture, but that autonomy is always in flux, always situated around the *idea* of the past, and finally validated only by showing how much *like* the past it really is. But the lack in the past has to be identified: Latin and Greek must be shown to be too privileged, not a true voice of the French humanist. He asks: "Why then are we such great admirers of others? Why are we so hateful to ourselves?" (Willet, *Poetry & Language,* 2.12.88).

Along with du Bellay, Ronsard was one of the most prominent and influential of the *Pléiade,* and his writing, like du Bellay's, reflects this classical crisis of the humanist program.[9] Ronsard's preface to his group of odes really takes to task the status of French, at the very least as a source of imitation:

> Imitating French Poets is so distasteful to me (since the language is still in its infancy) that I have distanced myself from them, creating a different style, a different meaning, a different body of work, and want nothing to do with such a monstrous mistake as they have made. (Willet, *Poetry & Language,* "Preface," 102)

The emphasis on being *different,* the need and desire to somehow become an autonomous literary voice, is noteworthy. Still, it is in the classical lyricists (at least in theory) that he seeks to find his own voice: "So, as I make my way along an unbeaten path, showing how to follow Pindar and Horace . . . " ("Preface," 102). And like du Bellay, he justifies or validates his purpose by positioning himself against precedent; he states that what Horace said "modestly" about himself applies to him as well: "Libera per uacuum posui uestigia princeps, non aliena meo pressi pede" (Horace, *Epistulae* 1.19.21–22). He also credits himself with the "resuscitation" of the classical lyricists because of his own "intervention" ("Preface," 102). Ronsard's positioning himself away from his fellow French writers and raising the classical lyricists from the dead, so to speak, is again typical of humanist identity formation. Like pulling up ruins from the past, he dusts off what he believes are the

---

9. See David Quint, "Petrarch, Ronsard, and the Seven-Year Itch," *Modern Language Notes* 124.5 (2009): 137–54; Lance Donaldson-Evans, "Ronsard's Folies Bergères: The Livret Des Folastries and Petrarch," *Neophilologus* 91.1 (2007): 1–17; Sara Sturm-Maddox, *Ronsard, Petrarch, and the Amours* (Gainesville: University Press of Florida, 1999); Jo Ann Della Neva, "Petrarch at the Portal: Opening Signals in 'Les Amours' de Ronsard," *Rivista di Letterature Moderne e Comparate* 50.3 (1997): 259–72; and Sharon Nell, "A Bee in Pindar's Bonnet: Humanistic Imitation in Ronsard, La Fontaine, and Rococo Style," in *Recapturing the Renaissance: New Perspectives on Humanism, Dialogue, and Texts,* ed. Diane S. Wood and Paul Allen Miller (Knoxville, TN: New Paradigm Press, 1996), 181–220.

forgotten writers of that past, situates his own work among them, and thus feels validated. However, he implies a lack in his sources, for he, just as du Bellay did more explicitly, writes in French, presumably for the French.

Ronsard's odes themselves are very much a mix, a blending, of classical sources with shades and hints of Petrarch. Ronsard's work obviously prioritizes any classical elements over French or Italian. There are places such as in this ode from *Le Cinquiesme Livre Des Odes,* where a clear instance of imitation is found—this one from Catullus and his counting of kisses:

Ma Maistresse, que j'aime mieux
Dix mille fois ny que mes yeux,
Ny que mon coeur, ny que ma vie,
Ne me donne plus, je te prie,
Des confitures pour manger,
Pensant ma fiévre soulager.
Car ta confiture, Mignonne,
Tant elle est douce, ne me donne
Qu'un desir de tousjours vouloir
Estre malade, pour avoir
Tes friandises en la bouche.

My Mistress, whom I idolize
Ten thousand times more than my eyes
Or than my heart, or than my very
Life, I beseech you, no more berry
Jellies and jams, no matter how
You think they cool my fevered brow!
For your preserves are sweet, my Pet;
So sweet that I would gladly let
Myself be ever ailing, thus
To eat and eat them, gluttonous. (1–11)

In other places, classical allusion to a god or motif or theme becomes relatively sacramental in its use. Such sacramental imitation does nothing to promote the kind of uniqueness of style that Ronsard had claimed was his purpose, except that it was not French or Italian:

De ma brebis ecorchée,
Morte entre les dens du lou,
À toi j'apen à ce clou

La dépouille pour trofée.
Ô Dieu Pan, si quelque grace
T'emeut en lieu de ceci,
Donne m'en cet an icy
Un cent d'autres en sa place.

As a tribute, Pan, to you,
My ewe's carcass here I hang,
She who fell to wolf's sharp fang,
Whom the beast held fast and slew.
Worthy god! If this scapegrace
Moves your heart to tenderness,
Pray give me this year no less
Than a hundred in her place. ("D'un Pasteur au Dieu Pan," *Le Bocage*, 1–8)

In both these examples there is very little that transcends the classical origins of their construction. This is from a Lacanian sense a kind of Imaginary self-positioning that does not deal with or even recognize a self separate from the Other. Ronsard seems to be comfortable in locating himself and his poetry within the past and not explicitly challenging the validity or even acknowledging the gap between his own ideological present and that valorized Other. Ronsard had characterized the French language as being in its infancy, and as with the infant there is no self-identity beyond its connection with that past.

Other poems within Ronsard's lyric corpus do begin to reflect a more "separate" sense of itself than these two poems, which capture very little of an identifiable self beyond its classical positioning, and thus move toward a more Symbolic mode of self-fashioning. In "D'une courtizanne à Venus," from *Le Bocage*, Ronsard seems to separate himself from the classical authority he uses. It is a playful poem, but one that clearly rises above simple eclectic imitation and tries to use the classical allusion only as a place from which to deviate and ultimately to mark a return to the present:

Si je puis ma jeunesse folle,
Hantant les bordeaus, garentir
De ne pouvoir jamais sentir
Ne poulains, chancre, ne verole,

Ô Venus, de Bacus compaigne,
À toi je promets en mes voeus

Mon éponge, et mes faus cheveus,
Mon fard, mon miroer, et mon paigne.

If, by whatever artifice,
You guard my youth, in brothel spent—
My foolish youth, on pleasure bent—
From sore, and scab, and syphilis,
I promise to bequeath to you,
Consort of Bacchus, Venus fair,
My puff, my artificial hair,
My rouge, my comb, my mirror too. (1–8)

Of course there were courtesans in ancient Rome, but this poem seems to situate this sacrifice to Venus in a more contemporary context. There is an underlying feeling that the court itself is being satirized here, with the "mes faus cheveus" and "mon éponge" and certainly with the references to venereal disease—"Ne poulains, chancre, ne verole"—which was always a topic of some amusement for Renaissance writers. There is a clear engagement here between present and past. The allusion to Venus serves as an anchor of valorization that gives Ronsard's statements about sixteenth-century sexuality and perhaps even sixteenth-century court behavior a kind of literary validity or resonance. Even beyond that, there is a feeling of the poet relinquishing the present to the past, giving up the present pomp to the glory of Venus. Ronsard's sixteenth-century sexuality is stained, is lacking in grandeur when compared to the beauty of Venus. The subtext of this rather light poem is that Rome has Venus, Bacchus, and the rich stories of love and sexuality; Ronsard's France has only fake hair, vain self-acclaimed beauty, and scabs and sores, all of which must be given up as sacrifice to the greatness of Venus. What is acknowledged here that is not in the first two poems quoted above is that Ronsard's world is *not* the classical world; difference is present, and difference defines. Although Ronsard essentially derides his own present for the past, in doing so he gives his present an identity. To construct that identity fully, however, he must then find a lack in the Other and validate the legitimacy and superiority of his own ideological reality.

Perhaps the best illustration—still in Ronsard's comic tone—of the anxiety that confronts him and humanist writers in general is his "Imitation de Martial" in *Les Poemes*. That Ronsard liked—and indeed imitated—Martial is obvious in Ronsard's opus, but this poem captures the cost of imitation and praise:

Ha mauditte nature! hé, pourquoy m'as tu fait
Si dextrement formé d'esprit et de corsage?
Que ne m'as tu fait nain, ou chevelu sauvage?
Niez, badin, ou fol, ou monster contrefait?

Si j'estois nain j'aurois toute chose à souhait,
J'aurois soixante sols par jour et d'avantage,
J'aruois faveur du Roy, caresse, et bon visage,
Bien en point, bien vestu, bien gras, et bien refait.

Ah! que vous fustes fols, mes parents, de me faire
Pauvre escolier Latin! vous deviez contrefaire
Mon corps, ou me nourrir à l'escole des fous.

Ah! ingrates chansons! ah! malheureuses Muses!
Rompez moy par depit fleuttes et cornemuses,
Puis qu'aujourd'huy les nains sont plus heureus que nous.

Au, cursed nature! Why did you decide
To fashion me so hale of mind and breast?
Why not a dwarf? Why not some beast unblest,
Shaggy, wild, daft; some monster ogrefied?

Were I a dwarf, naught would I be denied:
I would have sixty sous a day, caressed
By King and court; be plump, well dressed,
Bedecked, beprized, and much beloved beside.

Ah, foolish parents, who my youth misspent
With Latin! Best had they misshapen, bent
My limbs, or schooled me in stupidity!

Ah, useless songs! Ah, Muses, worthless brutes!
Dashed to bits be my damnèd pipes, my flutes,
Since dwarfs, today, are happier far, than we! (1–11)

This piece functions primarily as a contemplative poem about imitating classical writers, Martial in particular. This poem, as much as any other, obsesses over the dwarfing of the present in the presence of the past, but it also expresses a futility in approaching the classics and classical language at all ("Pauvre escolier Latin!"). The speaker cries out in the last stanza that basically his songs are useless, that for his own cursed and seemingly inadequate "fleuttes et cornemuses" the Muses are worthless to him, and his instruments should be tossed to the ground. The not so subtle implication here is that those flutes and pipes are dwarfed by the ancients, are incapable of living up to the past, and must live anxiously inferior in the reality of the present.

Marvell's Two Gardens: Rewriting the Roman *Hortus*[10]

Denying that language itself represents a crucial locus of identity is nearly impossible in today's critical climate. In fact, our modern experience itself makes clear the ties of language and identity. In south-central and southwestern Louisiana, Cajun French is considered the essence of an entire cultural and ethnic tradition, and as a result you can find Cajun and Creole French exclusively spoken in many homes and broadcast on certain radio stations in the Acadien area.[11] Similarly, the native Coushatta tribe, in which well less than a hundred still speak the language, is desperately trying to revitalize the Coushatta language and reeducate the tribe members about it, even pressuring the state of Louisiana to recognize Coushatta as a foreign language eligible to be taught in local schools. A resurgence in the language is considered by tribe elders to be integral to the survival and security of tribal identity. In the United Kingdom, Wales has been trying to regain its linguistic tradition for some time, with reasonable success; signage, publications, some public documents, and monuments typically include both English and Welsh. In all these cases, language is at least as much a cultural and identity signifier as spatial boundaries or even specific cultural practices or traditions. Physical borders are somewhat arbitrary; customs and traditions, though important and often lasting, can fade away and be replaced with new customs. However, language, despite its natural changes and developments, is at least *perceived* as a constant cultural marker, one that, once lost, can destroy the identity of an entire cultural consciousness.

10. A version of this section originally appeared as "Marvell's Two Gardens: Re-writing the Roman Hortus," *Andrew Marvell Newsletter* 2.2 (2011), http://academic.stedwards.edu/marvell/jacob-blevins-marvells-two-gardens—re-writing-the-roman-hortus/.

11. French in the region existed for some time as exclusively oral; see Barry Ancelet, *Cajun and Creole Folktales: The French Oral Tradition of South Louisiana* (Jackson: University Press of Mississippi, 1994); these trends to solidify the language itself are evident in such recent works as *Dictionary of Louisiana French: As Spoken in Cajun, Creole, and American Indian Communities* (Jackson: University Press of Mississippi, 2010).

The actual loss of language is not what is at issue in the early modern context with which this study is concerned; rather, this study focuses on the need for validating identity through language. We have already seen how writers such as du Bellay look to the vernacular as a way, as I argue here, to legitimize the autonomy of the writer's quest for poetic identity, to break from a past tradition that constantly threatens to envelop and consume any attempt at unique literary expression. Consistent with a kind of pervasive classical crisis for which I argue, du Bellay both attacks Latin (most notably in *Deffence et illustration de la langue françoyse*) and then turns around and writes in Latin himself elsewhere—and in some cases even translates his own Latin poetry *back* into French. Petrarch went back and forth from Latin to Italian (Petrarch wrote *Africanus* in Latin, the sonnets for Laura in Italian). And English writers certainly were concerned about exactly the same thing, as evidenced by Francis Meres and Richard Carew, who both argued in the early seventeenth century that the "excellency" of the English language compares favorably to that of the Latin and Greek. Although critics have always recognized the importance of the vernacular and the attempt to establish the vernacular as an authoritative mode of expression, there simply has not been enough discussion about the significance of writers choosing to forgo the vernacular and turning back to Latin. Neo-Latin poetry is often accepted as a kind of stable genre, and only the deviation from that genre through the vernacular is viewed as consequential. I would argue that the significance flows both ways. When these Renaissance writers choose to write in Latin, a language that fundamentally belongs to another cultural consciousness, there is significance to that; there is a statement of poetic identity present in that decision—conscious or unconscious. Kenneth Haynes has also recognized and, more uniquely in critical discussions of Neo-Latin, emphasized this:

> When authors choose the language in which they write, their choices should be investigated because the choice implies that the language of a work could have been different, and one of the things literary criticism may do is answer the question of why a work is as it is and not otherwise.[12]

Not only is "why" a work is as it is important, but also "how" it is what it is. What does the choice of language mean for the poem, and what would a *different* choice of language have meant? Unfortunately such conjecture is

---

12. Kenneth Haynes, *English Literature and Ancient Languages* (Oxford: Oxford University Press, 2003), 21.

usually just that; but there are examples of self-translation that can give us a glimpse into the significance of exactly the choice Haynes addresses. At this intersection of the vernacular and of the language of humanism's classical memory, we once again find a crisis of identity.

That English writers suffered from the same kind of crisis is clear. Andrew Marvell, particularly, offers a unique example and insight into the process of classical appropriation and the subsequent attempt at redefining the poet as a relevant, timely, and significant figure in his own ideological space. England seemed even one step further away from the (M)Other figure of the classical world, but its need to connect to and then separate from that world was as much a part of its writers' identity as it was for France's. Marvell's classicism deserves a comprehensive study; it is a classicism that is both complex and lucid, both explicit and implicit, and ultimately, much like Milton (though to a lesser degree), representative of humanism's pre-Enlightenment culmination of literary expression. This is not the time for such a thorough and comprehensive reading of Marvell's classicism, but a look at two of his garden poems will offer a useful example of his contribution to the topic at hand and help show the psychical dynamic to his classical appropriation. The interaction, or perhaps evolution, of Marvell's "twin" poems, "Hortus" and "The Garden," illustrates a method of imitation and influence that is indicative of the psychical processes of identity formation that were central to humanism and that were the cause of conflict and crisis in the assimilation of the classical and Christian in Renaissance texts. Marvell's "Hortus" represents a relatively simple form of eclectic or sacramental appropriation. Even though the poem as a whole is not a direct imitation of a specific classical source—though the Horatian components are obvious—it is an attempt at recreating a classical mode, a classical space, with no identification in the present, even in the actual language used. For the effective humanist writer, this kind of total reliance on tradition is unacceptable; it devalues the relevance of the writer's current context. In "The Garden," however, Marvell attempts to "rewrite" the classical space that dominates "Hortus," but he must do it in a way that both fixes his work in a tradition and then exposes what that tradition lacks. Marvell's garden poems contain the fissures and ideological repositioning that are characteristic of humanism's classical crisis, but they actually take us one step further in the writer's Symbolic self-construction.

Curiously, gardening and gardens themselves have proved to be a fascinating and well-explored topic of study. British classicist Diana Spencer has done work on the representation of the garden space in the Roman poets Statius and—and even more important to our purpose here—

Horace.[13] The early modern garden—obviously significant for Marvellians—is the topic of Rebecca Bushnell's 2004 book *Green Desire*. And any reader of Renaissance literature can recall many substantial "garden" passages in the early modern corpus (Shakespeare's *Richard II*, Milton's *Paradise Lost*, and so on). While the Christian garden draws much from its biblical origins, the *literary* garden seems to be grounded in the classical *hortus* and the pastoral tradition more generally. This sort of convergence of the classical and Christian in the garden image in many ways exemplifies the humanist program itself. Again, the Christian and the classical attempt to exist simultaneously, often anachronistically, with the literary grounded in the pagan and the ideological grounded in the Christian. The writer validates his poetic identity by engaging the classical, and his ideological identity by engaging the Christian. The problem is that this identifies a lack in the Christian tradition (i.e., the poet needs the achievement of the ancients; the Christian—despite many attempts by many writers—simply does not provide a suitable literary precedent). The result—at least in sophisticated, well-conceived imitation—is writers' identifying the lack in the classical world by showing, implicitly and explicitly, that the classical is nonetheless incomplete without the Christian despite its literary authority: the Christian fills the lack in the pagan past.

Marvell's two poems show us two distinct levels or modes of literary identification with that past. That both poems are connected to classical sources has been fairly well established. John M. Potter gives an excellent analysis of Horatian elements in the two poems.[14] Although Potter probably overstates the Horatian/Epicurean elements and underestimates the impact of the Judeo-Christian in "The Garden," his overall assessment of the classical in Marvell is solid and insightful. Potter believes that other critics, such as Stanley Stewart, H. E. Toliver, and Ruth Wallerstein, all take the poems too seriously and thus miss the greater significance of the classical, satiric, Horatian tone. My concern is less that the poems are classical but rather how Marvell attempts to make them classical.

13. Diana Spencer, "Singing in the Garden: Statius' plein air Lyric (after Horace)," in *Dialogism and Lyric Self-Fashioning: Bakhtin and the Voices of a Genre*, ed. Jacob Blevins (Selinsgrove, PA: Susquehanna University Press, 2008), 66–83.

14. See John M. Potter, "Another Porker in the Garden of Epicurus: Marvell's 'Hortus' and 'The Garden,'" *Studies in English Literature* 11 (1971): 137–51. See also Dominic Gavin, "'The Garden' and Marvell's Literal Figures," *Cambridge Quarterly* 37.2 (2008): 224–52; Andrew Barnaby, "The Politics of Garden Spaces: Andrew Marvell and the Anxieties of Public Speech," *Studies in Philology* 97.3 (2000): 331–61; Margaret Ann Carpenter, "Marvell's 'Garden,'" *Studies in English Literature* 10.1 (1970): 155–69.

With "Hortus" Marvell's attempt at creating a kind of classical, Epicurean pastoral ode hinges on the complete recreation of the classical space that was the norm in the original classical pastoral garden ode, on multiple levels. This starts with the mythological. "Hortus" is rooted in classical myth. Classical mythology is of course commonplace in Renaissance texts, but here the speaker pays full respect and commitment to the authority of that myth. Apollo and the Muses are invoked:

> Me quoque, vos Musae, et te conscie testor Apollo,
> Non Armenta juvant hominum, Circique boatus,
> Mugitusve Fori; sed me Penetralia veris,
> Horroresque trahunt muti, et Consortia sola. (16–19)

Apollo is here referred to as "testor Apollo," suggesting "all knowing," even "omniscient," which retains the original deific quality of Apollo. We have a full catalogue of other deities that reflects those classical figures associated with lovers and trees:

> Jupiter annosam, neglecta conjuge, Quercum
> Deperit; haud alia doluit sic pellice Juno.
> Lemniacum temerant vestigia nulla Cubile,
> Nec Veneris Mavors meminit si Fraxinus adsit.
> Formosae pressit Daphnes vestigia Phoebus
> Ut fieret Laurus; sed nil quaesiverat ultra. (41–46)

The identity of the poem's speaker is placed squarely within this mythological realm, and, even more important, the speaker is placed within the actual physical *space* of the classical world. Lines 17 and 18 situate the speaker in the peaceful green of the garden by differentiating it from the Roman Forum and from the Circus of Rome. "Hortus" is fundamentally different from a poem like "To His Coy Mistress," where Marvell's *carpe diem* motif is subtly situated in a much more contemporary world—there are elements of Catullus, Horace, and Ovid in "To His Coy Mistress," but the world of the poem remains fixed in the present. So in terms of "Hortus," despite the fact it is a fine Latin poem and a fine replication of a kind of Epicurean idealism, simply said, there is absolutely nothing English about it, nothing Christian, nothing that identifies or creates a seventeenth-century literary voice. Neither the speaker nor the writer has any real presence in the poem. The poem's Latin language and Latin meter remove it even further from the present. There certainly is nothing inherently wrong with this, but such imitation does force a reader to question the poem's purpose and makes clear that in it Marvell the poet is not reaching beyond the superficial sacramental rendering of his "source." As a humanist, Marvell the poet is at least implicitly paying a significant tribute to the classical Other that gives the humanist writer so much of his identity. To know and imitate the classics is admirable and demonstrates talent, but it is ultimately restrictive and ideologically void of a contemporary consciousness. The original folio printer of the volume containing this poem assumed (apparently based on Christian elements found in "The Garden") that something had to be missing (*desunt multa* was inserted right before line 50). It was almost as if he were saying: "Certainly there has to be something else to this."

In a way, Marvell imitates his own poem in "The Garden," and a primary goal in that imitation seems to be to redefine and ultimately reassess the valorization of the classical in the Latin version.[15] The opening of "The Garden" contains a passage that is very close to its Latin counterpart:

How vainly men themselves amaze
To win the Palm, the Oke, Or Bayes;
And their uncessant Labours see
Crown'd from som single Herb or Tree,
Whose Short and narrow verged Shade
Does prudently their toyles upbraid;
While all Flow'rs and all Trees do close
To Weave the Garlands of repose. (1–8)

The first two lines of the Latin "Hortus" read thus: "Quisnam adeo, mortale genus, praecordia versat? / Heu Palmae, Laruique furor, vel simplicis Herbae." The first two lines in both poems similarly question man's quest for public recognition. But subtle differences in the English declassicize the Latin version, which directly echoes certain commonplaces in classical literature. First, while the speaker of "Hortus" fears the "madness" (*furor*) of clinging to poetic fame or some other earthly glory, "The Garden" emphasizes the "vanity" of it. While the general classical "tone" in the English poem is present, the reference to vanity suggests a much more contemporary, Christian ideological concern. It is not the *furor* of an Orpheus, Pentheus, Ajax, or Heracles (all fallen to madness) from which the speaker suffers or could suffer, but of a self-serving interest in fame, in public approval and

15. Even though the Latin poem is commonly considered to have come first, if it were determined that that was indeed not the case, the interaction of the classicism in the two poems would still function similarly.

praise, all elements that challenge fundamental Christian humility. In addition, Marvell leaves out of his list of "Palm, Oak, and Bayes," the more classical "laurel" of Apollo that is part of the equivalent list in "Hortus" (*Palmae, Laurique*).

In stanza 4 of "The Garden" the mythological imagery is reduced to merely two classical episodes:

> The Gods, that mortal Beauty chase,
> Still in a Tree did end their race.
> Apollo hunted Daphne so,
> Only that She might Laurel grow.
>
> And Pan did after Syrinx speed,
> Not as a nymph, but for a reed. (27–32)

These are the only two classical "love stories" referenced—"Hortus" mentions several others, including Jupiter, Juno, Mars, and Venus. In both versions, the speakers pervert the original myths, suggesting that Apollo and Pan did not have any real desire for these nymphs but simply desired the trees they would become. The Latin version is even a bit more explicit than "Apollo hunted Daphne so / only that She might laurel grow." The Latin reads that Apollo pursued lovely Daphne for the laurel but "nil quaesiverat ultra" (but he sought nothing beyond this). This interpretation of the stories of Apollo and Pan in the *Metamorphoses* seems far-fetched—that is, that these deities wanted only the trees themselves, not the actual nymphs they chased. Nevertheless, regardless of the somewhat ludicrous reading of the myths by the speaker, both figures—Apollo and Pan—that do make it into "The Garden" are related closely to poetry and song, and therefore still relevant to the speaker's purpose.

A significant difference can be seen in "The Garden" in its reference to Gods that "mortal Beauty chase." The gods, Apollo and Pan, apparently are initially chasing some kind of "mortal beauty." Mythologically, that is not really true either; both Syrinx and Daphne are minor deities and thus immortal from the start, and it is not common for the beauty of a nymph to fade (i.e., to be mortal). This emphasis on mortal beauty is not at all addressed in "Hortus." The myth itself is used similarly in both poems, but "The Garden" contains a particular subtext, namely, that the natural love of the trees in the garden is somehow beyond simple earthly love and thus transcends the physical beauty perhaps implicit in "mortal beauty." The entire reference suggests a kind of Christian Neoplatonic notion of beauty, whereby the speaker's love of the green garden represents a greater love of something heavenly. The Christian comes in and really violates the integrity of the classical that was fully intact in "Hortus," and thus sets up the greater Christian implications in "The Garden" as a whole. In an essentially humanist move, the classical is recreated but only insofar as it can be undermined by the immediacy of the Christian and of the poet's own space and time. Here, the Circus Maximus and the Forum are nowhere to be found, but as if the writer cannot progress too far from the classical ode, the garden space here is left ambiguous.

Ultimately, instead of the speaker simply relishing the garden on its own terms, as one might find in a classical pastoral of private contemplation or as one *does* find in "Hortus," in "The Garden" the speaker anachronistically inserts the Christian as a means of validating the relevance of the largely classical garden that is the subject of the poem. With only the slight suggestion of a Christian presence earlier in "The Garden," such as the examples already mentioned, we the readers are brought strangely and abruptly within the Judeo-Christian realm as the speaker justifies his own celebration of peace and solitude:

> Such was that happy Garden-state
> While Man there walk'd without a mate:
> After a Place so pure, and sweet,
> What other Help could yet be meet!
> But 'twas beyond a Mortal's share
> To wander solitary there:
> Two Paradises 'twere in one
> To live in Paradise alone. (57–64)

Of course the seriousness of the passage is very doubtful, with the idea that man perhaps was in an even better paradise, a double paradise, before his mate arrived on the scene.[16] The satirical nature of the stanza indeed captures the essence of what Marvell does with the classical references in "Hortus"—lovers are better off carving the names of trees on trees than the names of lovers. But here somehow the sentiment of solitude needs a

---

16. Milton's Satan demonstrates the opposite sentiment in Book 4 of *Paradise Lost*, after he sees Adam and Eve embracing one another:

> Sight hateful, sight tormenting! thus these two
> Imparadis't in one another's arms
> The happier *Eden*, shall enjoy thir fill
> Of bliss on bliss. (505–8)

Christian precedent; somehow this places the virtue of solitude in the here and now and gives the speaker an actual identity—perhaps a Christian identity—that is missing in "Hortus."

In addition, the final stanza emphasizes the gardener rather than the maker of the garden, which in "Hortus" seems to be represented by Apollo and his association with the sun. But still the bee image in "The Garden"— "And, as it works, the industrious Bee computes its time as well as we"— directly echoes not just the closing of "Hortus" with its "Sedula Apis" (the officious or busy bee) that marks its work with thyme but even Horace himself in *Ode* 4.2, when he compares his own hard work of writing poetry to the hard-working Mantinian bee who busily gathers thyme. It is as if as quickly as the poet finds a Judeo-Christian image that works to move the ode forward, he turns back on himself, almost in doubt, and returns to a direct classical allusion—one that we have already seen used in "Hortus."

Catullus and the Sons of Ben[17]

One of few direct literary imitations I have mentioned to this point is Ronsard's imitation of Catullus ("Ma Maistresse, que j'aime mieux"), and it is not surprising to see such clear borrowing from Catullus in the French corpus. Many poets imitated Catullus during the Renaissance, particularly his Lesbia poems and wedding songs.[18] Catullus' *Carmina,* though relatively short for the most part, provide an array of styles, forms, themes, and emotional expression. As I, Micaela W. Janan, Paul Allen Miller, and others have discussed extensively, Catullus' poetry represents a complex ideological, poetic, and psychical notion of identity and subject positioning.[19] Catullus' speaker continually positions his desire and his conception of self within various sets of discursive signifiers: political, military, religious, and domestic. The result is a multilayered text that offers paradox, conflicting emotional subjectivity, and a lyric consciousness that is self-revising and always in flux. In the well-known Lesbia poems—those poems

17. This section on Catullus and the Sons of Ben is a revised version of a section in my *Catulllan Consciousness,* 114–22.

18. See Blevins, *Catullan Consciousness;* Julia Haig Gaisser, *Catullus and His Renaissance Readers* (Oxford: Oxford University Press, 1993); and James A. S. McPeek, *Catullus in Strange and Distant Britain* (Cambridge, MA: Harvard University Press, 1939).

19. Blevins, *Catullan Consciousness;* Miller, *Lyric Texts, Lyric Consciousness;* Miller, *Subjecting Verses;* Janan, *"When the Lamp Is Shattered";* William Fitzgerald, *Catullan Provocations: Lyric Poetry and the Drama of Position* (Berkeley: University of California Press, 1995); and R. O. A. M. Lyne, *The Latin Love Poets* (Oxford: Clarendon Press, 1980).

written about the speaker's specific lover affair with a mistress—the reader often finds a conflicting zone of desire, the articulation of which leads the speaker to define his affair with an unreliable, and uncommitted, mistress in terms of various Roman virtues, such as *pietas, amicitia, officium,* and *fides.* These concepts are related to Roman civic ideals, and the speaker justifies his own commitment to Lesbia by using these signifiers as a kind of linguistic and ideological validation of his desire. R. O. A. M Lynne states that at the time, Catullus' Rome did not have "a vocabulary for profound commitment in love . . . but it did have a highly developed code . . . of social commitment."[20] Similarly, William Fitzgerald calls the speaker's discourse of love a "rhetoric of aristocratic obligation," but that discourse is undermined by the inadequacy of the context to uphold the validity of the discourse itself: "The Catullan lover speaks with a great intensity a language that has been deprived of the social context that would render it efficacious; the poet's language, too, acquires much of its energy from the fact that it is withdrawn from the usual social contexts."[21] As the speaker continually attempts to define his desire in such terms, those terms often collapse on themselves as the idealism of the code itself becomes inapplicable to the realities of the affair. As I have argued elsewhere, there was a similar kind of ruptured discourse in Petrarchism and the Renaissance lyric as Neoplatonic idealism failed to provide a discourse that could adequately reflect desires that were antithetical to that idealism (the lovers in Wyatt, Shakespeare, Sidney, and Donne, for example). Such rupture is inherent in the lyric space and the lyric subject. These Petrarchan (or, perhaps, anti-Petrarchan) writers did not typically imitate the classics directly, but the written lyric genre, which Catullus helped develop, would influence the nature of genre for these early modern poets. Because of this, one might expect that a group of early modern lyric poets *explicitly* returning to Catullus as model would reflect the intricacies of Catullus' verses. Oddly enough for Ben Jonson and his followers, a return to the classics often meant doing serious violence to the poetic foundations of their sources. Jonson and the "Sons of Ben" return to direct borrowing of the classics, but their sources are declassicized, put into contexts that remove those sources from their classical origins.

Looking for Jonson's adoption of Catullus' Lesbia poems, one must turn to Jonson's three poems to Celia, two of which are close adaptations of the material found in Catullus' *Carmina* 5 and 7,[22] the two poems dealing

---

20. Lyne, *The Latin Love Poets,* 24.
21. Fitzgerald, *Catullan Provocations,* 16–17, 120.
22. For the relationship between these two poems and a reference to Jonson's use of Catullus

with the counting of kisses, the disregarding of envious, cranky old men, and the coming of a perpetual night. Catullus begins *Carmen 5*:

Vivamus, mea Lesbia, atque amemus,
rumoresque senum seueriorum
omnes unius aestimemus assis!
soles occidere et redire possunt:
nobis cum semel occidit breuis lux,
nox est perpetua una dormienda. (5.1–6)

Let's live, Lesbia mine, and love—and as for
scandal, all the gossip, old men's strictures,
value the lot at no more than a farthing!
Suns can rise and set ad infinitum—
for us, though, once our brief life's quenched, there's only
one unending night that's left to sleep through.[23]

Jonson writes a near translation of the original in his first "Song: To Celia":

Come my Celia, let vs proue,
While we may, the sports of loue;
Time will not be ours, for euer:
He at length, our good will seuer.
Spend not then his gifts in vaine.
Sunnes, that set, may rise again:
But if once we loose this light,
'Tis with vs, perpetuall night. (*Forest* 5.1–8)[24]

In isolation, these two passages are quite close. Jonson is certainly directly borrowing the rising and setting sun image, and he also captures the *carpe diem* motif that the lovers must love while they can.

Jonson, in his second song to Celia, "To the same," also directly imitates Catullus' reckoning of kisses. Immediately following the image of perpetual night, Catullus writes:

5 and 7, see Charles Segal, "Catullus 5 and 7: A Study in Complementaries," *American Journal of Philology* 89.3 (1968): 284–301.

23. The Latin text, and the verse translations for longer passages, are from Peter Green, trans., *The Poems of Catullus: A Bilingual Edition* (Berkeley: University of California Press, 2005).

24. All quotes from Ben Jonson are from *Ben Jonson,* 11 vols., ed. C. H. Herford and Percy and Evelyn Simpson (Oxford: Clarendon Press, 1925–73) and are cited by poem number and line number for the lyrics, and by act, scene, and line numbers for the plays.

da mi basia mille, deinde centum,
dein mille altera, dein secunda centum,
deinde usque altera mille, deinde centum.
dein, cum milia multa fecerimus,
conturbabimus illa, ne sciamus,
aut ne quis malus inuidere possit,
cum tantum sciat esse basiorum. (5.7–13)

Give me a thousand kisses, then a hundred,
then a thousand more, a second hundred,
then yet another thousand then a hundred—
then when we've notched up all these many thousands,
shuffle the figures, lose count of the total,
so no maleficent enemy can hex us
knowing the final sum of all our kisses.

Catullus continues the theme in *Carmen* 7 when he writes: "Qvaeris, quot mihi basiationes / tuae, Lesbia, sint satis superque" (1–2). Catullus goes on to explain just how many would be enough; he claims that they would be more than the number of Libyan sand and more than the stars. He writes:

tam te basia multa basiare
uesano satis et super Catullo est,
quae nec pernumerare curiosi
possint nec mala fascinare lingua. (9–12)

That's the number of times I need to kiss you,
that's what would satisfy your mad Catullus—
far too many tongues for the curious to figure,
or for an evil tongue to work you mischief!

Again, Jonson imitates the Catullan original:

Kisse againe: no creature comes.
Kisse, and score vp wealthy summes
On my lips, thus hardly sundred,
While you breath. First giue a hundred,
Then a thousand, then another
Hundred, then vnto the other
Adde a thousand, and so more:

. . .
That the curious may not know
How to tell 'hem, as they flow,
And the enuious, when they find
What their number is, be pin'd. (*Forest* 6.5–11, 19–22)

Jonson once again echoes the Catullan original, even though the final two lines, "And the envious, when they find / What their number is, be pin'd," imply a slightly different sentiment than does Catullus' *mala lingua* (evil tongues) that might want to bewitch (i.e., do harm to) those engaging in such kisses. Jonson, though still close to the original, stresses the idea that others will be jealous of their kisses, that they will yearn for them—"be pin'd." He does not stress explicitly, as Catullus does, that others might wish them harm because of their shared kisses. Even with these slight differences, the poems, looked at side by side with the Catullan originals, appear very faithful to the source.

However, Jonson's imitation of Catullus lacks the dramatic context that characterizes Catullus' poems. *Carmina* 5 and 7 are poems that illustrate the poet-lover's initial attempt to characterize his affair as one that transcends the criticism of others. He pleads with Lesbia to let them "live and love," to ignore those old men who criticize that love not simply from envy but because they see the flaws in the relationship from the outset. Nevertheless, the poet-lover says that if they simply ignore such judgments, concern themselves only with their own kisses (i.e., with their own love), the number of those kisses, which illustrate the magnitude and intensity of their love, will overpower the disparaging words of others and leave the critic unable to criticize. Later in the *Carmina,* Catullus' lover will realize that such criticism was perhaps valid after all; he will begin to see that any loyalty in the relationship was his and that his love for Lesbia is not the kind that is able to rise above criticism. However, at this point, within *Carmina* 5 and 7, the poet does not yet acknowledge the flaws—even if he does subconsciously know they are there—but rather focuses on what he hopes their love can be: something worthy of praise, not criticism.

While the dramatic context of Catullus' *Carmina* 5 and 7 depicts the speaker's desire for a worthwhile, virtuous love (even if that love never comes to a virtuous fruition), the dramatic context of Jonson's Celia poems demonstrates the speaker's explicit purpose to obtain satisfaction of sexual desire through deception and manipulation of the mistress and those around, all of which are motivations completely contrary to the Catullan original. Jonson's first song to Celia (and part of the second) first appears in 3.7 of

Jonson's *Volpone,* a play in which the titular character Volpone attempts to manipulate all those around him, including the married Celia. In hopes of acquiring Volpone's wealth—a scheme that Volpone has devised—Celia's merchant husband gives his wife to Volpone. Volpone, after listening to Celia beg that her honor be spared, clearly states his intention:

> I doe degenerate and abuse my nation,
> To play with oportunity, thus long:
> I should haue done the act, and then haue parleyed.
> Yeeld, or Ile force thee. (3.7.263–65)

It is in this context, earlier in this scene, that we find Jonson's imitation of Catullus' *Carmina* 5 and 7. Volpone himself sings the song to Celia: "Come, my Celia, let us prove." He uses the song as a typical early seventeenth-century *carpe diem* poem, one in which the lover tries to talk his mistress into forsaking her virtue and engaging in sex. In the song, again much like the Catullan original on the surface, lines such as "Why should wee deferre our ioyes? / Fame, and rumor are but toies" (3.7.173–74) (lines 9–10 of the poem found separately in *The Forest*) take on an entirely different meaning from what one finds in Catullus. Lesbia is a very willing participant; Celia is not. Rape is an option for Volpone; Catullus' lover claims that he wants a real relationship based on something more than physical desire. Celia and Lesbia, Volpone and Catullus' lover, the nature of their relationships—all these details could not be more different in the two poets, no matter how closely Jonson imitates the phrasing and images themselves. Unlike the poems in Catullus, there is no complexity of emotion, no emotional frustration, no conflict between a desired ideal love and a realistic love that fails in some way. Jonson's recontextualization of the passage demonstrates his ownership of, hence power over, the original text. As a poet, he can allude to, but undermine, the source of the appropriation.

Of Jonson's followers, Robert Herrick is the poet who demonstrates the most direct knowledge of Catullus and who imitates Catullus most often, namely, in his *Hesperides.* Herrick has received a great deal of critical attention concerning the influence of Catullus, beginning with the earliest editors and biographers. J. R. Lowell claims that Herrick was "the most Catullian of poets since Catullus," and the same sentiment is adopted by the early editors, A. B. Grosart, William Hazlitt, and George Saintsbury.[25]

---

25. J. R. Lowell, *Among My Books* (Boston: Houghton Mifflin, 1894), 391; Alexander B. Grosart, ed., *The Complete Poems of Robert Herrick* (London: Chatto & Windus, 1876), 1: 237; George Saintsbury, ed., *The Poetical Works of Robert Herrick* (London: George Bell & Sons, 1893), 1: 31.

Kathryn A. McEuen echoes the remarks of these early scholars, calling Herrick "the most Catullian of the Tribe of Ben," and Karl P. Harrington asserts that Herrick was "the seventeenth-century poet who drank deepest at the fount of Catullus."[26] These scholars imply Herrick's use of Catullus is "Catullan" in spirit as well as in phrasing; however, this is not the only critical stance. Although Herrick's biographer F. W. Moorman states that "of the Roman lyric poets, it is Catullus and Horace that have left the deepest impression upon [Herrick]," and although he notes the "striking superficial resemblance" in the loose arrangement of the *Hesperides* and the *Carmina,* Moorman qualifies his statement with regard to the love poetry of the two poets: "But it is as love poets that Catullus and Herrick have usually been compared, and here, it must be confessed, the difference between them is great. . . . The lack of the genuine fire of love makes Herrick's verses seem very different from those of the Roman poet."[27] The French critic Floris Delattre makes a similar assertion:

> In fact, nothing is more opposed to the gentle epicureanism of Herrick than the strong passion of Lesbia's lover. . . . Catullus tells the stories of his impetuous heart, from the beginning of proud and sweet love to the disgust that his tyrannical passion brought upon him and to the sarcasm and disgust of his goodbye letters. Herrick is incapable of understanding the grandeur (greatness) of that love. . . . He does not go beyond the elegant and somehow affected (mannered) style of some poems and does not get to the passionate simplicity that fills one's heart, a simplicity that is the essential source of the *Carmina.*[28]

James McPeek remarks that "Herrick never captures the grace, tenderness, and final beauty of Catullus."[29] The generalizations of Moorman, Delattre, and McPeek are correct, but these critics—as well as those advocating a "likeness" in spirit—never provide an adequate analysis of Herrick's imitation of Catullus' poems in his own work.[30]

---

26. Kathryn A. McEuen, *Classical Influence upon the Tribe of Ben* (Cedar Rapids, IA: The Torch Press, 1939), 167; Karl P. Harrington, *Catullus and His Influence* (Boston: Marshall Jones Co, 1923), 177.

27. F. W. Moorman, *Robert Herrick: A Biographical & Critical Study* (London: John Lane Company, 1910), 212–15.

28. M. Floris Delattre, *Contribution à l'étude de la poesie lyrique en Angleterre au dix-septième siècle* (Paris: F. Alcan, 1912), 408–10. Translated for the author by Dr. Sylvain Poosson (unpublished manuscript).

29. McPeek, *Catullus in Strange and Distant Britain,* 49.

30. See also Syrithe Pugh, "Ovidian Exile in the 'Hesperides': Herrick's Politics of Intertextual-

To a large extent, Herrick's imitation of Catullus is much like Jonson's in that Herrick borrows the phrasing of the original but sets it in a context quite different from the original. Herrick directly imitates *Carmina* 5 and 7, as Jonson does, and although Herrick does not have his poems originate in a morally questionable character like Volpone, he does focus on the playful, sometimes manipulative, aspects of the *carpe diem* theme, which characterizes so many of the Cavalier writers that come after Jonson. In one of Herrick's poems to Anthea, there is a direct imitation of *Carmen* 5:

> Ah my Anthea! Must my heart still break?
> (Love makes me write, what shame forbids to speak.)
> Give me a kisse, and to that kisse a score;
> Then to that twenty, adde an hundred more:
> A thousand to that hundred: so kisse on,
> To make that thousand up a million.
> Treble that million, and when that is done,
> Let's kisse afresh, as when we first begun.[31]

Other than line 2, which is from Ovid's *Heroides* 4.10 ("dicere quae puduit, scribere iussit amor"), this passage is a fine adaptation of Catullus' *Carmen* 5. However, the inclusion of the Ovidian reference is significant because it signifies the "shameful" topic about which the speaker is writing—although the reader does not know for sure the sexual nature of the poem until its conclusion. The speaker's request for kisses loses the affection of Catullus' original. Remember, Catullus' lover wanted simply to share such kisses as a sign of their affection and commitment to one another in spite of the grumbling of those who criticize; sexual desire is only implicit. Herrick does something different. Although his poet-lover begins with what appears to be the desire for a sincere show of affection, these millions of kisses are not really what the lover is after; he follows the request for kisses with a request for something better:

---

ity," *Review of English Studies*, n.s., 57.232 (2006): 733–65; A. B. Chambers, "Herrick, Corinna, Caticles, and Catullus," *Studies in Philology* 74.2 (1977): 216–27; A. B. Chambers, "Herrick and the Trans-Shifting of Time," *Studies in Philology* 72.1 (1975): 85–114; and Robert H. Deming, *Ceremony and Art: Robert Herrick's Poetry* (The Hague: Mouton, 1974); Deming, "Herrick's Funereal Poems," *Studies in English Literature* 9.1 (1969): 153–67; Deming, "Robert Herrick's Classical Ceremony," *English Literary History* 34.3 (1967): 327–48; and Paul Nixon, "Herrick and Martial," *Classical Philology* 5.2 (1910): 189–202.

31. *The Complete Poetry of Robert Herrick*, ed. J. Max Patrick (New York: Norton, 1968), 74.1–8. All subsequent quotes from Herrick's poetry are from this edition, cited by poem number (in the *Hesperides*) and line number.

But yet, though Love likes well such Scenes as these,
There is an Act that will more fully please:
Kissing and glancing, soothing, all make way
But to the acting of this Private play:
Name it I would; but being blushing red,
The rest Ile speak, when we meet both in bed. (74.9–14)

Herrick transforms the computation of kisses into a not so clever ploy to get a mistress into bed: kisses and glances are nice, but Love's real purpose is sexual. Herrick reflects in his imitation of Catullus the same sentiment we find more succinctly expressed in his epigram, "Kisses": "Give me the food that satisfies a Guest: / Kisses are but dry banquets to a feast" (797.1–2). Catullus' lover wants and appreciates physical love, which is evident in his desire for Lesbia's kisses, but it is not the lover's conscious purpose. Catullus' lover initially wants a love that reflects the loyalty and emotional commitment associated with *pietas*. For Catullus, physical affection is simply a part of that love. Nowhere in Herrick's poem is there a desire for anything but sexual conquest and the physical gratification that conquest brings.

Herrick ends up using *Carmen* 5 as a way to promote the attitude present in the expected Cavalier *carpe diem* motif adapted directly from Horace: lovers should love (physically) while they can. In "Corinna's Going a Maying," the lover, addressing the mistress, tries to convince her that the time is right for love. In typical fashion, the poet compares his mistress, who is obviously unwilling to engage in physical relations with the poet ("Many a jest told of the Keyes betraying / This night, and Locks pickt, yet w'are not a Maying," 178.55–56), to all the things in nature that are beautiful in spring, in youth. Herrick's last stanza, an imitation of Catullus' rising sun and perpetual night, summarizes the argument the lover hopes to use to seduce the addressee of the poem:

Come, let us goe, while we are in our prime;
And take the harmlesse follie of the time.
We shall grow old apace, and die
Before we know our liberty.
Our life is short; and our dayes run
As fast away as do's the Sunne:
And as a vapour, or a drop of raine
Once lost, can ne'r be found again:
So when you or I are made
A fable, song, or fleeting shade;

All love, all liking, all delight
Lies drown'd with us in endless night.
Then while time serves, and we are but decaying;
Come, my Corinna, come, let's goe a Maying. (178.57–70)

Catullus' *Carmen* 5 is definitely present in this poem: "soles occidere et
redire possunt: / nobis, cum semel occidit brevis lux, / nox est perpetua una
dormienda" (4–6). Catullus does convey a fundamental sense of *carpe diem:*
he and Lesbia will not live forever and must take advantage of the time they
have. However, his version of *carpe diem* is, unlike Herrick's, not a method
by which the lover might seduce an unwilling mistress. Lesbia *is* willing to
play and enjoy the moment. Echoes of *Carmen* 5, blended with the more
Cavalier concept of the *carpe diem* motif, can also be found in Herrick's "To
Sappho":

Let us now take time, and play,
Love, and live here while we may;
Drink rich wine; and make good cheere,
While we have our being here:
For once dead, and laid i'th grave,
No return from thence we have. (691.1–6)

Here Herrick reflects the "vivamus . . . atque amemus" (let us live . . . and
love) as well as the idea that once death comes there will be no chance for
loving anymore. However, this poem also transforms the original into a
"gather ye rosebuds" sentiment. Nowhere in Herrick's poem, or the *Hesperides* as whole, does Herrick reflect Catullus' initial description of an affair in
which the lover claims he desires an ideal relationship based on faithfulness,
and nowhere is the object of that love depicted as a flawed mistress who is
unable to give anything faithful at all.

Just like many Renaissance imitators, both Herrick and Jonson pull classical images and motifs out of their original context; as a result, in the case
of their Catullan imitation, they alter the underlying complexity present
in the Catullan original. Moreover, Jonson and Herrick most often choose
only two of the Lesbia poems, *Carmina* 5 and 7, to imitate substantially,
both of whose context can easily be altered and made to fit into the imitators' own purpose. Of course, there are some seventeenth-century poets who
literally translate Catullus (that is, they do not attempt to adapt the original
into any aspect of their own poetry, but simply translate it for its own sake).
Therefore, one would expect to find something more akin to the original
sentiment in these translations.

Richard Crashaw was not of the Jonsonian school, but he does offer one of the most impressive seventeenth-century translations of Catullus' *Carmen* 5. However, Crashaw still alters the meaning in places. The reckoning of kisses is quite close to Catullus:

> Then let amorous kisses dwell
> On our lips, begin and tell a thousand, and a hundred score,
> An hundred and a thousand more,
> Till another thousand smother
> That, and that wipe off another.
> Thus at last when we have numbered
> Many a thousand, many a hundred,
> We'll confound the reckoning quite
> And lose ourselves in wild delight. (376.9–18)[32]

This entire passage is similar to the original, but Crashaw adds to his translation of "conturbabimus illa, ne sciamus" (we will confuse them, so we will not know them [i.e., not know the number], 5.11) "And lose ourselves in wild delight." The "wild delight" implies the lovers are losing themselves in the ecstasy of the kisses themselves, the physical pleasure itself. Catullus' lover undoubtedly enjoys his physical relationship with Lesbia, but the lover never makes that the explicit focus of the kisses. He, however, does at least pretend that the focus of their kisses is to astonish their critics (i.e., show them how strong their union is). In the final two lines of Crashaw's translation, the difference between it and the original becomes clear: "While our joys so multiply / As shall mock the envious eye" (376.19–20). Whether Crashaw simply misreads the final lines or whether he consciously alters them, insightfully elaborating on the physical elements implicit in the original, the sentiment is slightly different from the original and gives the poem a different theme from Catullus' poem, which expresses the hope that such kisses will keep malicious men from bewitching the lovers; they are not trying to mock and make others jealous of their "wild delight."

The significance of this mode of imitation is noteworthy. Although their imitation may appear superficial at times, I would argue that there is a depth to that imitation that illustrates these poets' attempt to control, to dominate, their sources in a way that strips the literary other from its own ideological and poetic contexts. The closer the imitation of the specific source (the object itself), the more extreme is the decontextualization

---

32. "Out of Catullus," *The Complete Poetry of Richard Crashaw*, ed. George Walton Williams (New York: New York University Press, 1972), 522–25.

of that source. Jonson could have easily decided not to include a literal translation of Catullus in *Volpone,* but doing so directly confronts the force and influence of the literary Other on its own terms. By then stripping that source from the very contexts that make it a prioritized source of literary identity, Jonson and the others in a sense emasculate the potency of the source itself. Jonson, Herrick, and even Crashaw demonstrate their attempt to claim that potency as their own. They can take the source, manipulate it, make it part of their own poetic voice. That their imitation is so exact at times calls even more attention to the fact that they are challenging the very source of their own poetic history.

Chapter 4

Miltonic Elegy and the
Rebirth of a Roman (Split) Subject

⤫

> When someone else's ideological discourse is internally persuasive for us
> and acknowledged by us, entirely different possibilities open up. Such dis-
> course is of decisive significance in the evolution of an individual conscious-
> ness: consciousness awakens to independent ideological life precisely in a
> world of alien discourses surrounding it, and from which it cannot initially
> separate itself.
>
> —Mikhail Bakhtin, "Discourse of the Novel," *The Dialogic Imagination*

*C*riticism of John Milton during most of the twentieth century was, to
a significant degree, an example of simplification and literary idola-
try. This is not to say Milton studies has completely lacked insight or even
sophistication; however, there has been a recurring tendency in Milton
scholarship to approach Milton's corpus (poetry and prose) as a unified text
that is self-validating—supporting itself and its primary ideological sig-
nifications. Seeming contradictions have been explained away by scouring
the texts to find support and unification for a uniquely "Miltonic" theology,
political ideology, and poetic consciousness. As with a religious text, believ-
ers have twisted and shaped ambiguities and fissures in Milton in an effort
to demonstrate coherence in the text itself. Contradictions become wholeness misunderstood, a poetic vision simply unseen by the reader. The critic's
task was to bridge texts (sometimes written decades apart), to illuminate a
corpus certain in its own ideologies and a thinker committed to the task of
preaching his divinely inspired "word" to the masses. Milton's discourse has
been perceived, it could be argued, as a kind of authoritative discourse, one

that does not allow for response and subsequent dialogue—ironic, considering the massively allusive quality of his work.[1] Since the 1980s, however, there has been a growing movement to "destabilize" Milton, to use Peter Herman's phrase, and to show that ambiguity, doubt, paradox, and irreconcilable ideological splits are at the heart of Milton's work. Although this has at times sparked a virtual cry of critical blasphemy, the trend has continued, and an era of a more nuanced Milton criticism continues. Herman indentifies the problem in previous scholarship as a critical predilection to approach Milton as a poet of "certitude":

> While Milton studies encompasses God's plenty of approaches and topics, historical and non-historical, theoretical and non-theoretical, these studies have largely accorded with the paradigm that was established almost from the moment that *Paradise Lost* appeared on bookstalls in 1667, and that paradigm can be summarized as follows:
>
> * Milton is a poet of absolute, unqualified certainty;
> * *Paradise Lost* coheres;
> * and the critic's task is to make the poem cohere.[2]

Many traditional readers of Milton may reject Herman's assessment, but they cannot deny that newer attempts to read Milton's work as a more nuanced—and more ideologically shifting—text are becoming more prevalent in Milton studies.[3]

What Herman and others have begun to recognize is that the fissures and gaps in Milton's text account for its creative energy. Still, the text *is* subversive; it does often turn back on itself and undermine the very political, theological, and poetic ideologies it tries so desperately to promote.

---

1. The concept of an authoritative discourse that sets itself against dialogue is discussed by Bakhtin, *The Dialogic Imagination: Four Essays,* ed. and trans. Michael Holquist (Austin, TX: University of Texas Press, 1982), 43.

2. Peter C. Herman, "Paradigms Lost, Paradigms Found: The New Milton Criticism," *Literature Compass* 2.1 (2005): 1–2.

3. See, for example, Gordon Teskey, *Delirious Milton: The Fate of the Poet in Modernity* (Cambridge, MA: Harvard University Press, 2006); Peter C. Herman, *Destabilizing Milton: "Paradise Lost" and the Poetics of Incertitude* (New York: Palgrave, 2005); Michael Bryson, *The Tyranny of Heaven: Milton's Rejection of God as King* (Newark: University of Delaware Press, 2004); Joseph A. Wittreich, *Feminist Milton* (Ithaca, NY: Cornell University Press, 1987); John P. Rumrich, *Milton Unbound: Controversy and Reinterpretation* (Cambridge: Cambridge University Press, 1996); Rumrich, "Uninventing Milton," *Modern Philology* 87.3 (1990): 249–65; and Thomas Corns, "'Some Rousing Motions': The Plurality of Miltonic Ideology," in *Literature and the English Civil War,* ed. T. Healy and J. Sawday (Cambridge: Cambridge University Press, 1990), 110–26.

This should come as no surprise, considering the ideological crises that persisted in England during the seventeenth century. Milton witnesses the fall of monarchy, civil war, the blurring of religious lines within Christianity, the failure of the commonwealth he so desired, and finally a return to the monarchy he originally opposed. The projection of any individual wholeness during such historical rupture has to be questioned critically. Personally, Milton struggles with his desire for a poetic identity as he resigns himself to a world of political and ideological discourse that often conflicts with the humanist principles of creative expression. Consequently, Milton's text is wrought with rupture, and any attempt to unify the text violates the dynamics of that text: "The dominant paradigm of Milton studies does not allow for uncertainty, because it demands that critics find certainty even where the text does not supply it."[4] The attempt to stabilize Milton is an attempt to solder these ideological ruptures in his texts, and a failure to recognize the fundamentally split subject that emerges in nearly all of Milton's works. Despite the temptation one might have to base this "new Milton paradigm" on a biographical account of Milton's chaotic experiences, ultimately the incertitude present in Milton results not so much from personal experience as it does from a Symbolic referential system that disallows the Imaginary self-projection of wholeness the Miltonic subject seeks. Paul Allen Miller makes a similar case in his discussion of classical elegy: "Elegy is a symptom of the crisis in the Roman subject's self-conception. It does not so much reflect the lives and positions of a Tibullus or Propertius as it does a crisis in the categories of the Symbolic and the way the individual subject relates to them."[5] Miller argues that in a poet such as Catullus there is a "profound disassociation of the Imaginary and the Symbolic . . . a fundamental conflict between the subject's baseline self-identification in the world of Imaginary reflection and its recognition *as a subject* in the world of codified, signifying practices."[6] The critical result of this is a mixed reading of Catullus that, as in the case of Milton, is characterized by "critics [who] have tried to reduce a complex schizoid discourse to univocal phenomenon that directly reflects an extratextual political position."[7]

While Miller finds the most effective locus of this "profound disassociation" in the classical erotics of elegy, I believe that for Milton it is in the fabric of his intertextuality and the poetic consciousness of the Miltonic

---

4. Herman, "Paradigms Lost," 2.
5. Paul Allen Miller, *Subjecting Verses: Latin Love Elegy and the Emergence of the Real* (Princeton, NJ: Princeton University Press, 2003), 26.
6. Ibid., 43; original emphasis.
7. Ibid., 33.

speaking (writing) subject. As I have argued in chapters 1–3 of this study, the crisis of a Symbolically oriented classical appropriation amid the desire for creative wholeness ultimately leads to a self-alienating poetic identity and thus a text that undermines itself as an expression of that wholeness. The cultural and political realities of seventeenth-century England only amplify that undermining for Milton, who seems to struggle even more with the modes and codes of literary tradition than do the others discussed in this study. Although Bloom in his *Map of Misreading* uses Milton as a central figure of the anxiety of influence, Bloom can still not resist a final unification of the Miltonic text: "Milton's wit, his control of rhetoric, was again the exercise of the mind through all her powers, and not a lower faculty subordinate to judgment."[8] Nevertheless, the temporal and ideological differences that haunt Milton's self-assimilation into the classical tradition, into the Symbolic realm of literary law, make his work something of a case study in the humanist crisis. Just as Micaela W. Janan discusses in Catullus the dual desire of "preservation and abolition of difference" and the "endless substitutions" that keep the subject intact (partially, at least),[9] I propose that Milton's self-preservation in the humanist program is also dependent on a slippery movement between that Imaginary desire for poetic autonomy and the Symbolic limitations of expressing that desire within the boundaries of both tradition and the subject's own ideological realities. Milton must preserve the classical law that allows his poetic voice a theater, but he must also abolish the authority of that law to make room for a "unified" self. Of course, he can do neither, and the result is the manifestation of one of the greatest, and last, early modern humanists.

Milton's dialogue with past literature becomes an integral part of his self-construction as a poet—and his *Christian* ideological construction is constantly at odds with that.[10] Humanism's general negotiation between Christian and pagan is a battle that is waged throughout much of the early modern corpus, and Milton's work is an exemplary illustration of this battle. One well-known example of Milton directly engaging a primary text can be found in Book 4 of *Paradise Lost,* in the scene where Eve recalls her first moments of consciousness. As Milton describes these early moments

8. Harold Bloom, *A Map of Misreading* (Oxford: Oxford University Press, 1975).

9. Micaela W. Janan, *"When the Lamp Is Shattered": Desire and Narrative in Catullus* (Carbondale: Southern Illinois University Press, 1994), 141.

10. For one of the more nuanced discussions of Renaissance imitation in general, and Milton's imitation in particular, see G. W. Pigman, "Versions of Imitation in the Renaissance," *Renaissance Quarterly* 33 (1980): 1–32; Pigman, *Imitation and Pastoral Elegy* (New Haven, CT: Yale University Press, 1977).

after Eve's "birth" and her discovery of a pool, a "liquid Plain" that "stood unmov'd" (4.455), he directly calls on Ovid's description of Narcissus at the pool in Book 3 of the *Metamorphoses*.[11] In his allusion to Ovid, Milton not only imitates the image of Narcissus but also adopts the phrasing of the original, realizing perhaps that sophisticated imitation should reflect both sound and sense—as much as the difference between Ovid's dactylic hexameter and Milton's own blank verse would allow:

> As I bent down to look, just opposite,
> A Shape within the wat'ry gleam appear'd
> Bending to look on me, I started back,
> It started back, but pleas'd I soon returned,
> Pleas'd it returned as soon with answering looks
> Of sympathy and love; there I had fixt
> Mine eyes till now, and pin'd with vain desire. (4.460–66)[12]

Milton's general purpose here, in the larger context of *Paradise Lost,* is to show that Eve perhaps, from the moment of her creation, has a propensity for self-love, which will contribute to her final fall. These seven lines represent a kind of heuristic imitation. Ovid's Narcissus and Milton's Eve blend here seamlessly, but it is not merely sacramental imitation—it is not a retelling of the Narcissus myth. Milton's expression of Eve's vanity must be "sourced"; that is, Milton borrows as a way to legitimize his own assessment of the Judeo-Christian story of Eve, but his own Christian ideological system of images does not adequately provide a *literary* validation. Milton *needs* Ovid to fill the lack in his own prioritized Christian ideology, but to this point in the text his allusion to Ovid is not challenged. However, the poet now experiences the anxiety that is common in this sort of imitation; he fails to recognize a lack in the *objet a* itself (i.e., the source). Milton risks the devaluing of his own Christian identity (by relying so heavily on the

11. See Maggie Kilgour, "'Thy Perfect Image Viewing': Poetic Creation and Ovid's Narcissus in 'Paradise Lost,'" *Studies in Philology* 102.3 (2005): 307–39; Mandy Green, "The Virgin in the Garden: Milton's Ovidian Eve," *Modern Language Review* 100.4 (2005): 903–22; Kenneth J. Knoespel, "The Limits of Allegory: Textual Expansion of Narcissus in *Paradise Lost,*" *Milton Studies* 22 (1989): 79–100; Charles Martindale, *John Milton and the Ancient Epic* (London: Croom Helm, 1986), 186; Martindale, "Paradise Metamorphosed: Ovid in Milton," *Comparative Literature* 37.4 (1985): 301–33; Jonathan H. Collett, "Milton's Use of Classical Mythology in 'Paradise Lost,'" *Publications of the Modern Language Association* 85.1 (1970): 88–96; D. C. Allen, "Milton's Eve and the Evening Angels," *Modern Language Notes* 75 (1960): 108–9.
12. All quotations from Milton's English poetry are from Merrit Y. Hughes's edition, *John Milton: Complete Poetry and Major Prose* (Indianapolis and New York: Odyssey Press, 1957), cited by book number (where appropriate) and line number.

pagan source to situate his Christian purpose) and therefore immediately alters the source so that Eve does not suffer the same fate as Narcissus, and Milton can rise above his source and dialectically identify the lack therein:

> there I had fixt
> Mine eyes till now, and pin'd with vain desire,
> Had not a voice thus warn'd me, What thou seest,
> What there thou seest fair Creature is thyself,
> With thee it came and goes: but follow me,
> And I will bring thee where no shadow stays
> Thy coming, and thy soft imbraces, he
> Whose image thou art, him thou shalt enjoy
> Inseparably thine, to him shalt bear
> Multitudes like thyself, and thence be call'd
> Mother of human Race. (4.465–75)

No sooner has Milton used the Ovidian reference to validate his own description and evaluation of Eve than he undermines the source, identifies the lack in that source in light of his own religious identity. In the original, Ovid's narrator interjects himself into the text to comment on Narcissus and his misperception:

> credule, quid frustra simulacra fugacia captas?
> quod petis, est nusquam; quod amas, avertere, perdes!
> ista repercussae, quam cernis, imaginis umbra est:
> nil habet ista sui; tecum venitque manetque;
> tecum discedet, si tu discedere possis! (3.432–36)

> Foolish boy, why try to catch a fleeting image in vain.
> What you search for is nowhere; what you love, withdrawing, is gone!
> What you see is but a shadow of your own reflection:
> It is nothing it itself; with you to comes and stays;
> With you, it leaves, if you are able to leave![13]

However, in Milton, despite the fact that Milton's own narrator frequently interjects himself into *Paradise Lost,* in *this* case it is God, not the narrator, who guides Eve to the truth about the object of her gaze. Eve simply cannot have the fate of Narcissus; Christianity calls for a god that saves, leads,

---

13. This translation is my own.

nurtures, and Milton must acknowledge this lack in the same mythology he invokes.

Latin Elegy and the (New) Roman Subject

Of all of Milton's verse, some of his early Latin elegies are the most personal in tone. While much of the English poetry hinges on a certain detachment from the speaker—with occasional intrusions from the subject himself—Milton's Latin elegies often strive for a unified speaking subject that is coherent in its emotional and ideological self-positioning. This is not to say that the subject is not explicitly conflicted within the text; in fact, the tradition of Latin elegy from which Milton draws (Ovid, Propertius, Catullus) makes the conflicted subject a core characteristic of the genre itself. However, the conflict that the subject perceives is not always the conflict inherent in the text itself. Again, Miller proposes that in Roman elegy, the split subject falls victim to the limitations of the Symbolic codes that allow that subject to "speak" within the elegiac space. The result of this is a certain rupture in the subject's desire for unified self-projection. The subject's apparent conflicts are not always actual conflicts but the Symbolic manifestation of a more fundamental conflict in that subject's ability to self-project. Again, Miller finds the most intrusive ruptures in the discourse of erotics; for Milton, it is in the discourse of poetics, of poetic identity, of defining himself as a unique voice within a multitude of overheard voices he cannot quiet. Milton's elegiac positioning constantly revolves around the perceived center of a stable poetic consciousness; however, the articulation of that consciousness, the projection of that stability, he situates in a literary structure (of tradition) that promises the possibility of poetic autonomy but leads the subject to the reality of a closed system within which his voice must wander. Once again, we find that the "classical" becomes a perceived wholeness, and the closer the poet gets to that wholeness the more his own poetic voice suffers and fears its own insignificance.

Milton's engagement with the classical past exists on multiple levels. As I have discussed in previous chapters, the very decision to write in Latin suggests an attempt to legitimize the speaker's present voice through a language of a distinctly different set of cultural codes. Being able to express the self through the language of the Other, in this case, ironically confirms for the subject the authority of the present speech act. Milton even writes that amid all of his reading, elegy came easily to him:

I had my time, readers, as others have who have good learning bestowed upon them, to be sent to those places where, the opinion was, it might be soonest attained; and as the manner is, was not unstudied in those authors which are most commended. Whereof some were grave orators and historians, whose matter methought I loved indeed, but as my age then was, so I understood them; others were the smooth elegiac poets, whereof the schools are not scarce, whom both for the pleasing sound of their numerous writing, which in imitation I found most easy and most agreeable to nature's part in me.[14]

Milton might have attributed his writing elegy to his age and the "pleasing sound" of the verse, but the ability to emulate that pleasing sound (easily) is a statement about his own place in that tradition he admires.

Milton's Latin elegies (and odes) cover an array of material.[15] Again, many of them are the most personal of Milton's poetry, addressing his dear friend Charles Diodati and even his father. Still, regardless of the themes that the poet presses forward, there is a concern for situating the poetic self in the "now," and the subsequent intrusion of the past on that "now." *Elegia prima,* constructed as a letter to his dear friend Charles informing him of the mistreatment of a particular professor at Cambridge, has been seen as one of Milton's most important early poems, primarily for its autobiographical implications. The construction of the poem, however, also suggests the early crisis of filiation that will become even more significant in Milton's later work. The poem begins by firmly setting the subject within a temporal and spatial present:

> Tandem, chare, tuae mihi pervenere tabellæ,
> > Pertulit et voces nuntia charta tuas,
> Pertulit occidua Devae Cestrensis ab ora
> > Vergivium prono qua petit amne salum.

---

14. "Apology for Smectymnuus," 693. All prose quotations will be from the Hughes edition (above note 12), cited by page number.

15. Stella P. Revard's work with Milton's early poetry has been one of the most useful recent contributions to Milton's elegies and odes, including the *"Nativity Ode"* and *Lycidas.* See Stella P. Revard, *Milton and the Tangles of Neaera's Hair: The Making of the 1645 Poems* (Columbia: University of Missouri Press, 1997); and Revard, ed., *John Milton: Complete Shorter Poems* (Chichester: Wiley-Blackwell, 2009). See also Bruce Boehrer, "The Rejection of Pastoral in Milton's 'Elegia Prima,'" *Modern Philology* 99.2 (2001): 181–200; Gregory Chaplin, "'One Flesh, One Heart, One Soul': Renaissance Friendship and Miltonic Marriage," *Modern Philology* 99.2 (2001): 266–92; and John T. Shawcross, "Form and Content in Milton's Latin Elegies," *Huntington Library Quarterly* 33.4 (1970): 331–50.

Multum, crede, iuvat terras aluisse remotas
    Pectus amans nostri, tamque fidele caput,
Quodque mihi lepidum tellus longinqua sodalem
    Debet, at unde brevi reddere iussa velit.
Me tenet urbs reflua quam Thamesis alluit unda,
    Meque nec invitum patria dulcis habet.
Iam nec arundiferum mihi cura revisere Camum,
    Nec dudum vetiti me laris angit amor.
Nuda nec arva placent, umbrasque negantia molles.
    Quam male Phoebicolis convenit ille locus. (1–14)

At last, my friend, your letters made it through to me;
    the telling pages carried forth your words,
carried clear from the western shore of Dee by Chester
    where the stream falls headlong to the Irish Sea.
Trust me, it pleases me much that distant lands sustained
    A loving heart and so faithful a mind—
that a far land borrowed a charming friend from me, and yet
    quickly and willingly lends him back when asked.
That city keeps me which the tides of Thames lap at.
    This sweet homeland holds me—not unwillingly.
Now I've no care to revisit reedy Cam, nor am I
    pained by a love for a hearth long denied.
Stripped fields without gentle shade displease. That place,
    how poorly it suits followers of Phoebus![16]

The spatial markers, such as "Deae Cestrensis," "Vergivoium" (the Irish Sea), and "arundiferum Camum," set the voice of the subject within a space that is distinctly English and, considering the context of a letter moving through the English countryside, distinctly contemporary. These markers not only reflect the literal action of the poem; they also serve to separate the poet from the classical past that the form of the Latin elegy itself represents. The poet, however, can only sustain this separation for so long. The first classical allusion comes at the very point where the poet identifies himself as a poet: "Quam male Phoebicolis convenit ille locus" (How this place is not suited for the disciples of Phoebus, 14). This is a reference to himself as a follower of Phoebus, a poet who, not surprisingly, is viewing the present

---

16. The verse translations of Milton provided are by Lawrence Revard in Stella Revard's edition of Milton's short verse: *John Milton: Complete Shorter Poems*.

(literally his presence at Cambridge) as ill suited for the poet. After this anachronistic intrusion and self-identification as a kind of classical subject, he returns for the next several lines to a description of Cambridge that contains no classical allusions, until, once again, he identifies himself as an exiled poet (he was apparently asked to leave Cambridge), like the elegiac poet of Tomis: "O utinam vates nunquam graviora tulisset / Ille Tomitano flebilis exul agro" (21–22).

Thus in the first twenty-two lines of the poem, Milton makes two classical references, both identifying himself as a poet of the past set tenuously in the present. After the reference to himself as an exiled Ovid, the actual validation of that claim comes in a flurry of classical allusion: "Ionio Homero" (23), "victo Maro" (24), "placidis Musis" (25), the "sinuosi theatri" (27; see Ovid, *Ars Amatoria* 1.89; Propertius 4.1.15), "Pelopeia domus" (45), "aula Creontis" (46), among others. The poet's suggestion that he is like an Ovid cannot be grounded in the present that makes up the opening of the poem. Validation of poetic identity must root itself in the classical past; however, only by replacing that self in the present can the poet claim to be a structural equivalent to the world he invokes. Thus, after the speaker's classical digression, he returns, but only to undermine what he has just done by calling for a renunciation of that past, his own poetic history, to make room for his present. He asks the images and conventions of his classical past to yield ("Cedite") to his current locus, both spatial and ideological, in the *now:*

Cedite laudatæ toties Heroïdes olim,
  Et quaecunque vagum cepit amica Iovem.
Cedite Achaemeniae turrita fronte puellae,
  Et quot Susa colunt, Memnoniamque Ninon.
Vos etiam Danae fasces submittite Nymphae,
  Et vos Iliacae, Romuleaeque nurus.
Nec Pompeianas Tarpeia Musa columnas
  Iactet, et Ausoniis plena theatra stolis. (63–70)

Give way, Heroides, much praised once, and whichever
  girl took the roving Jove's fancy. Give way,
Achaemenian girls with turreted brows, or those
  who dwell in Susa or Memnonian Ninos.
And you—Danaan nymphs, even Romulan daughters
  and Trojan girls—lay down your signs of power.
Let the Tarpeian muse not boast of Pompey's colonnade
  and the theaters filled with Ausonian dresses.

Here, after his numerous classical allusions in the previous forty lines or so, the poet turns back on those allusions by asking that the most "elegiac" of those—the Heroides of Ovid, the Achaemenian maidens, the Danaan nymphs, the daughters of Romulus, and Trojan girls—give way. The speaker insists that Ovid (*"Tarpeia Musa"*) not glorify the theaters (i.e., the places, the spaces of Rome)—to yield to something else. And where should praise now be placed in this new Ovidian elegy in order to create this new elegiac space, this new elegiac subject? The poet usurps the images and symbols of the past and attempts a substitution of his own present; glory is now paid to maidens of Britain, not Rome ("Gloria virginibus debetur prima Britannis," 71) and those classical others should now follow, rather than be followed ("Extera sat tibi sit foemina posse sequi," 72). It is notable that initially the poet does not dismiss a specific ideology or explicit historical moment; the dismissal lies in a literary trope—the maidens of classical elegy. These generic tropes function as signifiers for the genre, and since the poet has chosen to write in the very genre that he is dismissing, he must deal with that genre within the terms of the genre itself. By dismissing the Roman maidens of elegy, the spatial markers of Latin erotic elegy (theaters, colonnades), he validates both the pressing significance of the form, which he is here imitating, and the need to transcend the form to account for his own historical and literary present. Still, the connection between that past and present cannot be so easily distinguished. Milton turns to a praise of London itself, initially the symbol that contrasted the plights he suffered as a student at Cambridge, as a new recreation of the past, but even here he must validate London as a product of "Dardaniis colonis":

Tuque urbs Dardaniis Londinum structa colonis
  Turrigerum late conspicienda caput,
Tu nimium felix intra tua moena claudis
  Quicquid formosi pendulus orbis habet. (73–76)

And then you, city of London, built by Dardanian
  colonists, your turreted crown widely visible,
you very happily enclose inside your walls
  whatever beauty the pendent world contains.

The poet states that Venus, who is firmly linked to this utterance as a mythological and generic signifier of Roman erotic elegy, now prefers London to Cnidos, Simois, Paphos, and Cyprus (83–84). The assertion of classical elegy's submissive position comes in a validation of London as the prioritized space through the classical signifier itself: Venus. Venus, the goddess associated with Latin erotic elegy, is not easily dismissed; her signification is transplanted onto the poet's validation of himself and his current poetic expression. Although the poem itself should have nothing to do with love or eroticism (based on the original "purpose" of the poem), the speaker ends by identifying with the tropes and symbols associated with erotic poetry because they are part of the system of generic identification. The poet cannot speak of elegy without addressing elegiac erotic discourse because that is the discourse of the genre itself.

Ultimately, in the final seven lines, the poet does return to the main thrust of the poem: for the speaker to express to his friend his disappointment in Cambridge. However, as we have seen, the majority of the text is a digression from this primary thread, and the digression functions as a battleground for the poet's self-negotiation with the classical form in which he is working, the tropes and signifiers that validate that form (including actual identification with classical poets), the authority of the past, and his attempt to validate the present. Even the final two lines in the poem accentuate the poem's engagement with the genre itself: "Interea fidi parvum cape munus amici, / Paucaque in alternos verba coacta modos" (91–92). Ironically, what seems to be one of the most personal of Milton's poems becomes more about humanism's attempt to place itself simultaneously in the past and present than about any personal account of the speaker's experience. The poet validates himself through both adherence to and subversion of the past, but there seems to be no clear "winner."

The one aspect of Milton's negotiation that does not emerge in *Elegia prima*—but that does become a primary issue in the major works—is the impact Christian ideological positioning has on the elegiac subject; however, the beginning of that subject position as it occupies a classical elegiac space does emerge in both *Elegia sexta* and *Epitaphium Damonis*. The intended purpose of the sixth elegy is to respond to a previous letter from Diodati, who apologized that his verses were not as inspired as usual because of his focus on entertaining and frivolity during the holiday season (December 13, 1629). The poet sets out, it appears, to do two things: to ensure Diodati that such celebration was appropriate, and to remind his friend that there is a more potent subject (the birth of Christ) that this time of year can inspire. These two themes become in the course of the poem a dialogue between the classical literary world and the contemporary Christian—though most of the poem remains in the realm of the classical past. The poet reminds his friend that the customary revels of the season, supplemented with French wine, are part of the celebration of Christ:

Quam bene solennes epulas, hilaremque Decembrim
    Festaque caelifugam quae coluere Deum,
Deliciasque refers, hyberni gaudia ruris,
    Haustaque per lepidos Gallica musta focos. (9–12)

How well you describe the customary revels, cheerful
    December, the feasts which have honored God come down
from heaven, the comforts and the joys of country winter
    and French wines drunk by pleasant firesides.

However, the poet wants his friend to understand that the "poor poetry," presumably about the celebrations themselves rather than the deeper significance of Christmas celebration, is appropriate within the context of classical verse. The speaker states that Bacchus, with all the implications of Bacchanalian celebration, and poetry belong together, and even Apollo could cut loose in the name of pleasure and comfort:

Quid quereris refugam vino dapibusque poesin?
    Carmen amat Bacchum, Carmina Bacchus amat.
Nec puduit Phoebum virides gestasse corymbos,
    Atque hederam lauro praeposuisse suae. (13–16)

But why complain that poems avoid the wine and parties?
    Song loves Bacchus; Bacchus loves songs.
It was no shame for Phoebus to dress in green ivy
    and to prefer the ivy to his laurel.

The significance of this initial statement by the poet is twofold. First, he acknowledges the Christian priority of the present; however, when he turns to writing itself he uses the standard stockpile of classical poetic symbols to begin his argument about *poetics*. It is as if the classical and Christian cannot occupy the same textual or psychical space.

In Milton's attempt to persuade the listener that celebration and poetry can function together, we find many of the same characteristics seen in *Elegia prima*. Once again, there is the association with the exiled Ovid, who in this case is presented as having written poorly at times even in solitude (i.e., without reveling and other distractions): "Naso Corallaeis mala carmina misit ab agris; / Non illic epulae, non sata vitis erat" (19–20). In contrast, he also invokes other classical poets who managed to produce quality work while either "celebrating" or writing about celebration: Anacreon, who wrote of flowers and wine, and Horace, who was known to get drunk on "the good stuff" ("Quadrimoque madens . . . Iaccho," 27). And most important is Bacchus himself, who, along with Erato, Ceres, and Venus, guides elegiac poetry: "Liber adest elegis, Eratoque, Ceresque, Venusque" (51). His case, therefore, is that poets should be afforded the opportunity to celebrate, even get drunk, at exactly the kinds of banquets of which Diodati is presumed to be a part. There is certainly a comic tone to the first fifty-five lines of this poem, and the speaker is basically telling his friend to relax and enjoy the festivities, but the subtext is the identification of poetry with the past, justifying the poet's moment by placing himself within the classical system of allusion and genre.

Just as this comic tone is achieved, the poem turns, and the poet returns to the ideological priorities of the present. The frivolity of the past (even though the case has just been made that the past can be and perhaps should be part of the present) must give way to the priorities of a Christian poetic voice. That turn begins by remaining tenuously rooted in the classical world; allusions turn to those classical voices that undermine the previous voices associating the classical world with what is fundamentally contrary to the seriousness of the Christian season. Frugal living, as taught by Pythagoras, is given as an alternative to the excessiveness of the poet's previous allusions. Now, the poet must recognize his own divine importance, and that recognition is also situated in a series of classical allusions, particularly to the epic voice of Homer. Homer becomes a Symbolic marker for divine inspiration and poetic responsibility, an idea the Christian Milton would cling to throughout his career: "Diis etenim sacer est vates, divumque sacerdos, / Spirat et occultum pectus et ora Iovem" (77–78). Once this identification is made, the poet can then move to the ideological priority of the present, the original "problem" the poem introduced:

> At tu si quid agam, scitabere (si modo saltem
>   Esse putas tanti noscere siquid agam)
> Paciferum canimus caelesti semine regem,
>   Faustaque sacratis saecula pacta libris;
> Vagitumque Dei, et stabulantem paupere tecto
>   Qui suprema suo cum patre regna colit;
> Stelliparumque polum, modulantesque aethere turmas,
>   Et subito elisos ad sua fana Deos.
> Dona quidem dedimus Christi natalibus illa;
>   Illa sub auroram lux mihi prima tulit.

Te quoque pressa manent patriis meditata cicutis,
    Tu mihi, cui recitem, iudicis instar eris. (79–90)

But you will ask if I do something (at least if you think it
    important to know if I am doing anything):
I sing of the peace-bringing king of heaven's seed, the lucky
    ages promised in sacred books, and the infant
cries of God, stabled in a poor house, who inhabits
    the heavenly kingdoms with his father—the new
star born in heaven, the throng singing in the air,
    the gods that instant shattered in their shrines.
Indeed we gave these presents for Christ's birth, these ones
    dawn's first light carried to me. For you
some studies readied on native reeds await as well.
    When I recite, you will act as judge for me.

In this final section, the classical world gives way to the priority of the present Christian world with which the poet ultimately wants to identify. The problem is that while the earlier allusive construction of Horace, Ovid, and Bacchus held together for the discussion of writing poetry in general, the later references to Pythagoras and Homer do not adequately set up the emphasis on Christ and the nativity. The question is, why does the poet need to root the Christian priority of the final lines in the classical through his allusions to the seriousness of and divine connection to past writers? The poet cannot rely solely on the present; even writing about Christ must be validated by a connection to the classical, which must then be left behind in order to address the Christian themes. While on the surface this may seem to be a natural "progression" of themes for the poet, the attempt to connect writing about the seriousness of the Christmas season with the seriousness of Pythagoras or the "divine voice" of Homer only accentuates the separation between that past and the present . . . and the poet's need for both.

Milton's need to recreate the past through his emulation of both form and contextual allusion finds a more organic expression in his *Epitaphium Damonis,* a pastoral elegy written after the death of Diodati. This poem is composed in anticipation of "The Nativity Ode" and *Lycidas,* both of which are written in English. The argument to the poem establishes explicitly the substitution of signifiers, with the actual subjects of the poem taking on the identities of a more traditional referential system: Thyrsis (from Theocritus) and Damon (from Virgil):

Thyrsis et Damon eiusdem viciniae Pastores, eadem studia sequuti a pueri-
tia amici erant, ut qui plurimum. Thyrsis animi causa profectus peregre
de obitu Damonis nuntium accepit. Domum postea reversus, et rem ita
esse comperto, se, suamque solitudinem hoc carmine deplorat. Damonis
autem sub persona hic intelligitur Carolus Diodatus ex urbe Etruriae Luca
paterno genere oriundus, caetera Anglus; ingenio, doctrina, clarissimisque
caeteris virtutibus, dum viveret, iuvenis egregius.

Thyrsis and Damon, shepherds of the same neighbourhood, having pursued from boyhood the same studies, were the firmest of friends. Thyrsis,
having traveled abroad to develop his mind, received the news of Damon's
death. Afterwards, returning home and finding that this was indeed the
case, he poured out a lament for himself and his loneliness in this song.
Here Charles Diodati is understood in the person of Damon, claiming
descent on his father's side from the Italian city of Lucca, in other respects
an Englishman; a young man, who in his lifetime was distinguished for his
character, learning, and other most splendid virtues.

The question that arises in this proclamation of the poem's purpose is,
within what ideological system will Damon's "virtutibus" be judged? If the
poem clearly transfers the contemporary reality of Diodati's virtues to a classical model, will the poet revert to a classical ideological construct or try to
impose the Christian ideology and the symbols of its privilege with which
he ended *Elegia sexta*? As we have seen in these previous elegies, Milton the
poet typically tries to do both. For Milton as a poet, the ability to construct
a "classical" poem, complete with a system of allusion, validates his poetic
abilities. The genre, the Latin language, and the use of allusion all function first to establish a poetic identity, one that is equivalent to the generic
models themselves. The Imaginary self-projection that the poet wants must
exist within the literary system, the established literary structure that gives
"voice" to that self-projection.

The poem begins immediately with a reference to the nymphs of Himera
in Theocritus 5.124 and 7.75, but those nymphs are asked to sing their
songs through the "Thamesina oppida," thus securing the context of the
poem both in the past and in the present. The poet moves through his elegiac mourning by recalling previous poets: clearly Theocritus, but also Virgil, whose "Ite domum, saturae, venit Hesperus, ite capellae" (*Eclogue* 10.77)
is adopted as a refrain for Milton's Damon: "Ite domum impasti, domino
iam non vacat, agni." Of all his poems in Latin, this is perhaps the most

sophisticated imitation. Milton appropriates a standard convention of the form, the refrain, but he does not imitate a specific refrain. The passage from Virgil is the final line of his lament for Gallus, one that is not repeated. More significant is what Milton does with the Virgilian reference. "Domino" (Master) takes the place of Hesperus, which declassicizes the original and even suggests the idea of God, the Judeo-Christian master, not having time to save Damon. In addition, "capellae" (goats), frequently a stock pagan image for Christians, is replaced with "agni" (lambs), suggesting the idea of the lamb as a Christian sacrificial object. Milton seems to assimilate the past and present into a more cohesive, yet subtler poetic expression. However, this is also accomplished through a more destructive rewriting of the past, one that gives a nod to the source but rewrites the source violently. Here the Symbolic necessity of the tradition is clear, but the Imaginary self-projection of the poet, a projection that is also impacted by the ideological necessities of Milton's present, is better negotiated with the Symbolic literary codes. Neither one can be given superiority at this point; they are both inevitable outcomes of the attempt to project an ideological subject in a past system that does not in itself contain the ideological signifiers necessary for the poet.

Even with the somewhat neutral prioritization at the beginning of *Damonis,* as the Christian ideological markers become more prevalent in the text, the stability of the classical context begins to break down. First, we begin to see the familiar emergence of Rome's ruins. The speaker feels a certain amount of guilt at passing up the opportunity to see his friend in order to witness a Rome in ruins:

> Heu! quis me ignotas traxit vagus error in oras
> Ire per aëreas rupus, Alpemque nivosam!
> Ecquid erit tanti Romam videsse sepultam?
> Quamvis illa foret, qualem dum viseret olim,
> Tityrus ipse suas et oves et rura reliquit;
> Ut te tam dulci possem caruisse sodale,
> Possem tot maria alta, tot interponere montes,
> Tot silvas, tot saxa tibi, fluviosque sonantes. (113–20)

> *Heu,* what fool delusion dragged me to foreign shores
> to travel past the towering cliffs and snowy Alps?
> Why was it so essential to see the buried Rome
> (even if it were great as what Tityrus once had seen

when he left his own flock and land behind) that I
could do without you, so beloved a friend—could put
so many deep oceans and mountains in between us,
so many forests, stones, and rushing rivers?

Literally, the speaker has chosen an excursion to Rome over time with his
friend; however, within this quote, the poet alludes to Virgil, Homer, and
Ovid. Still, the Rome the speaker chooses to connect to is a buried Rome.
There is the sense that his infatuation with the past is overtaking the privilege of the present. Damon represents not just a poet's friend, but a present
world that has been sacrificed with an obsessive need to revisit a past in
ruins, buried literally, but also psychically within the poet's own identity-
space. The spatial distance characterized by the woods and mountains and
rushing streams parallels a temporal distance represented by the image of a
buried Rome, and implicit in both is the ideological separation between a
disconnected pagan past and the Christian ideological codes that the entire
elegiac image of Damon seems to represent. The poem is one of loss, but it
is the loss not simply of a friend but of a perceived subject space.

   As in the two elegies previously discussed, there is eventually a movement to a specifically *poetic* statement, a declaration by the poet that he will
somehow leave the classical behind in favor of the Christian place and temporal space of a consciousness rooted in the present:

Ipse ego Dardanias Rutupina per æquora puppes
Dicam, et Pandrasidos regnum vetus Inogeniæ,
Brennumque Arviragumque duces, priscumque Belinum,
Et tandem Armoricos Britonum sub lege colonos;
Tum gravidam Arturo fatali fraude Iogernen,
Mendaces vultus, assumptaque Gorloïs arma,
Merlini dolus. O, mihi tum si vita supersit,
Tu procul annosa pendebis, fistula, pinu
Multum oblita mihi, aut patriis mutata camœnis
Brittonicum strides! Quid enim? omnia non licet uni
Non sperasse uni licet omnia. Mi satis ampla
Merces, et mihi grande decus—sim ignotus in ævum
Tum licet, externo penitusque inglorius orbi—
Si me flava comas legat Usa, et potor Alauni,
Vorticibusque frequens Abra, et nemus omne Treantæ,
Et Thamesis meus ante omnes, et fusca metallis
Tamara, et extremis me discant Orcades undis. (162–78)

I will tell of Dardanian ships on the Rutupian sea
and the ancient rule of Inogene, daughter of Pandarus,
of leaders Brennus, Arviragus, and old Belinus,
of Armoric settlers under British rule at last,
of Igraine pregnant with Arthur by a deadly fraud—
the counterfeited face and stolen arms of Gorlois,
Merlin's ruse. O, if I have life left over then,
my pipe, you will hang forgotten on an old pine far off,
or adapted to native muses, will sing a British theme—
and what of that? No one is permitted everything,
much less allowed to hope for it. Granted I may
be unknown for ages, wholly obscure to the rest of the world,
but I have enough reward, great honor, even, if
only blonde Ouse should read, and he who drinks the Alne,
the Humber full of whirlpools, every grove in Trent,
above all my Thames, the Tamar dark with minerals,
and if by the Orkneys' distant waters they learn of me.

The poet declares that he will tell the *English* story, though it is a story that
is grounded in the Roman. The previous classical iconography is replaced
by (or augmented with) a new English set of signifiers: "Armoricos Britonum sub lege colonos"; "Arturo"; "Gorlois arma"; and "Merlini dolus." In
essence, a new mythological system is introduced, and it is this system that
the poet is now proposing as one that holds more ideological significance.
However, the poet seems to question how effective this recreated set of codes
will be. If he were to go down this road, would his literary voice be part
of the structural Symbolic that is literary tradition? If he sings a British
song, will he be forgotten, unknown, completely obscured from the rest of
the world? Does this new theme—rooted retroactively in the present rather
than the past—cure the anxiety of literary significance? The answer is that
there is no one answer; the poet moves from states of stability to rupture.
And nowhere is this more apparent than in the closing lines, in which the
poet invokes again both the pagan and the Christian, seeming lost between
the two:

Ipse, caput nitidum cinctus rutilante corona,
Laetaque frondentis gestans umbracula palmæ
Æternum perages immortales hymenæos;
Cantus ubi, choreisque furit lyra mista beatis,
Festa Sionæo bacchantur et Orgia Thyrso. (215–19)

Yourself
ringed, radiant head with glittering crown, and bearing
the joyful shading of the branching palm, you will
forever act the timeless marriage out where song
and the lyres mingled with the blessed dances rave,
and under Sion's thyrsus the Orgies revel on.

Although Damon is associated with fadeless crowns of glory in 2 Peter 5.4
and the marriage of the lamb from Revelation, the poet seems to question
the literary possibilities of this as his ends not with a Christian image, but
one—ironically reminiscent of *Elegia sexta*—of Bacchus' revelers.

What emerges in Milton's Latin elegies is a humanist manifestation of
the elegiac split subject that Miller and others have identified in Roman
elegy. The genre itself, with a self-identified speaking subject engaged in
various modes of self-representation, seems to bring forth a voice that struggles to situate itself with ideological stability amid a structural set of signifiers that often runs against the self-projection of the speaking subject.
For the Latin elegists that Miller discusses, this struggle rests largely in the
ideological inferences of Roman political and social virtues and Latin erotic
discourse; for Milton, the struggle is situated in a poetic voice that has to
legitimize itself in a preexisting set of literary conventions and a system of
allusion that calls forth the authority of the classical past. However, those
signifiers (linguistic, generic, and allusive) cannot adequately reflect the
desire the poet has for autonomy and ideological separation from that past.
What we find in Milton is a speaker constantly invoking the past (through
genre, language, and allusion), but also undermining the priority of that
past as he makes room for his own present condition. The poet finds identity and validation by being part of the Symbolic structure of literary tradition, but there are inherent fissures in that structure when the poet seeks
true self-projection in the ideological present. He tries to quench the desire
to be relevant in the same structure that he subverts. This is the source of
the anxiety, and the result is an elegiac split subject that is a generic trait,
but also the condition of the Renaissance humanist.

"Christ's Nativity" and Exorcising the Pagan Past

Like his earlier French counterparts, Milton ultimately felt the need to
express himself in the vernacular. There were inherent conflicts in writing Latin elegy and undercutting the priority of the classical models from

which he drew. Part of Milton's poetic agenda seems to have been to find an authentic Christian poetic identity; we saw this in his Latin elegies, and we find it again in his English ode "On the Morning of Christ's Nativity."[17] The poem is an explicit attempt to celebrate the birth of Christ and the significance of Christ's presence in the world. Despite the immense implications the birth of Christ might have had for moral and ethical identity, the church, salvation, and social reconfiguration, Milton's focus slides into the relationship a post-Christ poet has to the classical past that prefigured him. Returning to English and the Spenserian Alexandrine form does not clear Milton from the crisis that he faces as a humanist writer. Just as he confronted in the Latin elegies, Milton is not able to rid himself of the crisis of identity. While the "Nativity Ode" should be an opportunity to project his Christian ideological present, he must still address the prioritized classical past. Only in this case, he explicitly and deliberately attacks the past—something, perhaps, that seems more authoritative in English—and it is only through that attack that he is able to situate himself as a poet of the present.

The critical corpus of Milton in general, and this poem specifically, have noted and considered this paradox of the classical and Christian that exists in Milton's texts. The problem lies in the fact that discussions too often drift to a success/failure dichotomous model that inadequately understands the humanist process: the process of identity formation and that of literary creation. Critics either deem Milton's text a success because the speaker succeeds in elevating Christ above the pagan world he is usurping, or a failure because that pagan legacy is a cornerstone of the poem's allusive structure, which undermines the poet's claim of a new age and hence a new literary orientation. Some critics insist that the conventional nature of Milton's allusiveness makes the blending of Christian and pagan part of a unified sense of history and of the self; others see the poet's self-evident reliance on the classical as a signal that his program fails, breaks down amid the conflict between the past and present. The fact is that both views are correct: humanism demands that the classical always be present, and the process of defining the self in such a present causes crisis. The failure exists

---

17. George William Smith, Jr., "Milton's Method of Mistake in the Nativity Ode," *Studies in English Literature* 18.1 (1978): 107–23; Richard Douglas Jordan, "The Movement of the 'Nativity Ode,'" *South Atlantic Quarterly* 38.4 (1973): 34–39; David B. Morris, "Drama and Stasis in Milton's 'Ode on the Morning of Christ's Nativity,'" *Studies in Philology* 68.2 (1971): 207–22; Lawrence W. Kingsley, "Mythic Dialectic in the Nativity Ode," in *Milton Studies,* ed. James D. Simmonds (Pittsburgh: Duquesne University Press, 1972), 163–76; and Shawcross, "Form and Content in Milton's Latin Elegies."

only insofar as the consciousness of the poet does not acknowledge the gap between the two literary positions, which is precisely when anxiety ensues. The poet feels such anxiety and attacks the literary orientation of the past in order to give precedent to the present. As I have illustrated throughout this study, this is neither success nor failure, but the humanist *process;* this process is how literary identity is constructed, and the literature itself is the manifestation of the process.

Milton's poem begins with what could be called its intended theme: to celebrate the birth of Christ. This is a theme not uncommon for seventeenth-century religious poets. This sort of nativity poem was fairly conventional. Similar poems were written by Thomas Traherne, Robert Herrick, Henry Vaughan, Richard Crashaw, and Robert Southwell.[18] However, of these English poets, only Milton grapples with the crisis between a classical and a pagan past and the emergence of a new Christian ideological poetic self as the major issue involved in the theme of Christ's birth. Milton's obsession with supplanting the classical past with a Christian present overwhelms the poem, and that obsession is what makes Milton's version of this convention fundamentally different from the others. At the beginning of the "Nativity Ode," as expected, we find no classical allusion, no conflict between form or purpose and the tenuous historical moment in which the poet finds himself:

> This is the Month, and this the happy morn
> Wherein the Son of Heav'ns eternal King,
> Of Wedded Maid, and Virgin Mother born,
> Our great redemption from above did bring;
> For so the holy sages once did sing,
>   That he our deadly forfeit should release,
> And with his Father work us as a perpetual peace. (1–7)

Although the poet is celebrating a historical moment in Christianity, this moment validates the religious, political, and moral moment of Milton himself. To celebrate Christ is to celebrate the present; to validate the authority of that historical moment is to validate the contemporary moment as well.

---

18. See Traherne's "On Christmas Day"; Herrick's "An Ode on the Birth of our Savior"; Crashaw's "In the Holy Nativity of our Lord God"; Vaughan's "Christ's Nativity"; and Southwell's "The Burning Babe." None of these English poets comments on the demise of the pagan world in light of the dawn of the Christian era that Christ's birth marks; however, Milton could have had Mantuan and Torquato in mind, as both do use the nativity to comment on the ruined past.

In this validation, Milton's ideological self-projection can be viewed as successful, but rather than continue the poem with continued praise of Christ, Milton returns to the identification of himself as poet, and with this comes the clash with the past.

As he does in many of his works, Milton uses but transposes classical convention. In the "Nativity Ode," he invokes the Muse according to classical precedent, but here he asks for a "Heav'nly Muse," seemingly undercutting the significance of the classical Muse that one might expect. However, there is a suggestion by the poet that the "heavenly Muse" might be insufficient; at least, the poet fears that will be the case:

> Say Heav'nly Muse, shall not thy sacred vein
> Afford a present to the Infant God?
> Hast thou no vers, no hymn, or solemn strain,
> To welcome him to this his new abode. (15–18)

The speaker questions the ability of the Christian heavens to inspire the song (the poem) necessary to praise properly the importance and significance of Christ's birth. While there is no explicit juxtaposition of classical allusion and contemporary Christian ideology, the passage suggests a movement from a classical convention (the invocation of the Muse), which has been anachronistically altered to reposition the convention in a contemporary context, to an immediate recognition of and response to the inadequacies of the revised convention to function in the same way that the original convention does.

As the ode itself begins, the poet continues with the celebration of the "Heav'n-born childe" (29), but the Christian theme is interrupted by a classically oriented description of the natural setting of such a birth. The personification of Nature—"Nature in aw to him / Had doff't her gaudy trim" (32–33)—is conventional enough in the Renaissance Christian tradition, but as the personification is developed, the classical precedent takes priority. According to the speaker, it was not time for Nature "To wanton with her Sun her lusty Paramour" (35). This reference invokes the classical *hieros gamos* of the earth and her sun lover (Apollo). Although the "sun"/"son" wordplay, which is often used in Christian poems of the period to connect metaphorically the light of the physical "sun" with the new light of the "son," is not explicitly at work here, such punning would naturally be recalled by the reader. However, in the case of this poem, Milton is adding to the physical sun and holy son connection the mythological "sun,"

Phoebus.[19] Ironically, it is Phoebus who is the first of the classical entities to flee from the new age and new mythology of Christ:

> And though the shady gloom
> Had given day her room,
>   The Sun himself withheld his wonted speed,
> And hid his head for shame, (80)
> As his inferior flame,
>   The new-enlight'n'd world no more should need;
> He saw a greater Sun appear
> Then his bright Throne, or burning Axletree could bear. (77–84)

This passage confirms the three-way punning of "sun" with the "greater Sun" from which the pagan sun hides his face in shame. Apollo is no longer needed in this new age of Christ; however, the initial use of Phoebus as a reference to the natural context of Christ's birth demonstrates the literary necessity of grounding the projection of Christ within the classical tropes of the past. Although one could argue that the initial allusions present in the poem are necessary in order for the poet to exorcise them, the construction of the poem challenges this. The opening and the subsequent stanzas already establish the presence of Christ; one would expect that Phoebus, for example, would immediately flee for shame. However, Milton utilizes the Phoebus/Earth marriage motif anachronistically before the exorcism takes place. The poet needs the image literarily but must dismiss it ideologically.

Milton not only associates (and then deassociates) the new "Sun" with Phoebus Apollo, but he also connects Christ with Pan in the next stanza, following Spenser's doing of the same in "May" of the *Shepheardes Calender*.[20]

---

19. See Mother M. Christopher Pecheux, "The Image of the Sun in Milton's 'Nativity Ode,'" *Huntington Library Quarterly* 38.4 (1975): 315–33.

20. Spenser references the "Great Pan," the gloss for which reads thus:

Great Pan is Christ, the very God of all shepheards, which calleth himselfe the greate and good shepherd. The name is most rightly (me thinkes) applyed to him, for Pan signifieth all, or omnipotent, which is onely the Lord Jesus. And by that name (as I remember) he is called of Eusebius, in his fifte booke *De Preparat. Evang.;* who thereof telleth a proper storye to that purpose. Which story is first recorded of Plutarch, in his booke of the ceasing of oracles, and of Lavetere translated, in his booke of walking sprightes. Who sayth, that about the same time that our Lord suffered his most bitter passion for the redemtion of man, certein passengers, sayling from Italy to Cyprus and passing by certain iles called Paxæ, heard a voyce calling alowde 'Thamus, Thamus!' (now Thamus was the name of an Ægyptian, which was pilote of the ship) who, giving eare to the cry, was bidden, when he came to Palodes, to tel that the great Pan was dead: which he doubting to doe, yet for that when he came to Palodes, there sodeinly was such a calme of winde, that the shippe stoode still

Milton constructs a traditional (classical) pastoral setting, using Pan as the expected classical artifact:

> The Shepherds on the Lawn,
> Or ere the point of dawn,
>   Sat simply chatting in a rustic row;
> Full little thought they then,
> That the mighty Pan
>   Was kindly come to live with them below;
> Perhaps their loves, or else their sheep,
> Was all that did their silly thoughts so busy keep. (85–92)

The scene is traditionally pastoral: shepherds relaxing on the lawn awaiting the pagan Pan. In this case, however, there is the transformation of the pagan Pan to the Christian Pan, an odd equivalency regardless of Spenser's explanation in the gloss of the *Shepheardes Calender*. The poet is establishing the presence of the classical world in order to dismiss it later in the poem, to demonstrate the implications of a new Christian age destined to usurp that past memory. The irony of course is that the literary priority of the pastoral is validated even by its dismissal. The Christian literary exists only within its relationship to the classical literary. Anxiety exists when there is lack of lack, when the gap and rupture between current consciousness and its connection to, in this case, a literary wholeness are not recognized. The need to connect the past and the present is the failure to recognize that inherent rupture, and the poet's conscious attempt to exorcise that past is his attempt to alleviate the anxiety. In this stanza, the classical shepherds are present, but they are clueless as to the enormity of the Great Pan that is coming. Their thoughts are "silly," focused on perhaps love or sheep, not the Christian savior himself.

After several stanzas suggesting the peace this child will bring to the world, the poem proceeds with a series of historical and mythological exorcisms, each of which address the secondary theme of the poem: to send

---

in the sea unmoved, he was forced to cry alowd, that Pan was dead: wherewithall there was heard suche piteous outcryes and dreadfull shriking, as hath not bene the like. By whych Pan, though of some be understoode the great Satanas, whose kingdome at that time was by Christ conquered, the gates of hell broken up, and death by death delivered to eternall death, (for at that time, as he sayth, all oracles surceased, and enchaunted spirits, that were wont to delude the people, thence-forth held theyr peace) and also at the demaund of the Emperoure Tiberius, who that Pan should be, answere was made him by the wisest and best learned, that it was the sonne of Mercurie and Penelope, yet I think it more properly meant of the death of Christ, the onely and very Pan, then suffering for his flock.

away the pagan world in order to make way for the new Christian era (I would say the primary theme, which has been largely abandoned, is to celebrate the actual birth and life of Christ). The wisdom and divine powers of Apollo are among the first to go. Despite the fact that the poet has invoked Apollo as a literary representation of the natural image of the sun, the significance of Apollo as divinity fades in the face of the new savior:

> The Oracles are dumb,
> No voice or hideous hum
> > Runs through the arched roof in words deceiving.
> *Apollo* from his shrine
> Can no more divine,
> > With hollow shriek the steep of *Delphos* leaving.
> No nightly trance, or breathed spell,
> Inspires the pale-ey'd Priest from the prophetic cell. (173–80)

The passage moves the poem to its most obvious theme of Christ replacing the divine nature of the pagan deities that existed before. Religiously, Apollo and the Delphic priests relinquish their prophetic significance; they will now be made "dumb," and Delphi will be silent from this point on. But this is not a literal reality; the poet does not *really* believe that Apollo had such influence, at least not in a purely religious sense. For a Christian, the pagan belief system even when accepted as such would have been "dumb." Similarly, a series of pagan deities are then depicted as fleeing from the power of Christ's birth: Lars and Lemures "moan with midnight plaint" (191); Peor and Baalim "Forsake their Temples dim" (198); Hammon "shrinks his horn" (203); Moloch "left in Shadows dread" (206); and Osiris is nowhere to be found (213–18). However, from a literary perspective the power of the pagan past has survived, has had a voice, and the poet is envisioning a new literary consciousness that is part of this new Christian age. Still, the literary past is validated in the poet's dismissal of that past. Its presence haunts the poem regardless of the poet's self-positioning within the poem. Anxiety and the alleviation of that anxiety is not a linear occurrence; the intrusion of the classical on the Christian suggests an anxious state that is continuously being "treated" by the poet's own fluctuating use of classical allusion as both a validating literary presence and an anachronistic, ideological misplacement of literary tropes. The poet still associates Satan with the classical image of Typhon and his "snaky twine" (226), and the infant Christ with the infant Heracles: "Our bab to shew his Godhead true, / Can in his swaddling bands controul the damned crew" (227–28). Although the poet wants to exorcise the religious significance of those pagan images through his poem—"Each fetter'd Ghost slips to his severall grave" (234)—poetically he cannot, and he returns again and again to the literary system, the literary structure, that gives his work validity.

Lycidas and Allusive Self-Consciousness

Milton's *Lycidas* may be considered the last of Milton's minor works or the first of his major works. The poem is a culmination of many of the themes and practices of the early verse and foreshadows many of the traits of *Paradise Lost, Paradise Regained,* and *Samson Agonistes. Lycidas* may be Milton's most allusive poem, both in its generic structure and in its imagery. Both a pastoral elegy in the tradition of Theocritus and Virgil and an occasional lament for Milton's former classmate Edward King, *Lycidas* orients itself in both past and present as fervently as any of Milton's verse.[21] Although the poem is often praised for its classical form, it has also been seriously criticized for being *too* dependent on those classical models, with accusations of insincerity and lack of innovation leveled at the poet. Samuel Johnson called the poem "easy, vulgar, and . . . disgusting,"[22] noting the anachronistic violence of a text that has classical shepherds mixed with contemporary religious and social dialogue: "It is . . . improper to give the title of a pastoral to verses, in which the speakers, after the slight mention of their flocks, fall to complaints of errors in the church, and corruptions in the government."[23] Because of this facile form and subject matter, according to Johnson, there is little legitimate passion in the poem, for "passion runs not after remote allusions and obscure opinions."[24] In varying manifestations, a parade of critics over the twentieth century have concurred with Johnson's eighteenth-century view of the poem, disagreeing with those who see the assimilation of past and present as a virtue of the poetic construction. But, again, this

---

21. In *Milton and the Tangles of Neaera's Hair,* chap. 6, Revard argues that *Lycidas,* like much of Renaissance elegy, is greatly influenced by the Pindaric ode. *See also* Revard, *Pindar and the Renaissance Hymn Ode: 1450–1700* (Tempe, AZ: Medieval and Renaissance Texts and Studies, 2001); and Steven Shankman, "The Pindaric Tradition and the Quest for Pure Poetry," *Comparative Literature* 40.3 (1988): 219–44.

22. *Lives of the Most Eminent English Poets,* ed. Roger Lonsdale (Oxford: Clarendon Press), 1: 278–79.

23. *The Yale Edition of the Works of Samuel Johnson* (New Haven, CT and London: Yale University Press, 1958–2005), 3: 204–5.

24. Lonsdale, *Lives,* 1: 278. For a recent, comprehensive study of Johnson's work on Milton, see Christine Rees, *Johnson's Milton* (Cambridge: Cambridge University Press, 2010).

success/failure dichotomy undercuts the actual process of how the humanist writer writes.

Lycidas is composed of what I would call three primary text threads—the pastoral, the occasional lament for a contemporary, and the ecclesiastical critique and commentary—and it is the inability of these three threads to hold the same temporal and ideological space at any given moment in the poem that leads to much of the fluidity and friction in the poem's themes. The idea that the poem is insincere is to a large degree a misplaced and irrelevant accusation. Milton himself didn't really know King;[25] *genuine* emotion over the death of a friend should never have actually been an expected result of the poem. Furthermore, Johnson's claim assumes that "sincerity" is some definable, quantifiable characteristic of a poem's intent, and that intent is directly tied to authorial intent, the success of the poem tied to the poem's ability to express the emotional state of its author. Determining whether or not the poem represents the true passion of the author is a fallacious enterprise; the fact is there *is* a sincerity inherent in the poem, but perhaps displaced into the artificiality of the form itself. The occasion of King's drowning served as a platform for the poet to establish himself as a pastoral poet in the tradition of Theocritus and Virgil. The poet vacillates, often violently, between form, tradition, convention, and content. *Lycidas,* and the conventions on which it is founded, provides a dialogic space for multiple speakers (Milton himself, perhaps, as one of those speakers) to effect the interaction with, engagement with, and disengagement from the tradition on which the poem draws. I would argue that there is no poem any more sincere than *Lycidas.* The sincerity of the poem, however, results not from a drowned classmate, but from a drowning humanist identity, a lost poetic self located on the fringes of two opposing but overlapping systems of identity construction.

One of the initial, and most obvious, signs that the poem will have to negotiate two cultural and ideological sets of signifiers comes in the published inscription of the poem itself. Below the title of *Lycidas,* the text reads: "In this Monody the Author bewails a learned Friend, unfortunately drowned in his passage from Chester on the Irish Seas, 1637; and, by occasion, foretells the ruin of our corrupted Clergy, then in their height." From this, it is clear (or seems clear) that the explicit purpose of the poet is indeed to "bewail a learned Friend" and, even more significant, to expose the ruin of a Christian clergy; although the poem's title, which the reader reads first,

---

25. See William Riley Parker's biography of Milton, *Milton* (Oxford: Clarendon Press, 1968), 1: 155.

wholly signifies a classical tradition of poetry, the description of the poem that immediately follows undercuts the reader's expectation that this is indeed a "classical" poem. Readers are being asked to reorient themselves and the identifying context of the poem. At this point there is no justification, no reason why the classical pastoral is necessary for a contemporary critique of the present. In the "Nativity Ode," the poet dismisses the priority of the pagan in order to discuss those things that are ideologically and temporally part of the poet's self-projection (the Christian), but here it appears as if the poet will be using the past in order to mark the present. There is an initial reconciliation to the fact that the priority of "Lycidas" as a signifier of a past literary ideal is the way in which the present can be told most effectively, and the poet at this point shows no apprehension about doing this. However, once the poem begins, the difficulty in representing both past and present in a simultaneous discursive space emerges. Mourning and loss remain at the poem's core, but what is actually being lost and mourned shifts throughout *Lycidas*. The reconciliation of what is lost comes only by exposing the lack that exists in both literary spaces and the inability of either the past or the present to provide a stable place for poetic consciousness to exist.

Milton draw heavily from both Theocritus and Virgil in terms of convention, and the opening of the poem explicitly employs the pastoral tradition to call attention to the fact that writing poetry itself is a theme the poem must explore. Conventionally, the poet invokes three symbols of poetic inspiration as he calls for aid in his lamentation:

> Yet once more, O ye Laurels, and once more
> Ye Myrtles brown, with Ivy never-sear,
> I com to pluck your Berries harsh and crude,
> And with forc'd fingers rude,
> Shatter your leaves before the mellowing year.
> Bitter constraint, and sad occasion dear,
> Compels me to disturb your season due. (1–7)

The initial allusion here to Virgil's *Eclogue* 2.54 ("et vos, o lauri, carpam et te, proxima myrte") is close to the original. The speaker plans to pluck those symbols of the three elegiac deities of Apollo, Venus, and Bacchus (all three of whom played a role in Milton's Latin elegies). "Once more" suggests that the poet has called on these symbols before (Milton literally did in the Latin elegies), but he also may be thinking that these symbols will, in terms of poetic history, have to be invoked once more. There is also a certain apologetic tone to "Yet"; it may be glossed as ("Here is a poem about an English student who has drowned and the corruption of the church, but, sorry, yet again, these classical symbols must be invoked before I can do that"). The poet is "forc'd" to call on the past for the current poem. His fingers have been "forc'd" to pluck the berries of these classical symbols, crush their leaves, and disturb their season, their time. On the surface of the poem, because Lycidas has prematurely died, the berries of poetic inspiration must be picked before they are ready. However, the fact that these plants are evergreens ["never-sear"] suggests that they should always be ready to inspire, that they should be permanent sources for the poet.[26] What seems more relevant and accurate in this opening is that the poet does not *want* to call on these classical deities. Their "season due" is not in the future, but in the past. The poet apprehensively identifies the need to invoke the past for this literary form, despite the fact that the stated themes of the poem are entirely in the "now." What this reading establishes is that the poet is following a tradition out of necessity, to ground his own poetic voice in the structure of tradition, not necessarily out of preference. This makes the violent imagery of appropriating the classical precedent a sign that the poem will be one that continuously seeks to justify its own form.

In addition, the choice of Lycidas as the pastoral shepherd addressed in this poem also brings contentiousness to the work. There were many classical literary shepherds from whom the speaker could draw. Gallus, from Virgil's *Eclogues,* would have been an obvious choice—since the Gallus poem is alluded to frequently in the poem—or even Propertius' Paetas (who actually drowned in 3.7.1–72 and, like Milton's Lycidas, "primo miser excidit aevo"). Although Milton might have chosen the name Lycidas arbitrarily, that seems unlikely considering how conscientious he is regarding his allusions. There is a good chance Milton knew the poem by Giles Fletcher the Elder, published by his son Phineus Fletcher in 1633, in which the speaker, Lycidas, mourns the drowning of a friend; the ties to Milton are even more closely observed in the fact that Fletcher's Lycidas questions Camus about the origins of Cambridge itself.[27] There appears to be a likely influence here; however, if Milton had remembered the Fletcher poem, he consciously decides to make Lycidas not the speaker, not the mourner,

26. Robert DeMaria and Robert Duncan Brown, *Classical Literature and Its Reception: An Anthology* (Oxford: Blackwell, 2007), 68 n. 2.

27. Giles Fletcher, *De literis antiquae Britanniae* (Cambridge, 1633). See David Norbrook's discussion of this in *Poetry and Politics in the English Renaissance* (Oxford: Oxford University Press, 2002), 260. See also an older article by Warren B. Austin, "Milton's Lycidas and Two Latin Elegies by Giles Fletcher, the Elder," *Studies in Philology* 44 (1947): 41–55.

but rather the mourned, the silent voice with which the speaker engages.[28] William C. Watterson makes, I feel, a more persuasive argument that since Theocritus' Lycidas is on the losing end of a singing competition, Milton is casting Edward King as a poet whom Milton battles and ultimately overcomes.[29] The problem with this specific reading is that Milton would hardly have considered Edward King a literary rival;[30] still, the notion that *Lycidas* represents literary rivalry in general and that Lycidas was on the losing end of such rivalry is consistent with Milton's continuous preoccupation with establishing himself and his poetic voice as prioritized. The use of "Lycidas" as the name of the dead shepherd who represents a failing poetic voice, and one that is grounded in and identified with the literary past, is the origin and basis for the poet's sincerity: he is, once again, trying to find his place in a literary tradition that is ultimately dead, but necessary to ground his own Symbolic construction of himself.

Although the poet begins his construction of the monodic speaker within the classical framework, he utilizes the violent nature of the allusions and signification of the classical symbols he invokes, which maintains the contentious and fragile nature of the literary structure itself. The speaker of the poem, after the first verse paragraph, appropriates the expected elements of pastoral poetry as a genre, thus establishing the literary structure on which the poem is constructed. He calls forth the "Sisters of the sacred well" (15) to "loudly sweep the string" of their lyre (17) in order to "favor" the poet's "destin'd Urn" (20).[31] The poet moves to an identification of himself with the dead poet Lycidas. Together they "drove afield" and "heard / What time the Gray-fly winds her sultry horn" (27–28) and fed their flocks late until "Heav'n's descent had slop'd his westering wheel" (31–?). Remembering these days together with Lycidas, working the fields, the speaker recalls the "Satyrs" and "Fauns with clov'n heel" who would appear shortly after their songs began on "th' Oaten Flute" (33). Consistent

---

28. Milton also likely knew the poem "Lycidas" by the sixteenth-century Neo-Latin poet Giovanni Baptista Amalteo, in which Lycidas says farewell to his homeland and hopes for a peaceful trip by sea; see J. W. Hales's letter in the *Athenaeum*, July 1891, 159–60. Lycidas is also the name of the shepherd in an eclogue written by Sannazaro entitled *Phillis* (1526). In both these poems Lycidas is a speaker, not the subject of the poem.

29. William Collins Watterson, "'Once More, O Ye Laurels': 'Lycidas' and the Psychology of Pastoral," *Milton Quarterly* 27 (1993): 48–57.

30. By all accounts, King was a liked and respected member of the Cambridge community, but although he did write a small amount of verse, he was not considered an accomplished writer. Casting King (through Lycidas) as Milton's literary rival does seem consistent with Milton's other writing, in which Milton typically compares himself to classical greats or recognized English writers, such as Spenser.

31. These conventions were common, most notably in Virgil's Eclogues 4.1 and 10.5–6.

with tradition, the two shepherds are also poets who isolate themselves within the pastoral world, blowing the pipes of Pan and celebrating the work of the day. Although Pan, as we have seen, has been associated with Christ in the "Nativity Ode," here there is no such subtext; the orientation is purely classical, the conventions completely drawing the reader into the systemic nature of the genre. Also, the reader is wholly outside the contemporary issues of the church that the poem purportedly will be addressing. At this point, the speaker *is* a classical shepherd; there is nothing here that fixes his identity as anything but that. There is no acknowledgment of the gap that exists between the referential system of the genre and the poet's temporal and spatial position—a gap that had been suggested in the opening lines with the harsh and crude berries of inspiration being rudely and violently plucked. Lycidas is the signifier of the poet's own identity; while alive and when they were together, the speaker's identity can be grounded in the generic system of the past; when Lycidas dies, so follows the speaker's self-identification. As in the "Nativity Ode," the pagan past must be silent before a new speaker, a new voice, can emerge. When the speaker considers the actual death of Lycidas, he questions where the classical deities themselves were and what they could have done:

> Where were ye Nymphs when the remorseless deep
> Clos'd o'er the head of your lov'd Lycidas?
> For neither were ye playing on the steep,
> Where your old Bards, the famous Druids, lie,
> Nor on the shaggy top of Mona high,
> Nor yet where Deva spreads her wizard stream:
> Ay me, I fondly dream!
> Had ye been there—for what could that have done? (50–57)

The poet's self-association with Lycidas and what he signifies makes his questions regarding the possible survival of Lycidas as much about the survival of the speaker's own poetic consciousness. When he follows this with the violent image of Lycidas as Orpheus, the archetypal poet, whose "gory visage down the stream was sent / Down the swift *Hebrus* to the *Lesbian* shore" (63), the poet has positioned himself as an Orpheus as well, one who suffers as much a death of identity as Lycidas suffers a physical death. Again, as in the "Nativity Ode," with the silence of the oracles introducing not just Christ but the new poet's capacity to express the ideological shift from pagan to Christian, it is the silence of Lycidas, "thy loss to Shepherd's ear" (49), that allows the current poet to leave the classical self-orientation that his connection with Lycidas signifies and be able to express something fresh and reidentify himself within a different ideological structure.

Once the speaker invokes the "gory visage" of the archetypal poet, Orpheus (Lycidas), he moves into an explicit discussion of the worth of the poetic enterprise, and the fame or literary acknowledgment it brings. The speaker, after a gasp of "Alas!," questions the relevance of tending the "Shepherd's trade" (65) and meditating on the "thankless Muse" (66). In this pastoral context, the shepherd's trade is poetry, contemplation, and reflection. Considering the fate of Lycidas, the speaker asks whether it were "not better done as others use, / To sport with *Amaryllis* in the shade, / Or with the tangles of *Neaera's* hair?" (67–69). This speaker suggests that frolicking with nymphs in the shade is a contrast to the contemplation of the shepherd's (poet's) life. Here, the speaker enters murky waters as the signifiers become conflated. In previous poems, those to Diodati, the poet argues that some amount of frolicking is appropriate for the poet and that Diodati should not be troubled by his desire for a serious commentary on Christmas and Christian ideals (*Elegia prima*). However, in *Lycidas* the classical signifies an ideological contrast to the contemplation of the poet—Milton's speaker in those cases tries to close the gap that exists by persuading Diodati that, in a sense, one can exist poetically in the classical and ideologically in the Christian. However, in *Lycidas,* the pastoral poet becomes the voice of the present, and the mythological markers are transformed anachronistically to signify something they originally were not. The movement in *Lycidas* from a classically inspired pastoral elegy to an ideological dialogue about the nature of poetic versus spiritual immortality marks a breakdown in the classical symbols themselves:

> *Fame* is the spur that the clear spirit doth raise
> (That last infirmity of Noble mind)
> To scorn delights, and live laborious days;
> But the fair Guerdon when we hope to find,
> And think to burst out into sudden blaze,
> Comes the blind Fury with th'abhorred shears,
> And slits the thin spun life. "But not the praise,"
> Phœbus repli'd, and touch'd my trembling ears;
> "Fame is no plant that grows on mortal soil,
> Nor in the glistering foil
> Set off to th'world, nor in broad rumor lies,
> But lives and spreads aloft by those pure eyes,
> And perfect witness of all judging Jove;

As he pronounces lastly on each deed,
Of so much fame in Heav'n expect thy meed." (70–84)

The shepherd is beginning to be transformed from a classically oriented
symbol to a Christian one. Poetic "fame" is contrasted here with the "shepherd's trade." The poet who leaves behind the pastoral (here, the Christian
sense of "pastoral" is invoked), who sports with Amaryllis, who seeks the
guerdon of poetic fame, is the one facing the ultimate slitting of a lightly
spun life. Phoebus, whom we have seen elsewhere taking on the Christ signification, enters the poem as a Christ figure, touches the speaker's "trembling ears," and explains that fame is a worldly pursuit, not a spiritual one.[32]
And "all judging Jove" is characterized more as the Christian Father than
the mythological king of the gods, as he is seen to be the final judge to
bequeath heavenly as opposed to worldly, poetic fame. Obviously, the poet
has made a conscious decision to structure his own poem as a classical pastoral, but what happens to the signifiers as the poem progresses marks the
inadequacies of the symbolic markers themselves. The "master signifier" of
Christianity—which functions as an ideological sublimation of the death
drive itself—overwhelms the symbolic structure of the poem and reorients
the classical symbols as referents for Christian immortality. The classical
system of signifiers to fulfill the desire of the speaker for both poetic and
spiritual immortality fails and becomes subservient to the symbolic revision
that the master signifier demands.

The element that critics simply do not adequately take into account is
the shifting of referential meaning in Milton's poetry. Rather than viewing
these shifts as intentional "strategies" of the poet, I would argue that the
shifts occur, at least initially, as unconscious symptoms of lack, manifesting
themselves through the poetic self-projection of the speaker. That Apollo and
Jove are reconceived in a Christian context is not a matter of simple convention; furthermore, the speaker does not stay committed to this transference
of meaning. Immediately after Jove is described as one who pronounces
heavenly fame, the poem shifts again as the poet admits that the voice of
Apollo was a "strain" of a "higher mood" (87), and he announces that fact
to "Fountain *Arethuse*" and "Smooth-sliding *Mincius*" (85–86), returning to
a more classically oriented reference, which allows him to continue with his
song: "But now my Oat proceeds" (88). The entrance and voice of pseudo-
Apollo, speaking against poetic fame, literally stop the poet's pastoral, and

32. Milton echoes in the swain's "trembling ears" a similar passage in Virgil, *Eclogue* 6.5–6:
"Cynthius aurem vellit, et admonuit: Pastorem, Tityre, pinguis / pascere oportet ovis, deductum
dicere Carmen."

the higher mood he brings—the Christian mood—interrupts the signifying structure of the pastoral itself. Now, the poet listens to "the Herald of the Sea / That came in *Neptune's* plea" (89–90), and the subsequent explanation as to why the swain, Lycidas, was allowed to die:

> He ask'd the Waves, and ask'd the Felon winds,
> What hard mishap hath doom'd this gentle swain?
> And question'd every gust of rugged wings
> That blows from off each beaked Promontory,
> They knew not of his story,
> And sage Hippotades their answer brings,
> That not a blast was from his dungeon stray'd,
> The Air was calm, and on the level brine,
> Sleek Panope with all her sisters play'd.
> It was that fatall and perfidious Bark
> Built in th'eclipse, and rigg'd with curses dark,
> That sunk so low that sacred head of thine. (91–102)

In this passage, the poem's Christian message is temporarily repressed as the poet returns to his classical orientation. The Christian interruption of Apollo's declaration is replaced with a more traditional and conventional procession of classical figures that simply comment on the literal death of Lycidas. One might expect that such a shift would either carry through the remainder of the poem or would never have occurred at all, that the poem would continue to build on the Christian ideology that the Apollo episode began.

The poet, however, in what is considered the main "digression" of the poem, shifts yet again to the present. Despite the many critical claims that the following passage is organic to the poem, the reality is that a major rupture occurs in the poem itself. Although the passage is consistent with the stated theme of the poem's inscription, it is not consistent with the pastoral continuity of the poem itself:

> Last came, and last did go,
> The Pilot of the *Galilean* lake,
> Two massy Keys he bore of metals twain,
> (The Golden opes, the Iron shuts amain)
> He shook his Miterd locks, and stern bespake:
> "How well could I have spar'd for thee, young swain,
> Enough of such as for their bellies' sake,
> Creep and intrude, and climb into the fold?

Of other care they little reck'ning make,
Than how to scramble at the shearers' feast,
And shove away the worthy bidden guest.
Blind mouths! that scarce themselves know how to hold
A Sheep-hook, or have learn'd ought els the least
That to the faithful Herdman's art belongs!
What recks it them? What need they? They are sped;
And when they list, their lean and flashy songs
Grate on their scrannel Pipes of wretched straw,
The hungry Sheep look up, and are not fed,
But swoln with wind, and the rank mist they draw,
Rot inwardly, and foul contagion spread:
Besides what the grim Woolf with privy paw
Daily devours apace, and nothing said,
But that two-handed engine at the door,
Stands ready to smite once, and smite no more." (108–31)

The significance of this passage as a reflection of Milton's own theological views has been well documented,[33] but what this so-called digression, presumably Saint Peter's sermon on the corruption of the seventeenth-century church, does to the pastoral signification of the poem is to introduce a violent anachronism. Even in the Apollo passage, classical symbols, inherent to the classical pastoral mode, are used even if their meaning is deferred to the ideological force of Christian ideology; here, the classical is completely absent. The poet's identification with the past is completely rejected in an attempt to reposition his self-identity in the ideological, political, and religious anxieties of the present. The poet has positioned his poetic identity within the generic system of the classical mode. Now, the poet is a split subject fluctuating between past and present self-identification, and poetic identity breaks down as the ruptures of the present invade and envelop the poet's identification with the past.

Familiarly, the poet's shift back to the classical comes with the exit of Saint Peter and an invocation to the classical symbols to return:

33. See, for example, M. J. Edwards, "The Pilot and the Keys: Milton's *Lycidas* 167–171," *Studies in Philology* 108.4 (2011): 605–18; Kathleen M. Swaim, "'The Pilot of the Galilean Lake' in *Lycidas*," *Milton Quarterly* 17.2 (1983): 42–45; Douglas Bush, ed., *Milton Poetical Works* (Oxford: Oxford University Press, 1965), 119; E. Tuveson, "The Pilot of the Galilean Lake," *Journal of the History of Ideas* 27 (1966): 44–58; Northrop Frye, "Literature as Context: Milton's *Lycidas*," *Studies in Comparative Literature* 23 (1959): 44–53; and Ralph E. Hone, "'The Pilot of the Galilean Lake,'" *Studies in Philology* 56.1 (1959): 55–61.

> Return *Alpheus*, the dread voice is past,
> That shrunk thy streams; Return *Sicilian* Muse,
> And call the Vales, and bid them hither cast
> Their Bells, and Flowrets of a thousand hues. (132–35)

There is no doubt that the poet slips back into the organic system of the genre itself, but the movement from the violent intrusion of the Saint Peter section back to the pastoral mode marks a more delicate interweaving of the classical and Christian that has been the root of the poet's anxiety. If we recall the basic Lacanian notion of anxiety, anxiety emerges when the subject fails to recognize the lack that is inherent in the referential nature of the subject's ego. To this point in *Lycidas*, the poet cannot simultaneously base his identity on the classical past and the present. Our subject is essentially split between what he must project as a poet, an orientation in the tradition he appropriates, and what he must project as a seventeenth-century religious subject, one who prioritizes the Christian signification above all other signifiers. Again, the shifts back and forth between ideological priorities have been to this point as harsh as the plucked berries in the opening suggest, but in this final section of the poem, the attempt of reconciliation and ultimate stabilization is more pronounced that it has been. The poet calls back Alpheus and a conventional listing of flowers that can now reappear, but that list contains the personified Amaranthus (149), the unwithering flower that both Spenser and Milton himself in *Paradise Lost* associates with the Garden of Eden.[34] The immortal nature of the amaranth was suggested in Aesop's fable about the rose and the amaranth, in which the rose bemoans its own temporal beauty and comments on the everlasting blooms of the amaranth, even when it has been cut back. This allusion is connected to the fate of Lycidas, who has been literally cut down but who will emerge as an immortal figure later. The poet also references the "stormy *Hebrides*" (156), a group of islands located off Scotland, and Bellerus, who signifies both the mythological figure and the location of Bellarium, the ancient Roman name of Land's End in England, where the "Guarded Mount" of Saint Michael protects:

> Whether beyond the stormy *Hebrides*,
> Where thou perhaps under the whelming tide
> Visit'st the bottom of the monstrous world;
> Or whether thou to our moist vows denied,

---

34. Spenser, *Faerie Queene* 3.6.45; Milton, *Paradise Lost* 3.353–57.

Sleep'st by the fable of *Bellerus* old,
Where the great vision of the guarded Mount
Looks toward *Namancos* and *Bayona's* hold. (156–62)

The poet enjoins the "angel" to "Look homeward . . . now, and melt with
ruth" (163); however, it is not exactly clear who the angel is.[35] What is clear
from the passage is that the speaker is requesting a return home, and the
references to the Hebrides, Bellerus, and the "guarded Mount" all demonstrate the poet's own return to images of home. With this return home, the
speaker can now, rather than simply mourn Lycidas, ask the Shepherds to
"weep no more, / For Lycidas your sorrow is not dead" (165–66). The poet
explicitly states that although Lycidas "has sunk low," he is now "mounted
high, / Through the dear might of him that walk'd the waves" (172–73), an
unnamed reference to Christ, who "hears the unexpressive nuptial Song, /
In the blest Kingdoms meek of joy and love" (176–77). The poem neither
assigns Christ a pagan avatar (as earlier with Phoebus) nor does it simply call
out Christ by name (as the poet did fundamentally with Saint Peter, as the
"Pilot of the Galilean lake," in the clerical digression). Both these strategies
were riddled with problems of signification. Now, through a more subtle,
but more psychically acceptable disconnect between the two worldviews the
poem represents, the poet can call forth Lycidas himself and announce him
as a transformed signifier. No longer simply a symbol of pastoral poetry, he
himself becomes a savior for those lost:

Now *Lycidas,* the Shepherds weep no more;
Henceforth thou art the Genius of the shore,
In thy large recompense, and shalt be good
To all that wander in that perilous flood. (182–85)

Lycidas takes the role of a Genius, an attendant spirit, of those wandering
amid the perilous waters of world. For the speaker, he becomes the reconfig-
ured symbol of rebirth, but for the reader a symbol of transference.

One of the most surprising elements of Milton's poem comes in the final
few lines. It is here that the speaker of the poem, the pastoral poet himself,
is revealed not to be the actual narrator of the poem. Milton shifts point of

---

35. Most critics believe that it is Lycidas who is being addressed in this passage; however, Saint
Michael is another possibility. See Lawrence Lipking, "The Genius of the Shore: Lycidas, Adamastor, and the Poetics of Nationalism," *Publications of the Modern Language Association* 111 (1996):
205–21.

view to a third-person narrator who comments not on Lycidas, on whom the poem is focused, but rather on the poet singing about Lycidas:

> Thus sang the uncouth Swain to th' Oaks and rills,
> While the still morn went out with Sandals gray,
> He touch'd the tender stops of various Quills,
> With eager thought warbling his *Doric* lay:
> And now the Sun had stretch'd out all the hills,
> And now was dropt into the Western bay;
> At last he rose, and twitch'd his Mantle blue:
> Tomorrow to fresh Woods, and Pastures new. (186–94)

Again, the entire perspective of the poem changes with this shift in point of view. We can no longer—if we were indeed tempted to do so in the first place—take the "uncouth swain" as completely reliable, nor can we immediately associate the primary voice of the swain of the poem with Milton himself. The swain is now seen as a character, one who becomes not just the teller of Lycidas's story, but the actual subject of the poem itself. The third-person narrator at the end of the poem says nothing of Lycidas; the speaker's remarks are directed solely to the uncouth swain and his fate, not the fate of Lycidas. This speaker does not explicitly discuss the religious implications of the swain's song; the focus is on the song of the poet: "thus sang the uncouth swain"; "He touch'd the tender stops of various quills"; warbled "his Doric lay"; and "twitch'd his mantle blue." The stretching out over the hills in line 190 certainly calls attention to a possible "sun"/"son" pun; however, in the context, as the sun is seen as fading in the west, the connotation with Christ does not seem applicable here. In addition, the frequently interpreted last line, in which our poet is described as now ready to seek new woods and pastures, does not in the context of the final lines suggest a spiritual search. What it does suggest is that the pastoral poet has finished his song and is ready to search for new songs.

The closing gives at least some affirmation that the poem is primarily about poetry, about the swain negotiating the significance and meaning of his own poetic voice—finding it, struggling with it, losing it, finding it again—and with the realization that the solidity of that voice, that self, is not grounded in permanence, he as a poet/shepherd must move on to new woods and new pastures. The primary speaker in *Lycidas* is symptomatic of a split subject. Grounding himself both in the referential system of genre and in the ideological expectations of Christianity and seventeenth-century cultural forces, the subject that emerges is one who struggles to find a balance. However, it is exactly at those moments when such balance is demonstrated, when the subject fails to recognize and accept the fundamental lack inherent in both of those systems of discourse, that anxiety emerges, and along with it an intertextual poetic process that is most compelling.

Chapter 5

Milton's Heroic Action and Formal Falls

In literary fictions the plot consists of somebody doing something. The somebody, if an individual, is the hero, and the something he does or fails to do is what he can do, or could have done, on the level of the postulates made about him by the author and the consequent expectations of the audience. Fictions, therefore, may be classified, not morally, but by the hero's power of action, which may be greater than ours, less, or roughly the same.

—Northrop Frye, *An Anatomy of Criticism*

*I*t would be more than thirty years after *Lycidas* before Milton would write anything substantial in verse. The new pastures that Milton himself tended became the political, religious, and social landscape of seventeenth-century England. He was prolific, but most of his writing was prose aimed at debating various charged issues of the day: monarchy, divorce, censorship, and the commonwealth.[1] Although his poetic consciousness was somewhat repressed, the ideological issues in which he was immersed had a profound impact on the way he conceived of poetry and the way he would ultimately project his poetic consciousness onto his later work. During his virtual hiatus from poetry, Milton constantly *thought* about poetry, how the art might be used as a vehicle to express those ideological principles to which he was so strongly attached. But what we see in Milton is what we

---

1. On Milton's political and social prose, see David Loewenstein and James Grantham Turner, eds., *Politics, Poetics, and Hermeneutics in Milton's Prose* (Cambridge: Cambridge University Press, 1990). See also Brooke Conti, "'That Really Too Anxious Protestation': Crisis and Autobiography in Milton's Prose," *Milton Studies* 45 (2006): 149–86.

have seen continuously in humanism; Milton's concern was how he could project a unique voice that represented the ideological realities of his own contemporary world while situating his voice within a literary structure that would ultimately threaten to make his voice derivative. Humanism required that its voices be sourced, validated through precedent and a structure of poetic tradition in which a writer's own voice could find a place. In "The Reason of Church Government" (1642), Milton expresses his desire to hold a position similar to the classical and Judeo-Christian authors of the past:

> That what the greatest and choicest wits of Athens, Rome, or modern Italy, and those Hebrews of old did for their country, I, in my proportion, with this over and above of being a Christian, might do for mine; not caring to be once named abroad, though perhaps I could attain to that, but content with these British islands as my world; whose fortune hath hitherto been that if the Athenians, as some say, made their small deeds great and renowned by their eloquent writers, *England* hath had her noble achievements made small by the unskilfull handling of monks and mechanics. (Preface, Book 2, 668)

Milton understands the importance of a writer's structural place within tradition. He does not simply want to be like past writers superficially, but to occupy the same place in tradition: to do for his "country" and his own historical moment what those previous writers did for theirs. But the searching out of the past was necessary for Milton's poetic self-projection in the present. Even the most pressing ideological concerns Milton first considers and situates in the past, in the artifacts of a classical memory that will allow him to fill the lack in the ruinous past as well as the lack in England's own "unskilful . . . monks and mechanics," who have made England's achievements pale in comparison to the past. Milton puts forth ideologically relevant themes through his own self-identity, but that identity comes only in its differential relation to the same past in which he seeks to take a place.

One of the dominant themes that fermented during the mid-seventeenth century for Milton was that of the Christian hero, and more specifically what literary models would best facilitate the ideal hero with whom he was concerned. In 1642, decades before the publication of *Paradise Lost, Paradise Regained,* and *Samson Agonistes,* Milton was already struggling to find a model for this Christian hero:

> Time serves not now, and perhaps I might seem too profuse to give any certain account of what the mind at home in the spacious circuits of her

musing hath liberty to propose to her self, though of highest hope and hardest attempting, whether that epic form whereof the two poems of Homer, and those other two of Virgil and Tasso are a diffuse, and the book of Job a brief model: or whether the rules of Aristotle herein are strictly to be kept, or nature to be follow'd, which in them that know art and use judgment, is no transgression but an enriching of art: and lastly what king or knight before the conquest might be chosen in whom to lay the pattern of a Christian hero. ("Reason of Church Government," Preface, Book 2, 668–69)

Not only does this passage make it very explicit that Milton, at least initially, was indeed looking for a model to depict the "Christian hero," but it also demonstrates the crisis at hand. Does he return to the classical epic, especially those of Homer and Virgil, or perhaps the brief biblical epic of Job? There were actually several examples of the biblical epic in sixteenth- and seventeenth-century verse, such as Cowley's *Davidies* (1656), Giles Fletcher's *Christ's Victorie and Triumph* (1610), and Thomas Robinson's *The Life and Death of Mary Magdalene* (1569).[2] Eventually, Milton would engage multiple genres during his quest to create the Christian hero, and he would consider if the more recent history of Europe might serve as an adequate source or whether the ancients simply provide the noblest models:

if to the instinct of nature and the emboldening of art aught may be trusted, and that there be nothing adverse in our climate, or the fate of this age, it haply would be no rashness from an equal diligence and inclination, to present the like offer in our own ancient stories: or whether those dramatic constitutions, wherein Sophocles and Euripides reign, shall be found more doctrinal and exemplary to a nation. ("Reason of Church Government," Preface, Book 2, 669)

Sure enough, Milton considers writing an epic based on King Arthur, but he ultimately abandons this more historically contemporary figure. Milton confronts all the pertinent crises in his poetic enterprise: he wants to depict a Christian hero, he needs established literary models to validate and facilitate his depiction of this hero, he seems to understand that there is an ideological and temporal difference from the classical world, but he also realizes that those antique models may indeed be the most validating literary

---

2. For a discussion of the rise of the biblical epic, see Thomas Greene, *The Descent from Heaven: A Study in Epic Continuity* (New Haven, CT: Yale University Press, 1963).

apparatus for his contemporary concerns. Milton desires an authentic literary voice that functions similarly to the voices that have come before. He understands that it is the *function* of those previous writers that he wants to adopt, but that function can be obtained only by association with the material and textual markers that define the tradition.

Having a statement from Milton that explicitly announces his desire to write a Christian hero opens up numerous problems of interpretation and understanding of Milton's heavy reliance on classical models. To a large degree the ancient hero was incidental to the heroic *action* of the form. Aristotle, for example, never identifies an "epic hero" as a defining quality of the epic. Aristotle is much more concerned with the narrative action: the manifestation of Achilles' wrath, the wanderings of Odysseus, and, later, to which Aristotle could be applied, Aeneas's quest. The characteristics of what we now call the epic hero are mere vehicles for the epic action that drives the narrative. Even in Aristotle's discussion of tragedy, in which he does propose certain necessary qualities of the *tragic* hero, those qualities are necessary not for any moral status of the hero himself/herself, but rather because those qualities enable the play's action to function in a particular way. The imitation about which Aristotle consistently writes as a defining characteristic of the form is manifested not by a particular hero, but by the imitation of an action, of which the protagonist is a part. The form of epic and tragedy simply does not have the kind of hero that we commonly associate with the term itself.[3] Therefore, Milton's dilemma is rooted in his desire to project his own vision of a Christian hero, but his classical models (as well as his biblical models) do not provide the generic conventions to accomplish that task easily. D. C. Feeney is only half correct to assert: "'Who is the hero of Paradise Lost?' is not a significant question within the terms of Milton's generic allegiance and professed intent."[4] Although Milton's "generic allegiance" does not imply the presence of the hero, Milton's intent to eventually give the reader a "Christian hero" does. And that is the crisis Milton faces.

The Hero Is in the Form

As was the case with some of Milton's early verse, in both *Paradise Lost* and *Samson Agonistes*, Milton uses the foreword material as an opportunity to

---

3. See D. C. Feeney, "Epic Hero and Epic Fable," *Comparative Literature* 38.2 (1986): 137–58.
4. Feeney, "Epic Hero and Epic Fable," 158.

establish a formal context for the poems. The form is directly connected to the nature of the heroic theme the poet will explore. Although there are Christian ideological projections in the poems' themes, Milton firmly and definitely makes the necessity of a classical orientation clear; in the case of *Paradise Lost,* he wants to justify his specific use of blank verse, which he does by relating it directly to his classical heroic models and differentiating contemporary writers with that prioritized form:

> The measure is *English* Heroic Verse without Rime, as that of *Homer* in *Greek,* and *Virgil* in *Latin;* Rime being no necessary Adjunct or true Ornament of Poem or good Verse, in longer Works especially, but the Invention of a barbarous Age, to set off wretched matter and lame Meter; grac't indeed since by the use of some famous modern Poets, carried away by Custom, but much to thir own vexation, hindrance, and constraint to express many things otherwise, and for the most part worse then else they would have exprest them. Not without cause therefore some both *Italian,* and *Spanish* Poets of prime note have rejected Rime both in longer and shorter Works, as have also long since our best English Tragedies, as a thing of itself, to all judicious ears, trivial, and of no true musical delight; which consists only in apt Numbers, fit quantity of Syllables, and the sense variously drawn out from one Verse into another, not in the jingling sound of like endings, a fault avoided by the learned Ancients both in Poetry and all good Oratory. This neglect then of Rime so little is to be taken for a defect, though it may seem so perhaps to vulgar Readers, that it rather is to be esteem'd an example set, the first in *English,* of ancient liberty recover'd to Heroic Poem from the troublesome and modern bondage of Riming. ("The Verse," Prefatory note to *Paradise Lost,* 210)

Although this defense of blank verse is on the surface an isolated statement about the form, its implications for the positioning of Milton's epic among his classical models is significant on multiple levels. Milton seeks to differentiate himself and his own poetic identity from his contemporaries or near contemporaries. Spenser, for whom Milton had great respect and who influenced Milton's work in numerous ways, wrote *The Fairie Queene* (1590) in a nine-line rhymed stanza (*ababbcbcc*):

> Gentle Knight was pricking on the plaine,
> Y cladd in mightie armes and siluer shielde,
> Wherein old dints of deepe wounds did remaine,
> The cruell markes of many' a bloudy fielde;

Yet armes till that time did he neuer wield:
His angry steede did chide his foming bitt,
As much disdayning to the curbe to yield:
Full iolly knight he seemd, and faire did sitt,
As one for knightly giusts and fierce encounters fitt. (1.1–9)

Cowley used rhymed couplets in the *Davideis* (1656):

I sing the *Man* who *Judahs Scepter* bore
    In that right hand which held the *Crook* before;
Who from best *Poet,* best of *Kings* did grow;
    The two chief *gifts Heav'n* could on *Man* bestow.
Much danger first, much toil did he sustain,
Whilst *Saul* and *Hell* crost his strong fate in vain.
Nor did his *Crown* less painful work afford;
Less exercise his *Patience,* or his *Sword;*
So long her *Conque'ror Fortunes* spight pursu'd;
Till with unwearied *Virtue* he subdu'd
All homebred Malice, and all forreign boasts;
Their strength was *Armies,* his the *Lord of Hosts.* (1.1–12)

For writers such as Spenser and Cowley, using distinctive rhyme in English functions in a significant way to make their own epic vision unique to English. Milton, however, is more hesitant and more apprehensive about formally veering off the heroic model of the ancients too radically. Or perhaps a better way to view Milton's attitude is this: Milton wants to remain connected to the formal validity of the classical models despite the fact that he will be writing in English on a theme that is distinctively nonclassical. Despite Milton's acknowledgment that the use of rhyme has been done well by "famous modern Poets," he emphasizes that this "Invention of a barbarous Age" has done harm to the heroic form itself. He justifies his unrhymed verse as an "ancient liberty recover'd," and the result will be the rescuing of heroic poetry "from the troublesome and modern bondage of Riming."

Milton's closet drama, *Samson Agonistes,* also defends the poet's reliance on classical genre,[5] but more subtly challenges the manner in which Milton's

---

5. The fundamental work on *Samson* as a classical drama remains William R. Parker, *Milton's Debt to Greek Tragedy in "Samson Agonistes"* (Baltimore: Johns Hopkins University Press, 1937). Other important studies of *Samson* include Mark R. Kelley and Joseph Wittreich, eds., *Altering Eyes: New Perspectives on "Samson Agonistes"* (Newark: University of Delaware Press, 2002); Stanley Fish, "Spectacle and Evidence in 'Samson Agonistes,'" *Critical Inquiry* 15.3 (1989): 556–86; Barbara

near contemporaries (Marlowe and Shakespeare, for example) undermine that genre. Milton prioritizes the classical conception of the form and the psychical principles that originally surrounded the form. Before his drama begins, Milton states his views "Of that sort of Dramatic Poem which is call'd Tragedy":

> Tragedy, as it was anciently compos'd, hath been ever held the gravest, moralest, and most profitable of all other Poems: therefore said by *Aristotle* to be of power by raising pity and fear, or terror, to purge the mind of those and such like passions, that is to temper and reduce them to just measure with a kind of delight, stirr'd up by reading or seeing those passions well imitated. Nor is Nature wanting in her own effects to make good his asser-tion: for so in Physic things of melancholic hue and quality are us'd against melancholy, sour against sour, salt to remove salt humors. Hence Philoso-phers and other gravest Writers, as *Cicero, Plutarch* and others, frequently cite out of Tragic Poets, both to adorn and illustrate thir discourse. The Apostle *Paul* himself thought it not unworthy to insert a verse of *Euripides* into the Text of Holy Scripture, I *Cor.* 15.33, and *Paraeus* commenting on the *Revelation,* divides the whole Book as a Tragedy, into Acts distinguisht each by a Chorus of Heavenly Harpings and Song between. Heretofore Men in highest dignity have labour'd not a little to be thought able to com-pose a Tragedy. Of that honor *Dionysius* the elder was no less ambitious, then before of his attaining to the Tyranny. *Augustus Caesar* also had begun his *Ajax,* but unable to please his own judgment with what he had begun, left it unfinisht. *Seneca* the Philosopher is by some thought the Author of those Tragedies (at lest the best of them) that go under that name. *Gregory Nazianzen* a Father of the Church, thought it not unbeseeming the sanctity of his person to write a Tragedy, which he entitl'd, *Christ Suffering.* This is mention'd to vindicate Tragedy from the small esteem, or rather infamy, which in the account of many it undergoes at this day with other common Interludes; happ'ning through the Poets error of intermixing Comic stuff with Tragic sadness and gravity; or introducing trivial and vulgar persons, which by all judicious hath bin counted absurd; and brought in without

K. Lewalski, "'Samson Agonistes' and the 'Tragedy' of the Apocalypse," *Publications of the Mod-ern Language Association* 85.5 (1970): 1050–62; Alan Rudrum, *A Critical Commentary on Milton's "Samson Agonistes"* (London: Macmillan, 1969); John Carey, *Milton* (London: Evans Bros., 1969); James Waddell Tupper, "The Dramatic Structure of Samson Agonistes," *Publications of the Modern Language Association* 35.3 (1920): 529–51. Alan Rudrum gives a thorough overview of the critical debates in "Milton Scholarship and the 'Agon' over 'Samson Agonistes,'" *Huntington Library Quar-terly* 65.3–4 (2002): 465–88.

discretion, corruptly to gratify the people. And though ancient Tragedy use no Prologue, yet using sometimes, in case of self defense, or explanation, that which *Martial* calls an Epistle; in behalf of this Tragedy coming forth after the ancient manner, much different from what among us passes for best, thus much before-hand may be Epistl'd; that *Chorus* is here introduc'd after the Greek manner, not antient only but modern, and still in use among the *Italians*. In the modelling therefore of this Poem, with good reason, the Ancients and *Italians* are rather follow'd, as of much more authority and fame. The measure of Verse us'd in the Chorus is of all sorts, call'd by the Greeks *Monostrophic*, or rather *Apolelymenon*, without regard had to *Strophe, Antistrophe* or *Epod*, which were a kind of Stanza's fram'd only for the Music, then us'd with the Chorus that sung; not essential to the Poem, and therefore not material; or being divided into Stanza's or Pauses, they may be call'd *Allæostropha*. Division into Act and Scene referring chiefly to the Stage (to which this work never was intended) is here omitted. It suffices if the whole Drama be found not produc't beyond the fifth Act.

Of the style and uniformity, and that commonly call'd the Plot, whether intricate or explicit, which is nothing indeed but such economy, or disposition of the fable as may stand best with verisimilitude and decorum; they only will best judge who are not unacquainted with *Æschylus, Sophocles*, and *Euripides*, the three Tragic Poets unequall'd yet by any, and the best rule to all who endeavor to write Tragedy. The circumscription of time wherein the whole Drama begins and ends, is according to ancient rule, and best example, within the space of 24 hours. ("Of that Sort of Dramatic Poem Which Is Called Tragedy," Prefatory note to *Samson Agonistes*, 549–50)

Two aspects of Milton's description stand out. Although Milton justifies traditional ancient tragedy on its own terms, he uses scripture and the Christian tradition to validate it as well—Paul's reference to Euripides and Nazianzen's use of the form in *Christ Suffering*. Also, Milton implies an inferiority in the kinds of tragedy written by the greatest English playwrights as he criticizes the mixture of tragic and comic and the violation of the Aristotelian unities (both common in Shakespeare and Marlowe). Again, this position by Milton is more than just a formal issue. Considering what will be the topics of *Paradise Lost and Samson Agonistes*, Milton's invocation to classical form before the poems even begin provides an initial identification with the classical past that will soon be usurped and challenged by his poetic projection within the poems. Milton's desire is not for an other, but rather for the desire of the Other; again, he desires to do for his own his-

torical moment what the ancients did for theirs. However, the classics exert
enough pressure on him that Milton expresses the belief that it is through
the form of those classical remnants that his own poetic self can be projected
onto the present and made to *do* what those classical others do. What is
not revealed by these introductions to the two poems is whether or not the
ancient forms can be transplanted into a different historical and ideological
context; whether the heroic narratives of the past can simply be replaced
by something else, without doing violence to either the form or the ideology Milton consciously or unconsciously projects. The crisis Milton faces
is evident at the very beginning of *Paradise Lost*. As he sets up his explora-
tion into and justification of God's providence—his explicit purpose of the
epic—by invoking his "Heav'nly Muse," he states:

> I thence
> Invoke thy aid to my advent'rous Song
> That with no middle flight intends to soar
> Above th' Aonian Mount, while it pursues
> Things unattempted yet in Prose or Rhyme. (12–16)

By calling on his muse, he clearly engages the classical convention but
immediately undercuts it by claiming to do more, to go beyond the Aonian
mount of classical inspiration and to do something new. But those things
yet unattempted Milton squarely places within the tradition. It can only be
made "new" and "original" by placing it in the very tradition that it seeks
to exceed. Milton's poetic dilemma is essentially a psychical one: he needs
the past to validate his own poetic consciousness, but the initial failure to
recognize the rupture that exists between the past and present brings forth
an anxiety that Milton remedies by announcing that he will transcend and
exceed the same poetic models that validate his own work.

Epic Action and Tragic Falls

Paradise Lost has historically caused Milton critics tremendous problems.
Romantics such as Shelley viewed Satan as the glorious rebellious hero who
defies the supreme monarch of heaven. C. S. Lewis was horrified by such
a notion. Later critics have split (the Satanists and anti-Satanists); others
claim that Satan is a *kind* of hero, perhaps an antihero, who displays some
traditional epic hero qualities, but only in a perverted and unheroic context.
The fact is that nearly every permutation of the "hero" in *Paradise Lost* has

been presented by critics: Satan is the hero; Satan is the antihero; Christ is the hero; Adam is the hero; Eve, in her final tragic recognition, becomes the hero; God the father, in his mercy and willingness to sacrifice his own son, is the hero; or there is no true hero at all, and so on.[6] Regardless of which position one takes, two things are certain: Milton structures his heroic poem as a classical epic, and heroism is at the center of Milton's proposition.

Following both the poem's introductory material, which establishes the classical precedent of nonrhyming verse and the priority of heroic poetry more generally, and the opening proposition that his poem will soar "Above th' Aonian Mount, while it pursues / Things unattempted yet in Prose or Rhyme" (*PL* 1.15–16), we begin the poem's narrative with the epic poet. To a large degree, this reference undercuts the association with classical heroic verse that Milton established in the header material, with the reconciliation being that he is conforming to the form but rising above the subject matter. The poet announces his theme: to "assert Eternal Providence / And justify the ways of God to men" (1.25–26). Declaring the subject matter of the epic to follow is conventional (e.g., the rage of Achilles in the *Iliad;* the story of Odysseus' wanderings and homecoming in the *Odyssey;* the destiny of Aeneas in the *Aeneid.* In addition to the poet's declaration that his intent is to justify God's providence, the action of the epic is set up initially as the story of humankind's disobedience, the fall from Eden:

> Say first, for Heav'n hides nothing from thy view
> Nor the deep Tract of Hell, say first what cause
> Mov'd our Grand Parents in that happy State,
> Favor'd of Heav'n so highly, to fall off

---

6. For just a brief selection of these various perspectives, see Feeney, "Epic Hero and Epic Fable"; Christopher Bond, *Spenser, Milton, and the Redemption of the Epic Hero* (Lanham, MD: Rowan and Littlefield, 2011); John Carey, "Milton's Satan," in *The Cambridge Companion to Milton,* ed. Dennis Danielson (Cambridge: Cambridge University Press, 1999), 160–74; John T. Shawcross, "The Hero of *Paradise Lost:* One More Time," in *Milton and the Art of Sacred Song,* ed. J. Max Patrick and Roger H. Sundell (Madison: University of Wisconsin Press, 1979), 137–47; T. J. B. Spencer, "*Paradise Lost:* The Anti-Epic," in *Approaches to Paradise Lost,* ed. C. A. Patrides (London: Edward Arnold, 1968), 81–98; Stella P. Revard, "The Heroic Context of Book IX of Paradise Lost," *Journal of English and Germanic Philology* 87.3 (1988): 329–41; Francis C. Blessington, *Paradise Lost and the Classical Epic* (Boston and London: Routledge, 1979), especially 1–18; Patrick Colm Hogan, "Lapsarian Odysseus: Joyce, Milton, and the Structure of Ulysses," *James Joyce Quarterly* 24.1 (1986): 55–72; David Loewenstein, *Milton: Paradise Lost* (Cambridge: Cambridge University Press, 1993), especially 58–70; S. Musgrove, "Is the Devil an Ass?" *Review of English Studies* 21.84 (1945): 302–15; C. S. Lewis, *A Preface to "Paradise Lost"* (London: Oxford University Press, 1942), especially 92–100; Elmer Edgar Stoll, "Give the Devil His Due: A Reply to Mr. Lewis," *Review of English Studies* 20.78 (1944): 108–24.

From thir Creator, and transgress his Will
For one restraint, Lords of the World besides? (*PL* 1.27–32)

The convention Milton adopts, while on the surface mirroring that of the ancient models, functions very differently. In all three classical models I have listed, the theme of the epic is tied directly to the actions of the "hero" and to the narrative that will ensue. Achilles's rage will be played out through his actions (and inaction); Odysseus' cunning and his journey home, his centripetal and centrifugal paradox, will be manifest in the actual details of his travels; and Aeneas' Roman destiny will be played out in the choices he faces and the decisions he makes.[7] This interplay between the declared theme and the actions of the protagonist is the structural device that drives the epic narrative. In *Paradise Lost,* however, the theme of justifying God's ways is largely disconnected from the actions of a specific protagonist (a specific hero). The epic action does not dictate the theme, as is largely the case in Milton's three ancient models, but rather the theme is meant to dictate the action. Stated another way, the ancient epic themes are denotative, while Milton's theme is connotative. The result of this functional difference is that the poet's perception of epic conventions is often removed from the epic context that originally defined them. The poet's identification with the classical Other, through the formal structure, breaks down when faced with the ideological positioning of the poet's desire to project his Christian identity onto the form.

The discord that exists relates directly to the critical issues surrounding the character of Satan and the identification and understanding of heroism in the epic. Its stated purpose is to justify God's ways, and the primary narrative theme is the fall of humankind from the Garden of Eden. However, the fall from the garden does not provide the narrative structure to support Milton's epic form. The action in the garden occurs in an isolated location, and both Adam and Eve are somewhat passive from an epic point of view, their fate more a result of a tragic fall than an epic journey. Milton needs a source of narrative movement that the fall itself cannot provide. Following the convention of beginning *in medias res,* the poem commences with Satan, whose past, current, and future actions are better able to sustain the narrative movement necessary for a true classical epic. The poet therefore shifts the initial focus from Adam and Eve to the predicament and actions of Satan:

---

7. See William B. Stanford, *The Ulysses Theme: A Study in the Adaptability of a Traditional Hero* (Oxford: Basil Blackwell, 1954); and William B. Stanford and J. V. Luce, *The Quest for Ulysses* (London: Phaidon Press, 1974).

> say first what cause
> Mov'd our Grand Parents in that happy State,
> Favor'd of Heav'n so highly, to fall off
> From their Creator, and transgress his Will
> For one restraint, Lords of the World besides?
> Who first seduc'd them to that fowl revolt?
> Th' infernal Serpent; hee it was, whose guile
> Stirr'd up with Envy and Revenge, deceiv'd
> The Mother of Mankinde, what time his Pride
> Had cast him out from Heav'n, with all his Host
> Of Rebel Angels, by whose aid aspiring
> To set himself in Glory above his Peers,
> He trusted to have equall'd the most High,
> If he oppos'd . . . (*PL* 1.28–41)

Although the negative characteristics of Satan are made clear in this shift of focus, the description of Satan and his legion of fallen angels that follows echoes the opening descriptions of the hero's situation in Homer and Virgil:

> Him the Almighty Power
> Hurl'd headlong flaming from th' Ethereal Sky,
> With hideous ruin and combustion, down
> To bottomless perdition, there to dwell
> In Adamantine Chains and penal Fire,
> Who durst defy th' Omnipotent to arms.
> Nine times the space that measures Day and Night
> To mortal men, hee with his horrid crew
> Lay vanquished, rolling in the fiery gulf,
> Confounded though immortal. But his doom
> Reserved him to more wrath; for now the thought
> Both of lost happiness and lasting pain
> Torments him: round he throws his baleful eyes,
> That witness'd huge affliction and dismay,
> Mixt with obdúrate pride and steadfast hate.
> At once as far as Angels ken he views
> The dismal Situation waste and wild.
> A Dungeon horrible, on all sides round,
> As one great furnace flam'd; yet from those flames
> No light; but rather darkness visible
> Serv'd only to discover sights of woe,

Regions of sorrow, doleful shades, where peace
And rest can never dwell, hope never comes
That comes to all, but torture without end
Still urges, and a fiery Deluge, fed
With ever-burning Sulphur unconsumed. (*PL* 1.44–69)

Rage—Goddess, sing the rage of Peleus' son Achilles,
murderous, doomed, that cost the Achaeans countless losses,
hurling down to the House of Death so many sturdy souls,
great fighters' souls, but made their bodies carrion,
feasts for the dogs and birds,
and the will of Zeus was moving toward its end. (*Iliad* 1.1–6)[8]

Many were those whose cities he saw, whose minds he learned of,
many were the pains he suffered in his spirit on the wide sea,
struggling for his own life and the homecoming of his companions.
Even so he could not save his companions, hard though
he strove to; they were destroyed by their own wild recklessness,
fools, who devoured the oxen of Helios, the Sun God. (*Odyssey* 1.3–8)[9]

I sing of arms and the hero who, from Trojan shores,
a fated exile, first set foot on Italian soil
and the Lavinian coast; driven on land and sea
by force of Heaven's gods and the unremitting anger
of cruel Juno; he suffered also much in war
to found his city and to bring his gods to Latium,
whence Latins, and Alban Fathers, and walls of mighty Rome.
Tell me the reasons, Muse, what slight to her will divine,
suffering what hurt did Heaven's Queen drive on a man
so righteous, to endure so many woes and afflictions?
Can gods harbor such resentment in their immortal breasts?
    (*Aeneid* 1.1–11)[10]

Although there are no specific classical allusions in the passage from Milton,
much of his description of Satan's orientation at the beginning of the epic
mirrors the opening passages of the classical epics. The description of Satan
includes images of being cast down, of being victimized by a deity, of hav-

---

8. Homer, *The Iliad*, trans. Robert Fagles (New York: Penguin, 1990).

9. Homer, *The Odyssey*, trans. Richard Lattimore (New York: Harper Collins, 1991).

10. Vergil, *The Aeneid*, trans. James H. Mantinband (New York: Ungar Publishing, 1964).

ing responsibility for "companions" (who are either dead or suffer because of a kind of "recklessness" toward the gods), and of a hero who is or will be consumed by excessive wrath. Satan certainly takes on the heroic role here, the epic poet's statement that Satan is the villain and the cause of humankind's fall is definitive:

> Who first seduc'd them to that fowl revolt?
> Th' infernal Serpent; he it was, whose guile
> Stird up with Envy and Revenge, deceiv'd
> The Mother of Mankind. (*PL* 1.32–36)

Because of the villainous role he plays, Satan's function as the epic hero does not directly further the epic's moral theme—at least not at this point—but it does provide the heroic action to allow the epic to progress. The various "heroic" traits and descriptions the poet uses to describe Satan and his followers might be considered by Thomas Greene (see note 2 above) as a form of eclectic imitation, an amalgamation of sources that neither seeks to distinguish itself from those sources nor identify with them. However, Milton was very aware of character perspective in his work (Satan speaks of God's tyranny in terms that Milton himself might have used against the English monarch, for example—he, who "Sole reigning holds the Tyranny of Heav'n" (*PL* 1.124)[11]—and the Greek and Roman heroes certainly could be considered villainous depending on the perspective of the one making the characterization. The demons themselves produce the same kind of heroic verse depicting their own fall that the epic poet is writing about in *Paradise Lost* to describe that of humankind:

> Others more mild,
> Retreated in a silent valley, sing
> With notes Angelical to many a Harp
> Thir own Heroic deeds and hapless fall
> By doom of Battel; and complain that Fate
> Free Virtue should enthrall to Force or Chance. (*PL* 2.546–51)

In this way, the poet in the first three books of *Paradise Lost* links Satan and his legion in various ways to the protagonists of classical epic, which gives Milton's work an identifying context from which it can proceed.

---

11. For an insightful study of Satan's antimonarchy rhetoric, see Michael Bryson, *The Tyranny of Heaven: Milton's Rejection of God as King* (Newark: University of Delaware Press, 2004).

The initial depiction of Satan is one of a battle-worn, but glorious hero of war; it is a description that helps to contextualize him physically in his heroic and quasi-divine role:

> Thir dread commander: he above the rest
> In shape and gesture proudly eminent
> Stood like a Tow'r; his form had yet not lost
> All her Original brightness. (*PL* 1.589–92)

Echoing the descriptions of Achilles' and Aeneas' shields (*Iliad* 18.478–608 and *Aeneid* 8.608–728), the poet describes Satan's shield and spear in typical heroic fashion, complete with epic simile:

> He scarce had ceas't when the superior Fiend
> Was moving toward the shore; his ponderous shield
> Ethereal temper, massy, large and round,
> Behind him cast; the broad circumference
> Hung on his shoulders like the Moon, whose Orb
> Through Optic Glass the *Tuscan* Artist views
> At Ev'ning from the top of *Fesole,*
> Or in *Valdarno,* to descry new Lands,
> Rivers or Mountains in her spotty Globe.
> His Spear, to equal which the tallest Pine
> Hewn on *Norwegian* hills, to be the Mast
> Of some great Ammiral. (*PL* 1.283–94)

Without the religious contextualization of Satan and with such descriptions of Satan's heroic stature, the first third of *Paradise Lost* casts Satan as a typical hero: brave, illustrious, semidivine, purposeful, respected, and committed to his epic task. The heroic nature of this figure, who seems "A Pillar of State" (2.302), "Majestic though in ruin" (305), "With *Atlantean* shoulders fit to bear / The weight of mightiest Monarchies" (306–7), sets the action of an epic hero setting out on a journey. Even later, in Book 6, where Satan is remembered as a warrior in heaven who battles Michael in a very Achilles- and Hector-like moment, his heroic prowess is evident. Nonetheless, the epic tradition provides Milton with enough of a paradoxical hero that Satan's moral deficiencies can at least be put into the same epic context he uses to build Satan up.

Milton most notably connects Satan's journey to that of Odysseus. Milton would have been quite familiar with the varied tradition of Odysseus, which depicted him at times as a wily, deceptive trickster, as well as one whose heroism is often challenged.[12] If it can be said that Milton's Satan is truly an epic hero, it is in this tradition that Satan's "heroism" functions. As he sets out on his journey to destroy humankind (after clever manipulation of the council of demons in Book 2), Satan is explicitly cast as an Odyssean figure:

> But glad that now his Sea should find a shore,
> With fresh alacrity and force renew'd
> Springs upward like a Pyramid of fire
> Into the wild expanse, and through the shock
> Of fighting Elements, on all sides round
> Environ'd wins his way; harder beset
> And more endanger'd, then when *Argo* pass'd
> Through *Bosporus* betwixt the justling Rocks:
> Or when *Ulysses* on the Larboard shunn'd
> *Charybdis*, and by th'other whirlpool steer'd. (*PL* 2.1011–20)

The additional reference to Jason is also appropriate, considering Jason's own epic sea voyage as well as his questionable moral compass. When Satan encounters the monstrous figure of Sin, the poet again connects Satan to Odysseus as the dogs protruding from the womb of Sin are said to be "Farr less abhorr'd than . . . / Vex'd *Scylla* bathing in the Sea that parts / *Calabria* from the hoarse *Trinacrian* shore (2.659–61). Through his verbal skills, he is able to trick Death into opening the gates of hell, which allows him to sail the abyss and continue on with his quest, as does his ability to alter his shape into that of a minor angel and then trick Uriel at the end of Book 2. Verbal ingenuity and shape shifting are both traits associated with Odysseus, and they serve for both Odysseus and Satan as a means to continue their epic journeys. However, although Satan's possession of both traits ultimately furthers his mission, his shape shifting also results in a decline in the physical appearance that earlier marked his heroic stature—as he changes from angel to bird to toad to serpent—and his verbal ingenuity becomes outright deception and guile when he corrupts Eve in Book 9. But the heroic nature

---

12. A large part of the tradition casts a very negative light on Odysseus. In Euripides, for example, Odysseus is described as "*shifty-hearted butcher knife, that sweet-coaxing, pandering son of Laertes*" (*Hecuba*, trans. Janet Lembke and Kenneth J. Reckford [Oxford: Oxford University Press, 1991], 31) and "*monster of wickedness whose tongue twists straight to crooked, truth to lies, friendship to hate, mocks right and honours wrong!*" (*The Women of Troy*, in *Euripides: The Bacchae and Other Plays*, trans. Philip Vellacott [London: Penguin Classics, 1954], 99).

of *Paradise Lost* as a whole makes clear that Milton's desire to depict a Christian hero does not manifest itself in the poem. The epic poet, though quite expository at times, never tries to suggest that the moral heroism of *Paradise Lost* resides in *any* hero. He understands that heroism is action and makes that claim clear in the opening of the climactic Book 9, in which the reader will witness Satan's success in the Garden of Eden and humankind's failure. The poet must write of humankind's fall as a "sad task" but one that is

> Not less but more Heroic then the wrath
> Of Stern *Achilles* on his Foe pursu'd
> Thrice Fugitive about the *Troy* Wall; or rage
> Of *Turnus* for *Lavinia* disespous'd,
> Or *Neptune's* ire or *Juno's,* that so long
> Perplex'd the *Greek* and *Cytherea's* Son. (*PL* 9.13–19)

This passage is significant, first, because it shows Milton clearly defending his poetic vision against the authority of classical epic. However, perhaps even more importantly, he demonstrates his own perception of what is heroic in the tradition itself, and that helps us understand the heroic quality of Milton's own epic. The wrath of Achilles and the wrath of angry gods targeting the hero are both indicative of Satan's own heroic quest. (Satan was earlier in Book 3 explicitly compared in an epic simile to both Odysseus and Jason as he headed out on his epic journey through chaos toward the garden of Eden.) Satan is not morally but functionally heroic. Milton attempts to place his own poem above that of his predecessors, but the genre requires a heroism that is allusive in quality (identifying the hero's action with that of past heroes) and founded on action, not character. Milton may have once wanted to depict a Christian hero, but he needs a classical hero to make his epic work, and Satan serves that role—morality is irrelevant to the function. Still, as Satan degenerates physically (and thus the poetic description of him becomes less heroic), his function as a morally corrupt character emerges and allows the portrayal of Adam and Eve as tragic figures, whose hubris results in a self-imposed doom. The poet has paid careful attention to the heroic construction of the action, but ideologically the epic must change; it must become something other than a classical epic. This change, this ideological gap between the "form" and the poet's projection of himself and his prioritized present, is defined in terms of what the new heroic must be:

> Since first this Subject for Heroic Song
> Pleas'd me long choosing, and beginning late;

Not sedulous by Nature to indite
Wars, hitherto the only Argument
Heroic deem'd, chief maistry to dissect
With long and tedious havoc fabl'd Knights
In Battels feign'd; the better fortitude
Of Patience and Heroic Martyrdom
Unsung; or to describe Races and Games,
Or tilting Furniture, emblazon'd Shields,
Impreses quaint, Caparisons and Steeds;
Bases and tinsel Trappings, gorgeous Knights
At Joust and Tournament; then marshall'd Feast
Serv'd up in Hall with Sewers, and Seneschals;
The skill of Artifice or Office mean,
Not that which justly gives Heroic name
To Person or to Poem. Mee of these
Nor skill'd nor studious, higher Argument
Remains, sufficient of it self to raise
That name. (*PL* 9.25–44)

Milton acknowledges that the heroic poem to which he had so long aspired could not exist in the battles and artifice of past conventions. He must attend to the "higher Argument" of his purpose. The irony is that for nearly nine books the artifice is exactly what he relied on, and the anxiety of a largely heuristic imitation that attempts to unite the ideologies and laws of convention, of past and present, surfaces in a moment of explicit renunciation of the heroic past as he attempts to reorient his epic and his own poetic consciousness in a present that is ideologically removed from the past.

To a large degree, the initial intention of *Paradise Lost* is similar to that of *Samson Agonistes,* a drama that tells of Samson's last hours, blind, in captivity at Gaza, and eventually prepared to destroy himself and all the pagan Philistines. Milton's choice of genre (a narratorless poem, in which the characters' knowledge is restricted by their historical context) makes it appropriate that there really are no classical allusions—just a creative retelling of an Old Testament story. However, Milton still places this heroic drama in the context of the classical tradition in two clear ways: (1) The play is very much modeled on Aeschylus' *Prometheus Bound*—the bound and suffering tragic hero Samson plays host to visitors (and an ever-present chorus) that mourn his anguish, pity his pain, and offer "advice" on how to relieve that suffering; (2) Milton's prologue explicitly praises the Aristotelian model of tragedy. He goes on to suggest the noble nature of tragedy, the "unequalled" accomplishments of Aeschylus, Sophocles, and Euripides, and he even refers to a proverb ("evil communications corrupt good manners") believed to be from Euripides, about which he states: "The Apostle Paul himself thought it not unworthy to insert a verse of Euripides into the Text of Holy Scripture." We see, in essence, a dialogue between *Samson* and *Paradise Lost;* in *Samson Agonistes,* Milton chooses to adopt the conventions and structure of, in this case, classical tragedy (just as he adopted the structure of epic in *Paradise Lost*), but he also avoids simple reproductive imitation of the classics by avoiding classical allusion and any direct comparison with classical heroes of the tradition. However, what the poet does do is to suggest that Samson is a hero and that the poem represents a mode of heroism that can be both classical and Christian simultaneously:

> Or do my eyes misrepresent? Can this be hee,
> That Heroic, that Renown'd,
> Irresistible *Samson?* whom unarm'd
> No strength of man, or fiercest wild beast could withstand;
> Who tore the Lion, as the Lion tears the Kid. (*SA* 124–28)

This initial reference to the heroism of Samson is primarily given in terms of his physical abilities. The allusion to tearing the lion is a direct reference to Judges 14.5–6, but there is a classical subtext that echoes the myth of Heracles defeating and skinning the Nemean Lion. Samson is also considered heroic as a committed leader, willing to sacrifice even his own moral vows to protect his people:

> Nor in respect of th'enemy just cause
> To set his people free,
> Have prompted this Heroic *Nazarite,*
> Against his vow of strictest purity,
> To seek in marriage that fallacious Bride. (*SA* 316–20)

Again, this passage stays fully and directly connected to the narrative of Judges but parallels Oedipus' saving the people of Thebes, as well as his boasting of his own heroic deeds:

> when in strength
> All mortals I excell'd, and great in hopes
> With youthful courage and magnanimous thoughts
> Of birth from Heav'n foretold and high exploits,

Full of divine instinct, after some proof
Of acts indeed heroic. . . . (*SA* 522–26)

The characteristics of the dramatic hero here are not much different from
those in epic. Samson was a warrior, whose past deeds defined his physical
heroism. However, the physical nature of the hero begins to shift as Samson's heroic traits are tied to a state of mind, one that is equally heroic—
"And feats of War defeats / With plain Heroic magnitude of mind / And
celestial vigor arm'd (*SA* 1278–80)—and one that is described in similar
terms to Milton's reconsideration of the heroic in Book 9 of *Paradise Lost:*
"the better fortitude / of Patience and Heroic Martyrdom" (31–32).

In the passage from *Paradise Lost* at the opening of Book 9 as well as
in the previous quotation from *Samson Agonistes,* Christian action becomes
not action at all but rather patience, contemplation, and sacrifice. With this
idea, Milton more closely approaches the Christian projection he desires
as a poet. Nevertheless, the most clearly stated reference to Samson's heroism comes immediately after a blatant act of physical "heroism," after Samson destroys himself and the Philistines (offstage, of course), and his father
Manoa glorifies the heroic act:

Come, Come, no time for lamentation now,
Nor much more cause: *Samson* hath quit himself
Like *Samson,* and heroicly hath finish'd
A life Heroic. (*SA* 1708–11)

This passage and the action to which it refers are complex. Based on the
early description of heroism as being an act of mind, is Samson's suicide
and destruction of his enemies the real act of heroism the poet wants to
emphasize? Does the heroism really lie in the fact that Samson, blind and
captive, must remain patient and must come to terms with his own failures
and regain his faith in God? Or he is just sort of a suicide bomber who
forgets the lessons of an inner heroism and takes revenge on his enemies in
Medea-like fashion?[13] As in *Paradise Lost,* the heroic is at the center of the

---

13. The violent, vengeful nature of the final action in Samson has long been discussed; however,
contemporary discussions have been affected by the events of September 11. See Michael Lieb and
Albert Labriola, eds., *Milton in the Age of Fish: Essays on Authorship, Text, and Terrorism* (Pittsburgh:
Duquesne University Press, 2006); Feisal G. Mohamed, "Confronting Religious Violence: Milton's
'Samson Agonistes,'" *Publications of the Modern Language Association* 120.2 (2005): 327–40; John
Carey, "A Work in Praise of Terrorism?: September 11 and *Samson Agonistes,*" *Times Literary Supple-
ment* 6 (September 2002): 15–16; Derek N. C. Wood, *Exiled from Light: Divine Law, Morality, and
Violence in Milton's "Samson Agonistes"* (Toronto: University of Toronto Press, 2001); Clay Daniel,

play, but *Samson Agonistes* executes a different way of positioning it within the tradition of classical heroism.

⁓

Milton's identification with the past is intricate, and through the few examples I have given—as well as the framework through which I propose such intricacy should be viewed—what seems clear is that Milton's "classicism" is not a seamless blending of his past and present, but rather an active, anxious attempt at finding a balance between the system of tradition that validates his accomplishments as a writer and the Christian ideology that is found to be inherently opposed to that tradition. We know that Milton variously adopts the structure of his classical models, and rejects such structures; embraces the images and myths of the ancients, and consciously avoids them. At times he praises the learning and worthiness of classical models; conversely, he deplores their inferiority. These conflicts are the basis of the complexities that make Renaissance art and literature so powerful, but it is a power that comes—historically as in the case of most great works of art—from discord, not unity.

"Lust and Violence in 'Samson Agonistes,'" *South Central Review* 6.1 (1989): 6–31; Anthony Low, "'No Power but of God': Vengeance and Justice in 'Samson Agonistes,'" *Huntington Library Quarterly* 40.4 (1977): 313–24.

Epilogue

The story goes that Thomas Ellwood, a friend of Milton's, read *Paradise Lost* and responded in this way: "Thou hast said much here of Paradise lost, but what hast thou to say of Paradise found?"[1] Milton then decides to write a four-book epic—modeled *not* on the classical epic but more in the tradition of the Job story of the Old Testament.[2] Interestingly, Milton stays committed to his 1642 consideration of various modes of epic: "whether that epic form whereof the two poems of *Homer,* and those other two of *Virgil* and *Tasso* are a diffuse, and the book of *Job* a brief model." Milton has tried a Homeric epic poem; he has tried an Aristotelian tragedy. Now, he puts a biblical model to the test. With such a nonclassical structure and relatively few classical allusions, this brief epic (as it has been called) seems very much a rebuttal not just of Satan's success at causing the fall, but of the very models Milton adopted to depict that fall. *Paradise Regained* depicts Satan's temptation of Jesus in the desert. Milton's initial invocation mirrors that in Book 9 of *Paradise Lost*—specifically the desire to sing something new, something heroic, but not yet attempted. His purpose is

---

1. David Masson, *The Life of John Milton* (London, 1859–94), 6: 654–55. Barbara Lewalski notes that this story is "probably apocryphal" (4; see note 2 below).

2. See Barbara K. Lewalski, *Milton's Brief Epic: The Genre, Meaning, and Art of "Paradise Regained"* (Providence, RI: Brown University Press, 1966); Lewalski's book remains one of the most important and influential studies of *Paradise Regained.*

With prosperous wing full summ'd to tell of deeds
Above Heroic, though in secret done,
And unrecorded left through many an Age,
Worthy t' have not remain'd so long unsung. (*PR* 1.14–17)

Here, as in *Paradise Lost,* the poet expresses his desire to write a heroic tale that is in fact above heroic, and though there is no explicit reference to muses, no comparison to the heroic tales of the past, no reference to previous heroes—just below the surface of the text, all those elements are present.[3] Only now Milton does not invoke what he must reject. But why the change in poetic process? Why change a method that proved infinitely rich in the case of *Paradise Lost?* Perhaps for the anxiety of the writer, such richness comes at cost. Jesus is clearly the hero; he, while thinking about his first trips to the temple as a child, says that in his mind and heart he sensed the heroism to come:

victorious deeds
Flam'd in my heart, heroic acts; one while
To rescue *Israel* from the *Roman* yoke,
Then to subdue and quell o'er all the earth
Brute violence and proud Tyrannic pow'r,
Till truth were freed, and equity restor'd. (*PR* 1.215–20)

Just as he does in *Paradise Lost* and *Samson Agonistes,* the poet makes "heroic acts" a defining component of the hero. Ironically, Jesus, like Satan in *Paradise Lost,* seeks to rescue his own people from "Tyrannic pow'r." The heroism of Jesus and Satan is spoken of in similar terms, but the structure in which that heroism occurs impacts the ideological moral significance of those "heroic acts." Jesus' heroic deeds (though they are forthcoming) are not derived from those of the classical heroes in the past but are placed squarely and directly within a closed Judeo-Christian tradition—both in the narrative but also in the form used to drive that narrative. The epic model of Homer works only if the heroic figure is classically heroic; the Job model provides a model that is more organic to the Christian hero.

---

3. Early studies on the heroic theme of *Paradise Regained* include Merrit Y. Hughes, "The Christ of *Paradise Regained* and the Renaissance Heroic Tradition," *Studies in Philology* 35 (1938): 254–77; Frank Kermode, "Milton's Hero," *Review of English Studies,* n.s., 4 (1953): 317–30; Don M. Wolfe, "The Role of Milton's Christ," *Sewanee Review* 51 (1943): 467–75; A. S. P. Woodhouse, "Theme and Pattern in *Paradise Regained,*" *University of Toronto Quarterly* 25 (1956): 167–82.

Epilogue

As already mentioned, staying largely true to his purpose of writing a nonclassical epic, Milton in *Paradise Regained* seems to avoid classical structure and for the most part classical allusion. However, in Book 4, after two previous failed temptations of Jesus in the desert, Satan makes his last attempt. Oddly enough, the final temptation speaks volumes about not just Jesus, but also Milton's entire poetic methodology. Book 4 begins with Satan bringing Jesus to a mountaintop; from there he asks Jesus to look upon the glory of Rome:

> The City which thou seest no other deem
> Then great and glorious *Rome,* Queen of the Earth
> So far renown'd, and with the spoils enricht
> Of Nations; there the Capitol thou seest,
> Above the rest lifting his stately head
> On the *Tarpeian* rock, her Citadel
> Impregnable, and there Mount *Palatine*
> Th' Imperial Palace, compass huge, and high
> The Structure, skill of noblest Architects,
> With gilded battlements, conspicuous far,
> Turrets and Terraces, and glittering Spires. (*PR* 4.44–54)

The image of Rome that so often served as the symbol of humanism is glorified by Satan but quickly renounced by Jesus: "Nor doth this grandeur and majestic show / Of luxury, though call'd magnificence, / More than of arms before, allure mine eye" (4.110–12). Jesus is not taken at all with the glory of Rome; the new world that Jesus brings is oriented "On *David's* Throne" (147) and from that seat, "it shall be like a tree / Spreading and overshadowing all the Earth" (147–48). Satan offers Jesus the knowledge of the ancients, stating that "All knowledge is not couch't in *Moses'* Law" (225), and invites Jesus to spend his time learning the knowledge and arts of Greece. He mentions the Stoics, Epicurus, Homer, Socrates, and many others. Jesus, as we know of Milton himself, admits to already having this knowledge: "Think not but that I know these things" (286); and he then systematically explains his rejection of this knowledge, including the classical arts: "Or if I would delight my private hours / With Music or with Poem, where so soon / As in our native language can I find / that solace" (331–34).[4] His reasoning

---

4. See Howard Schultz, *Milton and Forbidden Knowledge* (New York: Modern Language Association of America, 1955); Irene Samuel, "Milton on Learning and Wisdom," *Publications of the Modern Language Association* 64 (1949): 708–23; and George F. Sensabaugh, "Milton on Learning," *Studies in Philology* 43 (1946): 258–72.

is that the biblical Jewish tradition is rich in its knowledge and arts and is more virtuous, more heroic, because it is directed to and by the light of God. The fact is, in *Paradise Regained,* Milton is following his own Jesus' example by turning to the Old Testament for his model rather than to classical epic—seemingly in a clear rejection of his own poetic methodology in *Paradise Lost.* Still, the reality is that Milton cannot help but acknowledge all those classical philosophers and arts, and the very nature of classical heroism that he is now trying to outdo. Milton's own heroic vision must be shown to be what it is not. The classical, in light of the Christian context, must be rejected, but even as it is rejected, it must be acknowledged, and its importance therefore affirmed. But even more importantly, *Paradise Regained* explicitly supports the presence of a classical crisis in *Paradise Lost* and, in a different way, *Samson Agonistes.* Milton revises his own conception of the heroic. From the standpoint of a poet actively engaging past models, the Satan of *Paradise Lost* is not an antihero because of his moral status; in many ways, the Jesus of *Paradise Regained* is the classical antihero in Milton's corpus as a whole—precisely because of his own moral status. Christ rejects not only Satan, but also the poet of *Paradise Lost.*

This study's focus on the early modern period and the humanist obsession with the past is grounded in my belief that this period represents a pivotal moment of modern poetic identity. A psychical interplay exists between a desired association with the classical past and an evolving sense of self that is founded on both an emerging humanism and an evolving Christian theology. The core of this relationship has long been recognized. However, critically, the fundamental psychical crisis on which this relationship is based is ignored on the grounds either that the phenomenon of literary appropriation is primarily historical or that the psychical processes of subjectivity are the result of a stable assimilation of past and present. But neither critical stance is complete. The historical forces that dictate the practice of literary filiation are themselves manifestations of psychical rupture, and the weaving together of a past, prioritized literary tradition and a desired poetic self-projection oriented in the present is riddled with contradiction and ideological violence. Subjects who desire an authentic, self-defining creative act are ultimately caught in the referential labyrinth of systems of the Symbolic—literary, historical, ideological. However, these systems are first and foremost manifestations of the subject's desire for wholeness, personal and cultural attempts at replacing what is irreplaceable. Like the subject itself, the early modern period is not separate from its past, its history, but an extension of it. But negotiating that past is fundamentally a negotiation with the self. Freud, Bloom, Greene, and Lacan all provide certain concepts that can aid the critic in dealing with the anxieties of influence that are inherent in the humanist tradition. Freud not only gave us the essential notion of anxiety and sublimation and the literal family romance that shapes the development of the ego, but he imagined the potential power that ancient Rome could have as a determining factor of selfhood. Bloom picked up on the family romance as a representation of a writer's interaction with precursors; he found the anxiety of influence an elemental crisis the writer-to-be must overcome in order to be a strong poet with an autonomous voice. Greene revises Bloom to offer a more thoughtful analysis of imitation and worldview. Greene finds that the practices of imitation can be classified according to a writer's positioning of his work with that of his predecessors according to a challenge or conflation of the worldviews that imitation represents. And Lacan, I have argued, provides a further nuanced understanding of anxiety and the relationship the poetic self has with a ruptured sense of wholeness that original identification with the past sought to restore, a split subject seeking to locate a decentered center of its identity.

For early modern identity, the fissures in an authentic self-projection were partially the result of a past that existed in literal ruins. The humanist searching for a connection to the classical past had to reconstruct that past from the material remains found around him—broken stones, crumbling roads, fragmented texts—or had to imitate, recreate from these artifacts of memory, a newly constructed vision of the past that compensated for what was materially lacking, but also ideologically lacking. Writers such du Bellay, Shakespeare, and Jonson all explicitly dealt with the reality of a split Rome, one that must be valorized and shown as destructive within itself. The material realities left from the ancient world were only partially complete. And the humanist's task was to identify that incompleteness and to offer a new sense of unity that a humanist reinvention of the past could bring.

While the literal inadequacies of a fractured Rome—evident in the ruins themselves—were of great concern to the humanist, within their texts writers negotiated the priority of the past and the need to reorient that past through a contemporary sense of identity. French poets of the Pléiade, such as Pierre de Ronsard, Joachim du Bellay, and even Montaigne acknowledge both explicitly and through their appropriations of classical topoi that the classical world was a source of poetic validation, but these poets could establish through the vernacular, they believed, a unique identity that prioritized their identification as French poets. Still, the association with the past could not be abandoned; their ultimate desire was the desire of the classical Other: to do for French what the Latin writers did for Rome. Of course, Roman writers were undergoing a similar crisis of identity with regard to their relationship to Greece. Andrew Marvell in his twin *hortus* poems—one in English, one in Latin—demonstrates the need for the vernacular to project a subjectivity that transcends the perceived limitations of the classical, but like the French poets, Marvell can neither completely abandon the past nor fully embrace it. Jonson and his followers directly imitate their classical predecessors, but as seen in their imitation of Catullus, they often do extreme violence to the contextual pressures that give those original Latin poets their voice. In doing so, Jonson and his followers empower themselves by demonstrating that they own the texts they appropriate; they are not indebted to the ideological realities of those ancient texts. They can use them and destroy them at will—and those poetic acts attest to the power to define themselves through their own poetic self-projections; it is their ability to destroy the texts they imitate that gives them their voice.

All these examples, and the various crises they demonstrate, culminate in a writer like John Milton. Milton is both immensely allusive but also firmly situated in the contemporary superstructures that dictate identity in seventeenth-century Europe. Milton desires to be a poet whose scope and substance rival his classical predecessorss, but he also places his core identity within the ideological realities of a Christian ideal that makes him a kind of prophet of contemporary religious and political ideologies. In Milton's early elegies, the adoption of both the Latin language and the generic form of elegy places the poet's sense of poetic self in a tenuous position. Milton's elegiac subject consistently positions his self-identification between the past and present, frequently seeking a voice that is validated by the literary priority of the classical Other it seeks to usurp with a contemporary Christian ideology. Milton's attempt to rewrite a heroic poem that transcends the classical models of heroic verse hinges on his ability to invoke those models and then quickly undermine the very models to which he has given priority. There is an immense intratextual dynamic to Milton's three major works, *Paradise Lost, Samson Agonistes,* and *Paradise Regained.* All three poems explicitly comment on the importance of "the heroic," but a dialogue exists between them. *Paradise Lost* adopts a functional hero in Satan, who takes on the characteristics of epic in order to drive the epic narrative that allows the poem to progress. However, the allusive nature of the poem consistently calls attention to the fact that the epic hero cannot function also as the moral, Christian hero. *Samson Agonistes* conforms to the major principles of classical drama and the tragic hero, and the genre allows for a structural nod to the classics while avoiding direct allusion, a kind of anxious resistance to the gap that exists between the classical form and the Christian subject matter. Ultimately, Milton acknowledges that gap in *Paradise Regained* as he abandons classical form and explicitly, through the mouth of Christ, claims that neither Rome nor the classical world of the past can adequately reflect the ideological realities of the present and his own need to break from his connection with that past.

A psychical understanding of classical imitation need not be confined to the early modern period; however, that "moment" in history required a dependence on the past that would historically begin to change. For later writers the classical world became primarily a source of difference; the need to validate through the past was not as prevalent. Still, the manner in which writers connected to and used the classical world as a means of self-projection remains important. Although not consumed with exactly the same Christian ideological pressures faced by Milton, Tennyson's later, romantic engagement with classical mythology—specifically, classical heroism—was equally problematic. In his well-known poem "Ulysses," Tennyson challenges the very perception of classical heroism as a construct, a perception born from classical texts themselves as well as the subsequent appropriation and reappropriation of those texts. "Ulysses" is a kind of confessional monologue in the voice of Ulysses as the years have passed, as age has set it, and as the world itself has proceeded, in a sense, without him. The melancholy nature of the romantic mind-set weighs heavily on this reading of the Ulysses myth. Ulysses represents in this poem a kind of romantic "Everyman," one who signifies the grandeur and immense potential of humanity as well as the sadness over the often static nature of human beings. Tennyson recognizes the dualistic centripetal/centrifugal nature of Ulysses as a hero—one who seeks the stability of home as well as values the adventurous, wandering, boundless human spirit. And while Tennyson adopts this classical figure as a validation, a model of this romantic ideal, he also acknowledges this as an incomplete myth, one that fails to reveal the equally important romantic understanding of human deterioration:

> Come, my friends,
> 'Tis not too late to seek a newer world.
> Push off, and sitting well in order smite
> The sounding furrows; for my purpose holds
> To sail beyond the sunset, and the baths

Of all the western stars, until I die.
It may be that the gulfs will wash us down:
It may be we shall touch the Happy Isles,
And see the great Achilles, whom we knew.
Tho' much is taken, much abides; and tho'
We are not now the strength which in old days
Moved earth and heaven, that which we are, we are;
One equal temper of heroic hearts,
Made weak by time and fate, but strong in will
To strive, to seek, to find, and not to yield. ("Ulysses" 56–70)[5]

Tennyson establishes his own poetic and ideological visions by succumbing to the literary past, but the lack in the ideological construction of the past has to be exposed as well. Tennyson has to view himself both as part of the past and as distinct from it.

W. B. Yeats in "Leda and the Swan" even better illustrates a poet who dialectically undermines the structurality of classical mythology and the ideology it signifies. Yeats clearly acknowledges the beauty and power of the poem's classical origins; however, he attempts to fill the lack in what might be perceived as a twentieth-century realism regarding the violence and destruction inherent in such so-called beauty:

How can those terrified vague fingers push
The feathered glory from her loosening thighs?
And how can body, laid in that white rush,
But feel the strange heart beating where it lies? ("Leda and the Swan" 5–8)[6]

The result of the rape of Leda was Helen of Troy. Yeats here plays on the image of a violent rape—Leda is "mastered by the brute blood of the air" (13)—as the source of what is considered the epitome of classical beauty. That beauty in turn results in even more violence and ultimately a classical world again in ruins:

A shudder in the loins engenders there
The broken wall, the burning roof and tower
And Agamemnon dead. ("Leda and the Swan" 9–11)

---

5. "Ulysses," in *The Complete Works of Alfred Tennyson* (New York: R. Worthington, 1880), 61–62.

6. "Leda and the Swan," in *The Collected Poems of W. B. Yeats* (London: Wordsworth Editions, 2000), 182.

Yeats invokes the imminence and power of the classical world, clearly feeling himself, or rather establishing himself as, a part of that grand poetic tradition, but that tradition is one of violence, of destruction, and the poet here finds his own identity by exposing the weakness, the frailty, the ruins of that ancient world he summons. Yeats must show the ancient world and its power as somehow lacking the constancy and creative potency it represents. Bloom most likely would be uninterested in such a poem with regard to the anxiety of influence, for it does not challenge a single identifiable source. Still, Yeats engages what amounts to a signifier for an entire structure of influence. He is battling with mythology as a structural force, trying to be part of the structure by revealing the gaps in the structure. Again, this is not a misreading nor an intentional misinterpretation of a predecessor, but an ideological repositioning of the classical world that the myth signifies. By gazing back to the past, Yeats is able to identify himself in the present, and the cyclical nature of destruction and the birth of beauty that the poem depicts becomes the system of the poet's own existence, a validation of his own poetic self.

The current study should also open up the possibilities of considering imitation in light of other psychoanalytic theories of the self. Thinkers such Julia Kristeva and Luis Irigaray, for instance, offer a feminist perspective on the unconscious that could be applied to the manner in which women or other marginalized groups of writers position their poetic self against the authority of tradition.

There is, in fact, much this study does not do, but what I hope to have accomplished is to offer a framework for the continued study of the classical tradition and the poetic crises that determine its function.

Selected Bibliography

Allen, D. C. "Milton's Eve and the Evening Angels." *Modern Language Notes* 75 (1960): 108–9.

Althusser, Louis. "Ideology and Ideological State Apparatuses." In *Lenin and Philosophy and Other Essays,* trans. Ben Brewster, 127–88. New York: Monthly Review Press, 1971.

———. "Ideology and the State." In *Essays on Ideology,* 1–60. London: Verso, 1984.

———. *Writings on Psychoanalysis: Freud and Lacan.* Ed. Olivier Corpet and François Matheron. Trans. Jeffrey Mehlman. New York: Columbia University Press, 1996.

Ancelet, Barry. *Cajun and Creole Folktales: The French Oral Tradition of South Louisiana.* Jackson: University Press of Mississippi, 1994.

Anselmi, Gian Mario. *Le frontiere degli umanisti.* Bologna: CLUEB, 1988.

Armstrong, Richard H. *A Compulsion for Antiquity: Freud and the Ancient World.* Ithaca, NY: Cornell University Press, 2005.

Atkinson, James B. "Naïveté and Modernity: The French Renaissance Battle for a Literary Vernacular." *Journal of the History of Ideas* 35.2 (1974): 179–96.

Austin, Warren B. "Milton's 'Lycidas' and Two Latin Elegies by Giles Fletcher, the Elder." *Studies in Philology* 44 (1947): 41–55.

Bailey, Cyril, ed. *The Legacy of Rome.* Oxford: Clarendon Press, 1923.

Bakhtin, Mikhail. *The Dialogic Imagination: Four Essays.* Ed. Michael Holquist. Trans. Caryl Emerson and Michael Holquist. Austin: University of Texas Press, 1982.

———. *Problems of Dostoevsky's Poetics.* Ed. and trans. Caryl Emerson. Minneapolis: University of Minnosota Press, 1984.

Barkan, Leonard. *Transuming Passion: Ganymede and the Erotics of Humanism.* Stanford, CA: Stanford University Press, 1991.

———. *Unearthing the Past: Archaeology and Aesthetics in the Making of Renaissance Culture.* New Haven, CT and London: Yale University Press, 1999.

Barnaby, Andrew. "The Politics of Garden Spaces: Andrew Marvell and the Anxieties of Public Speech." *Studies in Philology* 97.3 (2000): 331–61.

Baron, Hans. *The Crisis of the Early Italian Renaissance: Civic Humanism and the Republican Liberty in an Age of Classicism and Tyranny.* Princeton, NJ: Princeton University Press, 1966.

Belsey, Catherine. *Culture and the Real.* London: Routledge, 2005.

Black, Robert. *Humanism and Education in Medieval and Renaissance Italy: Tradition and Innovation in Latin Schools from the Twelfth to the Fifteenth Century.* Cambridge: Cambridge University Press, 2001.

Blessington, Francis C. *"Paradise Lost" and the Classical Epic.* Boston and London: Routledge, 1979.

Blevins, Jacob. *Catullan Consciousness and the Early Modern Lyric: From Wyatt to Donne.* Aldershot, UK: Ashgate, 2004.

———. "Influence, Anxiety, and the Symbolic: A Lacanian Rereading of Bloom." *Intertexts* 9.2 (2006): 123–38.

———. "Marvell's Two Gardens: Re-writing the Roman Hortus." *Andrew Marvell Newsletter* 2.2 (2011). http://academic.stedwards.edu/marvell/jacob-blevins-marvells-two-gardens—re-writing-the-roman-hortus/.

———. "Staging Rome: The Renaissance, Rome, and Humanism's Classical Crisis." In *The Sites of Rome: Time, Space, Memory,* ed. David H. J. Larmour and Diana Spencer, 271–94. Oxford: Oxford University Press, 2007.

Bloom, Harold. *The Anxiety of Influence.* New York: Oxford University Press, 1973.

———. *Kabbalah and Criticism.* New York: Seabury Press, 1975.

———. *A Map of Misreading.* New York: Oxford University Press, 1975.

———. *Poetry and Repression.* New Haven, CT and London: Yale University Press, 1976.

Boehrer, Bruce. "The Rejection of Pastoral in Milton's 'Elegia Prima.'" *Modern Philology* 99.2 (2001): 181–200.

Bond, Christopher. *Spenser, Milton, and the Redemption of the Epic Hero.* Lanham, MD: Rowan and Littlefield, 2011.

Booker, Keith M. *A Practical Introduction of Literary Theory and Criticism.* New York: Longman, 1995.

Bouwsma, William J. *The Waning of the Renaissance, 1550–1640.* New Haven, CT: Yale University Press, 2000.

Braden, Gordon. *Petrarchan Love and the Continental Renaissance.* New Haven, CT: Yale University Press, 1999.

Bryson, Michael. *The Tyranny of Heaven: Milton's Rejection of God as King.* Newark: University of Delaware Press, 2004.

Bush, Douglas, ed. *Milton Poetical Works.* Oxford: Oxford University Press, 1965.

———. *The Renaissance and English Humanism.* Toronto: University of Toronto Press, 1939.

Butler, Rex. *Jean Baudrillard: The Defence of the Real.* London: Sage, 1999.

Cantor, Paul A. *Shakespeare's Rome, Republic and Empire.* Ithaca, NY: Cornell University Press, 1976.

Carey, John. *Milton.* London: Evans Bros., 1969.

———. "Milton's Satan." In *The Cambridge Companion to Milton,* ed. Dennis Danielson, 160–74. Cambridge: Cambridge University Press, 1999.

———. "A Work in Praise of Terrorism?: September 11 and *Samson Agonistes.*" *Times Literary Supplement* 6 (September 2002): 15–16.

Carpenter, Margaret Ann. "Marvell's 'Garden.'" *Studies in English Literature* 10.1 (1970): 155–69.

Caruso, Carlo, and Andrew Laird, eds. *Italy and the Classical Tradition: Language, Thought, and Poetry.* London: Duckworth, 2009.

Castor, Grahame. *Pléiade Poetics: A Study in Sixteenth-Century Thought and Terminology.* Cambridge: Cambridge University Press, 1964.

Catullus. *The Poems of Catullus: A Bilingual Edition.* Trans. Peter Green. Berkeley: University of California Press, 2005.

Cavallini, Giovanni. *Polistoria.* Ed. Marc Laureys. Stuttgart: B. G. Teubner, 1995.

———. *Polistoria de Virtutibus et Dotibus Romanorum.* Biblioteca Apostolica Vaticana MS, Rossiano 728, fol. 1.

Chambers, A. B. "Herrick, Corinna, Caticles, and Catullus." *Studies in Philology* 74.2 (1977): 216–27.

———. "Herrick and the Trans-Shifting of Time." *Studies in Philology* 72.1 (1975): 85–114.

Chaplin, Gregory. "'One Flesh, One Heart, One Soul': Renaissance Friendship and Miltonic Marriage." *Modern Philology* 99.2 (2001): 266–92.

Chernaik, Warren L. "Ben Jonson's Rome." In *The Myth of Rome in Shakespeare and His Contemporaries,* 108–34. Cambridge: Cambridge University Press, 2011.

Clark, William Bedford. "Letters from Home: The Epistolary Aspects of Joachim Du Bellay's 'Les Regrets.'" *Renaissance Quarterly* 52 (1999): 140–79.

Coffin, David R. *Pirro Ligorio: The Renaissance Artist, Architect, and Antiquarian.* University Park: Pennsylvania State University Press, 2003.

Coldiron, A. E. B. "How Spenser Excavates Du Bellay's *Antiquitez;* or, The Role of the Poet, Lyric Historiography, and the English Sonnet." *Journal of English and Germanic Philology* 101.1 (2002): 41–67.

Collett, Jonathan H. "Milton's Use of Classical Mythology in 'Paradise Lost.'" *Publications of the Modern Language Association* 85.1 (1970): 88–96.

Conti, Brooke. "'That Really Too Anxious Protestation': Crisis and Autobiography in Milton's Prose." *Milton Studies* 45 (2006): 149–86.

Corns, Thomas. "'Some Rousing Motions': The Plurality of Miltonic Ideology." In *Literature and the English Civil War,* ed. T. Healy and J. Sawday, 110–26. Cambridge: Cambridge University Press, 1990.

Coward, David. *A History of French Literature: From Chanson de Geste to Cinema.* Oxford: Blackwell, 2002.

Cox, Virginia, and John O. Ward, eds. *The Rhetoric of Cicero in Its Medieval and Early Renaissance Commentary Tradition.* Leiden: Brill, 2006.

Crashaw, Richard. "Out of Catullus." In *The Complete Poetry of Richard Crashaw,* ed. George Walton Williams, 522–25. New York: New York University Press, 1972.

Daniel, Clay. "Lust and Violence in 'Samson Agonistes.'" *South Central Review* 6.1 (1989): 6–31.

Dannenfeldt Karl H., ed. *The Renaissance: Medieval or Modern?* Boston: D.C. Heath, 1959.

Dean, Paul. "Tudor Humanism and the Roman Past: A Background to Shakespeare." *Renaissance Quarterly* 41.1 (1988): 84–111.

Delattre, M. Floris. *Contribution à l'étude de la poésie lyrique en Angleterre au dix-septième siècle.* Paris: F. Alcan, 1912.

Della Neva, JoAnn. "Petrarch at the Portal: Opening Signals in 'Les Amours' de Ronsard." *Rivista di Letterature Moderne e Comparate* 50.3 (1997): 259–72.

————. *Unlikely Exemplars: Reading and Imitating beyond the Italian Canon in French Renaissance Poetry.* Newark: University of Delaware Press, 2009.

DeMaria, Robert, and Robert Duncan Brown. *Classical Literature and Its Reception: An Anthology.* Oxford: Blackwell, 2007.

Demerson, Guy. *La mythologie classique dans l'oeuvre lyrique de la Pléiade.* Geneva: Droz, 1972.

Deming, Robert H. *Ceremony and Art: Robert Herrick's Poetry.* The Hague: Mouton, 1974.

————. "Herrick's Funereal Poems." *Studies in English Literature* 9.1 (1969): 153–67.

————. "Robert Herrick's Classical Ceremony." *English Literary History* 34.3 (1967): 327–48.

Dictionary of Louisiana French: As Spoken in Cajun, Creole, and American Indian Communities. Jackson: University Press of Mississippi, 2010.

Dollimore, Jonathan. *Radical Tragedy: Religion, Ideology, and Power in the Drama of Shakespeare and His Contemporaries.* 3rd ed. Durham, NC: Duke University Press, 2004.

Donaldson-Evans, Lance. "Ronsard's Folies Bergères: The Livret Des Folastries and Petrarch." *Neophilologus* 91.1 (2007): 1–17.

Du Bellay, Joachim. *The Regrets.* Trans. Richard Helgerson. Philadelphia: University of Pennsylvania Press, 2006.

Edwards, Catherine. *Roman Presences: Receptions of Rome in European Culture.* Cambridge: Cambridge University Press, 1999.

————. *Writing Rome: Textual Approaches to the* City. Cambridge: Cambridge University Press, 1996.

Edwards, M. J. "The Pilot and the Keys: Milton's *Lycidas* 167–171." *Studies in Philology* 108.4 (2011): 605–18.

Eliot, T. S. *Selected Essays.* 3rd ed. London and Boston: Faber and Faber, 1951.

Enterline, Lynn. *The Rhetoric of the Body from Ovid to Shakespeare.* Cambridge: Cambridge University Press, 2000.

Euripides. *Euripides: The Bacchae and Other Plays.* Trans. Philip Vellacott. London: Penguin Classics, 1954.

————. *Hecuba.* Trans. Janet Lembke and Kenneth J. Reckford. Oxford: Oxford University Press, 1991.

Evans, Dylan. *An Introductory Dictionary of Lacanian Psychoanalysis.* London: Routledge, 1996.

Faisant, Claude. *Mort et résurrection de la Pléiade.* Paris: H. Champion, 1998.

Feeney, D. C. "Epic Hero and Epic Fable." *Comparative Literature* 38.2 (1986): 137–58.

Felluga, Dino. "Modules on Lacan: On the Structure of the Psyche." *Introductory Guide to Critical Theory.* January 31, 2011. Purdue University. December 2, 2011. <http://www.purdue.edu/guidetotheory/psychoanalysis/lacanstructure.html>.

Ferguson, Margaret W. "'The Afflatus of Ruin': Meditations on Rome by Du Bellay, Spenser, and Stevens." In *Roman Images,* ed. Annabel Patterson, 23–50. Baltimore: Johns Hopkins University Press, 1984.

————. "The Exile's Defense: Du Bellay's *La Deffence et illustration de la langue François.*" *Publications of the Modern Language Association* 93.2 (1978): 275–89.

Fink, Bruce. *The Lacanian Subject: Between Language and Jouissance.* Princeton, NJ: Princeton University Press, 1996.

Fish, Stanley. "Spectacle and Evidence in 'Samson Agonistes.'" *Critical Inquiry* 15.3 (1989): 556–86.

Fitzgerald, William. *Catullan Provocations: Lyric Poetry and the Drama of Position.* Berkeley: University of California Press, 1995.

Fletcher, Giles. *De literas antiquae Britanniae.* Cambridge, 1633.

Freud, Sigmund. *Civilization and Its Discontents.* Ed. and trans. James Strachey. New York and London: Norton, 1961.

———. *The Complete Psychological Works of Sigmund Freud.* New York: Norton, 1990.

———. *Inhibitions, Symptoms, and Anxiety.* Vol. 20. The Standard Edition, 1929.

———. *Introductory Lectures on Psycho-Analysis.* Vol. 15. The Standard Edition, 1916–17.

Fryde, E. B. *Humanism and Renaissance Historiography.* London: Continuum, 1984.

Frye, Northrop. "Literature as Context: Milton's *Lycidas.*" *Studies in Comparative Literature* 23 (1959): 44–53.

Fubini, Riccardo. *Humanism and Secularization: From Petrarch to Valla.* Durham, NC: Duke University Press, 2003.

Gaisser, Julia Haig. *Catullus and His Renaissance Readers.* Oxford: Clarendon Press, 1993.

Galbraith, David. "Petrarch and the Broken City." In *Antiquity and Its Interpreters,* ed. Alina Payne, Ann Kuttner, and Rebekah Smick, 17–26. Cambridge: Cambridge University Press, 2000.

Gallagher, Cormac. *The Seminar of Jacques Lacan X: Anxiety.* London: Karnac Books, 2002.

Garbero, Maria Del Sapio. *Identity, Otherness, and Empire in Shakespeare's Rome.* Farnham, UK and Burlington, VT: Ashgate, 2009.

Gavin, Dominic. "'The Garden' and Marvell's Literal Figures." *Cambridge Quarterly* 37.2 (2008): 224–52.

Gilbert, Sandra M., and Susan Gubar. *The Madwoman in the Attic: The Woman Writer and the Nineteenth-Century Literary Imagination.* New Haven, CT: Yale University Press, 1979.

Gilmore, Myron P. *The World of Humanism.* New York: Harper, 1952.

Giordani, Françoise. "Utilisation et description de l'espace dans *Les Antiquitez de Rome* de Joachim du Bellay." In *Du Bellay et ses sonnets romains,* ed. Yvonne Bellenger, 19–46. Paris: Champion, 1994.

Glidden, Hope, and Norman R. Shapiro, eds. *Lyrics of the French Renaissance: Marot, Du Bellay, Ronsard.* New Haven, CT and London: Yale University Press, 2002.

Gouwen, Kenneth. "Erasmus, 'Apes of Cicero,' and Conceptual Blending." *Journal of the History of Ideas* 71.4 (2010): 523–45.

Grassi, Ernesto. *Heidegger and the Question of Renaissance Humanism.* Binghamton, NY: Medieval and Renaissance Texts and Studies, 1983.

———. *Renaissance Humanism: Studies in Philosophy and Poetics.* Binghamton, NY: Medieval and Renaissance Texts and Studies, 1988.

Green, Mandy. "The Virgin in the Garden: Milton's Ovidian Eve." *Modern Language Review* 100.4 (2005): 903–22.

Greene, Thomas M. *The Descent from Heaven: A Study in Epic Continuity.* New Haven, CT: Yale University Press, 1963.

———. *The Light in Troy: Imitation and Discovery in Renaissance Poetry.* New Haven, CT: Yale University Press, 1982.

———. "Petrarch and the Humanist Hermeneutic." In *Italian Literature: Roots and Branches,* ed. Giose Rimanelli and Kenneth J. Atchity, 201–24. New Haven, CT: Yale University Press, 1976.

———."Resurrecting Rome: The Double Task of the Humanist Imagination." In *Rome in the Renaissance: The City and the Myth*, ed. P. A. Ramsey, 41–54. Binghamton, NY: Medieval and Renaissance Texts and Studies, 1982.

Hale, J. W. Letter. *Athenaeum*, July 1891, 159–60.

Hampton, Timothy. *Literature and Nation in the Sixteenth Century: Inventing Renaissance France*. Ithaca, NY: Cornell University Press, 2001.

Harari, Roberto. *Lacan's Seminar on 'Anxiety': An Introduction*. Trans. Jane Lamb-Ruiz. New York: The Other Press, 2001.

Harrington, Karl P. *Catullus and His Influence*. Boston: Marshall Jones Co, 1923.

Hay, Denys, and Nicolai Robinstein, eds. *The Age of the Renaissance*. New York: McGraw-Hill, 1967.

Haynes, Kenneth. *English Literature and Ancient Languages*. Oxford: Oxford University Press, 2003.

Herman, Peter C. *Destabilizing Milton: "Paradise Lost" and the Poetics of Incertitude*. New York: Palgrave, 2005.

———. "Paradigms Lost, Paradigms Found: The New Milton Criticism." *Literature Compass* 2.1 (2005): 1–26.

Herrick, Robert. *The Complete Poems of Robert Herrick*. 3 vols. Ed. Alexander B. Grosart. London: Chatto & Windus, 1876.

———. *The Complete Poetry of Robert Herrick*. Ed. J. Max Patrick. New York: Norton, 1968.

———. *The Poetical Works of Robert Herrick*. 2 vols. Ed. George Saintsbury. London: George Bell & Sons, 1893.

Hogan, Patrick Colm. "Lapsarian Odysseus: Joyce, Milton, and the Structure of Ulysses." *James Joyce Quarterly* 24.1 (1986): 55–72.

Homer. *The Iliad*. Trans. Robert Fagles. New York: Penguin, 1990.

———. *The Odyssey*. Trans. Richard Lattimore. New York: Harper Collins, 1991.

Homer, Sean. *Jacques Lacan*. New York: Routledge, 2005.

Hone, Ralph E. "'The Pilot of the Galilean Lake.'" *Studies in Philology* 56.1 (1959): 55–61.

Hubbard, Thomas K. *The Pipes of Pan: Intertextuality and Literary Filiation in the Pastoral Tradition from Theocritus to Milton*. Ann Arbor: University of Michigan Press, 1998.

Hughes, Merrit Y. "The Christ of Paradise Regained and the Renaissance Heroic Tradition." *Studies in Philology* 35 (1938): 254–77.

Jacks, Philip. *The Antiquarian and the Myth of Antiquity: The Origins of Rome in Renaissance Thought*. Cambridge: Cambridge University Press, 1993.

Jameson, Fredric. "Imaginary and Symbolic in Lacan: Marxism, Psychoanalytic Criticism, and the Problem of the Subject." *Yale French Studies* 55–56 (1977): 338–95.

Janan, Micaela. *"When the Lamp Is Shattered": Desire and Narrative in Catullus*. Carbondale: Southern Illinois University Press, 1994.

Johnson, Samuel. *Lives of the Most Eminent English Poets*. 4 vols. Ed. Roger Lonsdale. Oxford: Clarendon Press, 2006.

———. *The Yale Edition of the Works of Samuel Johnson*. Vol. 3. Ed. W. J. Bate and Albrecht B. Strauss. New Haven, CT and London: Yale University Press, 1958–2005.

Jonson, Ben. *Ben Jonson*. 11 vols. Ed. C. H. Herford and Percy and Evelyn Simpson. Oxford: Clarendon Press, 1925–73.

Jordan, Richard Douglas. "The Movement of the 'Nativity Ode.'" *South Atlantic Quarterly* 38.4 (1973): 34–39.

Kahn, Coppélia. *Roman Shakespeare: Warriors, Wounds, and Women.* London and New York: Routledge, 1997.

Kelley, Mark R., and Joseph Wittreich, eds. *Altering Eyes: New Perspectives on "Samson Agonistes."* Newark: University of Delaware Press, 2002.

Kennedy, William J. *The Site of Petrarchism: Early Modern Sentiment in Italy, France, and England.* Baltimore: Johns Hopkins University Press, 2003.

Kermode, Frank. "Milton's Hero." *Review of English Studies,* n.s., 4 (1953): 317–30.

Kilgour, Maggie. "'Thy Perfect Image Viewing': Poetic Creation and Ovid's Narcissus in 'Paradise Lost.'" *Studies in Philology* 102.3 (2005): 307–39.

Kingsley, Lawrence W. "Mythic Dialectic in the Nativity Ode." In *Milton Studies,* ed. James D. Simmonds, 163–76. Pittsburgh: Duquesne University Press, 1972.

Knoespel, Kenneth J. "The Limits of Allegory: Textual Expansion of Narcissus in Paradise Lost." *Milton Studies* 22 (1989): 79–100.

Kristeller, Paul O. *Renaissance Thought and Its Sources.* New York: Columbia University Press, 1979.

Lacan, Jacques. *Ecrits.* Trans. Bruce Fink. New York: Norton, 2006.

———. *The Ego in Freud's Theory and in the Technique of Psychoanalysis, 1954–1955. The Seminar of Jacques Lacan: Book II.* London: W. W. Norton & Company, 1991.

———. *The Four Fundamental Concepts of Psycho-Analysis.* Ed. Jacques-Alain Miller. Trans. Alan Sheridan. New York: Norton, 1978.

———. *Freud's Papers and Techniques, 1953–1954. The Seminar of Jacques Lacan: Book 1.* Ed. Jacques-Alain Miller. Trans with notes John Forrester. New York: Norton, 1988.

———. *The Psychoses, 1955–1956. The Seminar of Jacques Lacan: Book 3.* Ed. Jacques-Alain Miller. Trans. with notes Russell Grigg. New York: Norton, 1997.

———. *Seminar IV: Object-Relations.* 1956–57.

———. *Seminar VIII: Transference.* 1960–61.

———. *Seminar XXII: 'R-I-S.'* 1975–76.

———. *Le seminaire, Livre X: L'angoisse.* Trans. Cormac Gallagher. London: Karnac Books, 2002.

Laplanche, Jean, and J. B. Pontalis. *The Language of Psychoanalysis.* London: Hogarth Press, 1974.

Lee, Jonathan Scott. *Jacques Lacan.* Boston: Twayne Publishers, 1990.

Lewalski, Barbara K. *Milton's Brief Epic: The Genre, Meaning, and the Art of "Paradise Regained."* Providence, RI: Brown University Press, 1966.

———. "'Samson Agonistes' and the 'Tragedy' of the Apocalypse." *Publications of the Modern Language Association* 85.5 (1970): 1050–62.

Lewis, C. S. *A Preface to "Paradise Lost."* London: Oxford University Press, 1942.

Lieb, Michael, and Albert Labriola, eds. *Milton in the Age of Fish: Essays on Authorship, Text, and Terrorism.* Pittsburgh: Duquesne University Press, 2006.

Lipking, Lawrence. "The Genius of the Shore: 'Lycidas,' Adamastor, and the Poetics of Nationalism." *Publications of the Modern Language Association* 111 (1996): 205–21.

Loewenstein, David. *Milton: Paradise Lost.* Cambridge: Cambridge University Press, 1993.

Loewenstein, David, and James Grantham Turner, eds. *Politics, Poetics, and Hermeneutics in Milton's Prose.* Cambridge: Cambridge University Press, 1990.

Low, Anthony. "'No Power but of God': Vengeance and Justice in 'Samson Agonistes.'" *Huntington Library Quarterly* 40.4 (1977): 313–24.

Lowell, J. R. *Among My Books.* Boston: Houghton Mifflin, 1894.

Luna, B. N. *Jonson's Romish Plot: A Study of Catiline and Its Historical Context.* Oxford: Oxford University Press, 1976.

Lyne, R. O. A. M. *The Latin Love Poets.* Oxford: Clarendon Press, 1980.

Mackenzie, Louisa. *The Poetry of Place: Lyric, Landscape, and Ideology in Renaissance France.* Toronto: University of Toronto Press, 2011.

Macphail, Eric. "The Roman Tomb or the Image of the Tomb in Du Bellay's *Antiquitez.*" *Bibliothèque d'Humanisme et Renaissance* 48.2 (1986): 359–72.

———. *The Voyage to Rome in French Renaissance Literature.* Saratoga, CA: ANMA Libri, 1990.

Man, Paul de. "Literary History and Literary Modernity." In *Blindness and Insight: Essays in the Rhetoric of Contemporary Criticism.* 142–65. New York: Oxford University Press, 1971.

Martindale, Charles. *John Milton and the Ancient Epic.* London: Croom Helm, 1986.

———. *John Milton and the Transformation of Ancient Epic.* Bristol: Bristol Classical Press, 2002.

———. "Paradise Metamorphosed: Ovid in Milton." *Comparative Literature* 37.4 (1985): 301–33.

Martindale, Charles, and A. B. Taylor, eds. *Shakespeare and the Classics.* Cambridge: Cambridge University Press, 2004.

Masson, David. *The Life of John Milton.* 7 vols. London, 1859–94.

Maus, Katharine Eisaman. *Ben Jonson and the Roman Frame of Mind.* Princeton, NJ: Princeton University Press, 1984.

Mazzocco, Angelo. "The Antiquarianism of Francesco Petrarca." *The Journal of Medieval and Renaissance Studies* 7 (1977): 203–24.

———. "Rome and the Humanists: The Case of Biondo Flavio." In *Rome in the Renaissance: The City and the Myth,* ed. P. A. Ramsey, 185–95. Binghamton, NY: Medieval and Renaissance Texts and Studies, 1982.

McCanles, Michael. *Jonsonian Discriminations: The Humanist Poet and the Praise of True Nobility.* Toronto: University of Toronto Press, 1992.

McEuen, Kathryn A. *Classical Influence upon the Tribe of Ben.* Cedar Rapids, IA: The Torch Press, 1939.

McGowan, Margaret M. *The Vision of Rome in Late Renaissance France.* New Haven, CT: Yale University Press, 2000.

McKnight, Stephen A. *Sacralizing the Secular: The Renaissance Origins of Modernity.* Baton Rouge: Louisiana State University Press, 1989.

McLaughlin, M. L. *Literary Imitation in the Italian Renaissance: The Theory and Practice of Literary Imitation in Italy from Dante to Bembo.* Oxford: Clarendon Press, 1995.

McPeek, James A. S. *Catullus in Strange and Distant Britain.* Cambridge, MA: Harvard University Press, 1939.

Melehy, Hassan. "Du Bellay's Time in Rome: The *Antiquitez.*" *French Forum* 26.2 (2001): 1–22.

———. *The Poetics of Literary Transfer in Early Modern England.* Farnham, UK and Burlington, VT: Ashgate, 2011.

Miles, Geoffrey. *Shakespeare and the Constant Romans.* Oxford: Clarendon Press, 1996.

Miller, J. "Translator's Notes." In *The Four Fundamental Concepts of Psycho-Analysis,* ed. Jacques-Alain Miller, trans. Alan Sheridan, 279–80. New York: Norton, 1978.

Miller, Paul Allen. *Lyric Texts, Lyric Consciousness.* New York: Routledge, 1994.

————. *Subjecting Verses: Latin Love Elegy and the Emergence of the Real.* Princeton, NJ: Princeton University Press, 2003.

Milton, John. *The Complete Poems and Major Prose.* Ed. Merritt Y. Hughes. Indianapolis and New York: Odyssey Press, 1957.

Minta, Stephen. *Petrarch and Petrarchism: The English and French Traditions.* Manchester: Manchester University Press, 1980.

Miola, Robert S. *Shakespeare's Rome.* Cambridge: Cambridge University Press, 1983.

Mohamed, Feisal G. "Confronting Religious Violence: Milton's 'Samson Agonistes.'" *Publications of the Modern Language Association* 120.2 (2005): 327–40.

Montaigne, Michel de. *The Complete Essays of Montaigne.* Trans. Donald M. Frame. Stanford, CA: Stanford University Press, 1958.

Moorman, F. W. *Robert Herrick: A Biographical & Critical Study.* London: John Lane Company, 1910.

Morris, David B. "Drama and Stasis in Milton's 'Ode on the Morning of Christ's Nativity.'" *Studies in Philology* 68.2 (1971): 207–22.

Mouchel, Christian. *Cicéron et Sénèque dans la rhétorique de la Renaissance.* Marburg: Hitzeroth, 1990.

Musgrove, S. "Is the Devil an Ass?" *Review of English Studies* 21.84 (1945): 302–15.

Navarrete, Ignacio Enrique. *Orphans of Petrarch: Poetry and Theory in the Spanish Renaissance.* Berkeley: University of California Press, 1994.

Nell, Sharon. "A Bee in Pindar's Bonnet: Humanistic Imitation in Ronsard, La Fontaine, and Rococo Style." In *Recapturing the Renaissance: New Perspectives on Humanism, Dialogue, and Texts,* ed. Diane S. Wood and Paul Allen Miller, 181–220. Knoxville, TN: New Paradigm Press, 1996.

Nixon, Paul. "Herrick and Martial." *Classical Philology* 5.2 (1910): 189–202.

Norbrook, David. *Poetry and Politics in the English Renaissance.* Oxford: Oxford University Press, 2002.

Papazin, Mary A., ed. *The Sacred and Profane in English Renaissance Literature.* Newark: University of Delaware Press, 2008.

Parenti, Giovanni. *Benet Garret detto il Cariteo: Profilo di un poeta.* Florence: Olschki, 1993.

Parker, Barbara L. *Plato's Republic and Shakespeare's Rome: A Political Study of the Roman Works.* Newark: University of Delaware Press, 2004.

Parker, William Riley. *Milton: A Biography.* 2 Vols. Oxford: Clarendon Press, 1968.

————. *Milton's Debt to Greek Tragedy in "Samson Agonistes."* Baltimore: Johns Hopkins University Press, 1937.

Pecheux, Mother M. Christopher. "The Image of the Sun in Milton's 'Nativity Ode.'" *Huntington Library Quarterly* 38.4 (1975): 315–33.

Pigman, G. W. "Du Bellay's Ambivalence towards Rome in the *Antiquitez.*" In *Rome in the Renaissance: The City and the Myth,* ed. P. A. Ramsey, 321–32. Binghamton, NY: Medieval and Renaissance Texts and Studies, 1982.

————. *Imitation and Pastoral Elegy.* New Haven, CT: Yale University Press, 1977.

————. "Versions of Imitation in the Renaissance." *Renaissance Quarterly* 33 (1980): 1–32.

Potter, John M. "Another Porker in the Garden of Epicurus: Marvell's 'Hortus' and 'The Garden.'" *Studies in English Literature* 11 (1971): 137–51.

Prescott, Anne Lake. "Spenser (Re)Reading Du Bellay: Chronology and Literary Response." In *Spenser's Life and the Study of Biography,* ed. Judith Anderson, Donal

Cheney, and David A. Richardson. Amherst: University of Massachusetts Press, 1996. 131–45.

Pugh, Syrithe. "Ovidian Exile in the 'Hesperides': Herrick's Politics of Intertextuality." *Review of English Studies*, n.s., 57.232 (2006): 733–65.

Quillen, Carol Everhart. *Rereading the Renaissance: Petrarch, Augustine, and the Language of Humanism*. Ann Arbor: University of Michigan Press, 1998.

Quint, David. "Petrarch, Ronsard, and the Seven-Year Itch." *Modern Language Notes* 124.5 (2009): 137–54.

Ragland-Sullivan, Ellie. *Jacques Lacan and the Philosophy of Psychoanalysis*. Urbana: University of Illinois Press, 1986.

Rebhorn, Wayne A. "Du Bellay's Imperial Mistress: *Les Antiquitez de Rome* as Petrarchist Sonnet Sequence." *Renaissance Quarterly* 33.4 (1980): 609–22.

Rees, Christine. *Johnson's Milton*. Cambridge: Cambridge University Press, 2010.

Revard, Stella P. "The Heroic Context of Book IX of Paradise Lost." *Journal of English and Germanic Philology* 87.3 (1988): 329–41.

———, ed. *John Milton: Complete Shorter Poems*. Chichester: Wiley-Blackwell, 2009.

———. *Milton and the Tangles of Neaera's Hair: The Making of the 1645 Poems*. Columbia: University of Missouri Press, 1997.

———. *Pindar and the Renaissance Hymn Ode: 1450–1700*. Tempe, AZ: Medieval and Renaissance Texts and Studies, 2001.

Roche, Thomas P. *Petrarch and the English Sonnet Sequences*. New York: AMS Press, 1989.

Roudinesco, Elisabeth. "The Mirror Stage: An Obliterated Archive." In *The Cambridge Companion to Lacan*, ed. Jean-Michel Rabaté, 25–34. Cambridge: Cambridge University Press, 2003.

Rudrum, Alan. *A Critical Commentary on Milton's "Samson Agonistes."* London: Macmillan, 1969.

———. "Milton Scholarship and the 'Agon' over 'Samson Agonistes.'" *Huntington Library Quarterly* 65.3–4 (2002): 465–88.

Rumrich, John P. *Milton Unbound: Controversy and Reinterpretation*. Cambridge: Cambridge University Press, 1996.

———. "Uninventing Milton." *Modern Philology* 87.3 (1990): 249–65.

Samuel, Irene. "Milton on Learning and Wisdom." *Publications of the Modern Language Association* 64 (1949): 708–23.

Schultz, Howard. *Milton and Forbidden Knowledge*. New York: Modern Language Association of America, 1955.

Segal, Charles. "Catullus 5 and 7: A Study in Complementaries." *American Journal of Philology* 89.3 (1968): 284–301.

Sensabaugh, George F. "Milton on Learning." *Studies in Philology* 43 (1946): 258–72.

Serrano, Carlos Montes. *Cicerón y la cultura artística del Renacimiento*. Valladolid: Universidad de Valladolid, Secretariado de Puplicaciones e Intercambio Editorial, 2006.

Shakespeare, William. *The Riverside Shakespeare*. 2nd ed. Ed. G. Blakemore Evans. Boston and New York: Houghton Mifflin, 1997.

Shankman, Steven. "The Pindaric Tradition and the Quest for Pure Poetry." *Comparative Literature* 40.3 (1988): 219–44.

Sharpe, Matthew, and Geoff Boucher. *Žižek and Politics*. Edinburgh: Edinburgh University Press, 2010.

Shawcross, John T. "Form and Content in Milton's Latin Elegies." *Huntington Library Quarterly* 33.4 (1970): 331–50.

———. "The Hero of *Paradise Lost:* One More Time." In *Milton and the Art of Sacred Song,* ed. J. Max Patrick and Roger H. Sundell, 137–47. Madison: University of Wisconsin Press, 1979.

Shepherdson, Charles. Foreword to *Lacan's Seminar on 'Anxiety': An Introduction,* by Roberto Harari. New York: The Other Press, 2001.

Smith, George Gregory. Elizabethan Critical Essays. 2 vols. Oxford: Oxford University Press, 2004.

Smith, George William, Jr. "Milton's Method of Mistake in the Nativity Ode." *Studies in English Literature* 18.1 (1978): 107–23.

Spencer, Diana. "Singing in the Garden: Statius' plein air Lyric (after Horace)." In *Dialogism and Lyric Self-Fashioning: Bakhtin and the Voices of a Genre,* ed. Jacob Blevins, 66–83. Selinsgrove, PA: Susquehanna University Press, 2008.

Spencer, T. J. B. "Paradise Lost: The Anti-Epic." In *Approaches to "Paradise Lost,"* ed. C. A. Patrides, 81–98. London: Edward Arnold, 1968.

Spenser, Edmund. *The Poetical Works of Edmund Spenser.* Ed. J. C. Smith and E. De Selincourt. London: Oxford University Press, 1950.

Stanford, W. B. *The Ulysses Theme: A Study in the Adaptability of a Traditional Hero.* Oxford: Blackwell, 1954.

Stanford, W. B., and J. V. Luce. *The Quest for Ulysses.* London: Phaidon Press, 1974.

Stapleton, M. L. "Spenser, the Antiquitez de Rome, and the Developments of the English Sonnet Form." *Comparative Literature Studies* 27 (1990): 259–74.

Stoll, Elmer Edgar. "Give the Devil His Due: A Reply to Mr. Lewis." *Review of English Studies* 20.78 (1944): 108–24.

Sturm-Maddox, Sara. *Ronsard, Petrarch, and the Amours.* Gainesville: University Press of Florida, 1999.

Swaim, Kathleen M. "'The Pilot of the Galilean Lake' in *Lycidas.*" *Milton Quarterly* 17.2 (1983): 42–45.

Tennyson, Alfred, Lord. *The Poems of Tennyson.* London: Longman, 1969.

———. "Ulysses." In *The Complete Works of Alfred Tennyson.* New York: R. Worthington, 1880.

Teskey, Gordon. *Delirious Milton: The Fate of the Poet in Modernity.* Cambridge, MA: Harvard University Press, 2006.

Thomson, Patricia. "Wyatt and the School of Serafino." *Comparative Literature* 13 (1961): 289–315.

Tortoreto, Alessandro. *Lirici Cortigiani del Quattrocento: Il Chariteo, il Tebaldeo, l'Aquilano.* Milan: Leonardo, 1942.

Traversi, Derek. *Shakespeare: The Roman Plays.* Stanford, CA: Stanford University Press, 1963.

Tucker, George Hugo. *The Poet's Odyssey: Joachim Du Bellay and the Antiquitez de Rome.* Oxford: Clarendon Press, 1990.

Tudeau-Clayton, Margaret. *Jonson, Shakespeare, and Early Modern Virgil.* Cambridge: Cambridge University Press, 1998.

Tupper, James Waddell. "The Dramatic Structure of Samson Agonistes." *Publications of the Modern Language Association* 35.3 (1920): 529–51.

Tuveson, E. "The Pilot of the Galilean Lake." *Journal of the History of Ideas* 27 (1966): 44–58.

Ullmann, Walter. *Medieval Foundations of Renaissance Humanism.* Ithaca, NY: Cornell University Press, 1977.

Vergil. *The Aeneid.* Trans. James H. Mantinband. New York: Ungar Publishing, 1964.

Villani, Giovanni. *Cronica.* Ed. F. G. Dragomanni. 4 vols. Florence, 1844–45.

Vout, Caroline. "Sizing up Rome, or Theorizing the Overview." In *The Sites of Rome: Time, Space, Memory,* ed. David H. J. Larmour and Diana Spenser, 295–322. Oxford: Oxford University Press, 2007.

Watterson, William Collins. "'Once More, O Ye Laurels': 'Lycidas' and the Psychology of Pastoral." *Milton Quarterly* 27 (1993): 48–57.

Weiss, Robert. *The Dawn of Humanism.* New York: Haskell, 1970.

———. *The Renaissance Discovery of Classical Antiquity.* Oxford: Blackwell, 1969.

———. *The Spread of Italian Humanism.* London: Hutchinson, 1964.

Wells, Charles. *The Wide Arch: Roman Values in Shakespeare.* New York: St. Martin's, 1993.

Wilkins, Ernest H. "A General Survey of Renaissance Petrarchism." *Comparative Literature* 2.4 (1950): 327–42.

Willet, Laura, ed. and trans. *Poetry & Language in 16th-Century France: Du Bellay, Ronsard, Sebillet.* Toronto: Centre for Reformation and Renaissance Studies, 2003.

Witt, Ronald G. "Civic Humanism and the Rebirth of the Ciceronian Oration." *Modern Language Quarterly* 51 (2001): 167–84.

Wittreich, Joseph A. *Feminist Milton.* Ithaca, NY: Cornell University Press, 1987.

Wolfe, Don M. "The Role of Milton's Christ." *Sewanee Review* 51 (1943): 467–75.

Wolfe, Jessica. *Humanism, Machinery, and Renaissance Literature.* Cambridge: Cambridge University Press, 2004.

Wood, Derek N. C. *Exiled from Light: Divine Law, Morality, and Violence in Milton's "Samson Agonistes."* Toronto: University of Toronto Press, 2001.

Woodhouse, A. S. P. "Theme and Pattern in *Paradise Regained.*" *University of Toronto Quarterly* 25 (1956): 167–82.

Yeats, W. B. *The Collected Poems of W. B. Yeats.* 2nd ed. London: Macmillan, 1950.

———. "Leda and the Swan." In *The Collected Poems of W. B. Yeats,* 182. London: Wordsworth Editions, 2000.

Žižek, Slavoj. *Interrogating the Real.* London and New York: Continuum, 2005.

Index

CLASSICAL MEMORIES/MODERN IDENTITIES
Paul Allen Miller and Richard H. Armstrong, Series Editors

This series consistently explores how the classical world has been variously interpreted, transformed, and appropriated to forge a usable past and a livable present. Books published in this series will detail both the positive and negative aspects of classical reception and will take an expansive view of the topic. Therefore, it will include works that examine the function of translations, adaptations, invocations, and classical scholarship in the formation of personal, cultural, national, sexual, and racial identities. This series's expansive view and theoretial focus thus separate cultural reception from the category of mere *Nachleben*.

Tragic Effects: Ethics and Tragedy in the Age of Translation
  THERESE AUGST

Reflections of Romanity: Discourses of Subjectivity in Imperial Rome
  RICHARD ALSTON AND EFROSSINI SPENTZOU

Philology and Its Histories
  EDITED BY SEAN GURD

Postmodern Spiritual Practices: The Construction of the Subject and the Reception of Plato in Lacan, Derrida, and Foucault
  PAUL ALLEN MILLER

CPSIA information can be obtained
at www.ICGtesting.com
Printed in the USA
FFOW04n0621071016
28210FF